Media and
Globalization

Media and Globalization

Why the State Matters

Edited by
Nancy Morris and Silvio Waisbord

Epilogue by
Kaarle Nordenstreng

ROWMAN & LITTLEFIELD PUBLISHERS, INC.
Lanham • Boulder • New York • Oxford

ROWMAN & LITTLEFIELD PUBLISHERS, INC.

Published in the United States of America
by Rowman & Littlefield Publishers, Inc.
4720 Boston Way, Lanham, Maryland 20706
www.rowmanlittlefield.com

12 Hid's Copse Road, Cumnor Hill, Oxford OX2 9JJ, England

British Library Cataloging in Publication Information Available

Library of Congress Cataloging-in-Publication Data

Media and globalization : why the state matters / edited by Nancy Morris and Silvio
Waisbord.
    p.   cm.
    Includes bibliographical references and index.
    ISBN 0-7425-1029-8 (alk. paper)—ISBN 0-7425-1030-1 (pbk. : alk. paper)
    1. Mass media policy.   2. Internet (Computer network)—Government policy.
3. Communication, International.   I. Morris, Nancy, 1953–   II. Waisbord, Silvio
R. (Silvio Ricardo), 1961–
P95.8.M384   2001
302.23—dc21   2001019012

Printed in the United States of America

∞ ™ The paper used in this publication meets the minimum requirements of
American National Standard for Information Sciences—Permanence of Paper for
Printed Library Materials, ANSI/NISO Z39.48-1992.

Contents

Introduction

Rethinking Media Globalization and State Power

Silvio Waisbord and Nancy Morris

The idea that globalization erodes the power of the state has become conventional wisdom in globalization studies. As a process that supersedes geographical borders, the argument goes, globalization deals a powerful blow to the nature of the state. Governments claim to exercise authority over a territorial space but this becomes increasingly difficult, if not impossible, amid globalization. Regardless of which dimension of globalization is considered, according to some globalization theorists the result is the same. The rise of transnational organizations, the unprecedented worldwide expansion of corporations and market economies, the global capacity of military superpowers, the ability of technology to eliminate spatial barriers, and the consolidation of an international legal system, to mention a few dimensions of globalization, render obsolete the basis of stateness, the existence and protection of a sovereign territory (Wriston 1992; Featherstone, Lash, and Robertson 1995; Waters 1996).

These arguments are found across the social sciences, and they are central to communication and media studies. The impact of international forces on state sovereignty is a long-running theme in the field of international communication. The cultural imperialism and New World Information and Communication Order (NWICO) literature of the 1960s-1980s criticized the presence of foreign media, particularly from the United States, as a threat to cultural autonomy in the developing world (Dorfman and Mattelart 1972; International Commission for the Study of Communication Problems 1980). Several now-classic volumes have examined the challenges that international media flows pose to national autonomy. Kaarle Nordenstreng and Herbert I. Schiller's *National Sovereignty and International Communication,* published in 1979, laid the cornerstones for discussion of issues related to development communication, the "new international information order," and emerging communications technologies. Long before the explosion of megacorporate megamergers, the birth of the World Wide Web, or the coining of the term "globalization," Nordenstreng and Schiller noted that "powerful forces have been trespassing over national boundaries on an unprecedented scale. The central organizer of this border-crossing has been the business system, operating globally" (1979: ix). They highlighted "the vital importance of communication in the struggle to achieve meaningful national autonomy" (1979: xi. See also Hamelink 1988). In a follow-up edited volume published fourteen years later, Nordenstreng and Schiller noted that the concept of national sovereignty in international communications was "a continuing, though problematic, theme" (1993: xi).

As several authors (Alleyne 1995, Frederick 1993, Hamelink 1988, Mohammadi 1997a, Mowlana 1997) have argued, the coming of digital technologies and systems that transcend geographical limitations, coupled with the unfettered worldwide expansion of media and telecommunications companies, represents the latest assault on state sovereignty—that is, on the capacity of states to rule within a certain territory without intrusion from other states. The premise of sovereignty is that states have undivided power (Held 1989) to make decisions within their borders without interference from other states or organizations. Communication sovereignty refers to states' exercise of authority over flows of ideas and information inside their territories. The gap between the ideal of sovereignty and contemporary reality, a concern of globalization scholars in several fields, has been particularly evident in regard to communication and information. Although states have been endowed with the task of cordoning off communicative spaces, the control of these intangible borders is seen as a Sisyphean task in the face of media globalization.

While some observers celebrate the effects of media globalization on states, others find them deeply troubling. Optimists believe that cross-border technologies open up new possibilities for more people around the world to have better and faster access to more information. This position brings together Ithiel de Sola Pool's "technologies of freedom" (1983) argument with the antipathy to government intervention in communications that underlies, most clearly, the First Amendment to the United States Constitution. Media moguls, Western officials, neoconservative thinkers, and technology enthusiasts have repeatedly touted the benefits of media globalization for democratic prospects worldwide. From a perspective that sees the state as the bogeyman of information democracy, the globalization of media technologies makes it possible to bypass government control. The democratization of information undermines the attempts of authoritarian states to control information flows and to curb the entrance of ideas that autocrats might deem inappropriate. As catalysts of the breakup of government communications monopolies, market reforms coupled with wider access to media technologies usher in information democracy. Any individual connected to the global information superhighway has access to more information than any of his or her forebears could ever have imagined, and this access comes substantially without government regulation.

Other observers, in contrast, find such rosy promises unconvincing and alarming. They see such information utopias as myths rather than real prospects (Ferguson 1992). For critical political economists, media imperialism theorists, and antiglobalization activists, the process by which media corporations gain power and untrammeled market forces consolidate their hegemony is hardly a matter for democratic enthusiasm (McChesney and Herman 1997; Schiller 1996). In this view, the organization of global information flows along free-market lines signals the eclipse of state projects for self-determination and for the protection of autonomous information spaces, reducing states' historic grasp on communications sovereignty. With the possible exception of economic nationalists and cultural purists, proponents of this position do not romanticize state control of communications, even as they continue to warn against the damaging consequences of media globalization.

In the context of this ongoing debate, this book explores the role of the state in communications and cultural policymaking in a globalized world. Although there is substantial evidence that the forces of global media and commerce threaten the state in relation to communication and information, we seek to examine this argument more closely by asking what states can and cannot do. Certainly, states currently face changing and challenging conditions. The remarkable global expansion of media corporations, facilitated by liberalization and privatization of media systems worldwide and the development of cable and satellite technologies, has reduced states' ability to exercise power and maintain information sovereignty. It would be unwarranted, however, to conclude that the state no longer matters. Reports about the death of the state may be greatly exaggerated, as many contributors in this book suggest. Also, there is insufficient evidence for asserting the death of the state, because the state remains underanalyzed in the literature on media globalization. Pinned between the global and the local, states continue to be largely absent from current analyses in media and communications. A fundamental premise of this book is that a reevaluation of the notion that globalization erodes state power is necessary in studies of media globalization. As such, this book shares with recent works in the social sciences the idea that it is premature to conclude that the state is withering away and to assume, catastrophically or gleefully, a post-state world. With them, we agree that the interaction between globalizing forces and states is more complex than is usually recognized in the globalization literature, and that states retain important functions and are not likely to disappear (Evans 1997a; Hirst and Thompson 1995; Sassen 1998; Krasner 1991).

Our starting point is that the state still matters as an analytic category, despite the considerable confusion that surrounds it. As Nikhil Sinha discusses in chapter 4, the state remains a problematic and elusive concept in the social sciences. In recent decades, renewed intellectual interest has not put this matter to rest but, rather, has revealed the difficulty in reaching even a minimal definition of the state that is widely accepted. There is little consensus beyond agreement that the state is related to rulemaking and enforcement within geographical boundaries. In Zygmunt Bauman's (1998: 60) words, "States set up and enforce rules and norms binding the run of affairs within a certain territory." Despite this persistent confusion, the state remains a fundamental pillar of the international system and fundamental point of reference at individual, national, and supranational levels. "[A]s even the name of the United Nations reveals," Jürgen Habermas (1998: 105) points out, "world society today is composed politically of nation-states."

Convinced that the state merits analysis, we have asked a number of media scholars to consider the role of states in regard to media and information sovereignty. The contributors to this volume discuss various relationships between states and communications issues. They take different positions on the question of the erosion of state power amid globalization, but collectively they argue that states must be taken into account as actors in media and telecommunications.

STATES, LAWMAKING, AND POWER

The coercive and discursive powers of states to control communications increasingly come up against globalizing forces. Governments cannot escape confrontation with powerful transnational corporations and international organizations whose horizons extend far beyond the state. States remain fundamental political units in a world that continues to be divided along Westphalian principles of sovereignty according to which states are supreme authorities within their borders. Douglas W. Vick explores the concept of sovereignty in chapter 1.

Several contributors to this volume suggest that the growing prominence of international agreements has not eclipsed the most tangible power available to states: lawmaking. Globalization has challenged but not eliminated states as power centers (Garnham 1986)—sets of institutions where decisions are made regarding the structure and functioning of media systems. Just as states continue to assert and defend sovereignty by participating as autonomous organizations in international organizations, sovereignty is also expressed through a variety of media policies. Studies of media policies continue to demonstrate that, notwithstanding the strong combined pressures from external actors (global corporations, financial institutions, and international bodies), states ultimately hold the power to pass legislation that affects domestic media industries. The dynamics of media policymaking, whether policies adhere to or maintain distance from the neoliberal cornerstones of privatization, liberalization, and deregulation, suggest states' relevance as power containers (Giddens 1985). For many, the state remains the best hope for harnessing market-driven media globalization. While some authors see governments as guarantors of the interest of media capital (Winseck 1998), others hold democratic expectations and endow the state with important functions. For example, Oliver Boyd-Barrett (1997: 25) writes, "there is no other credible route [than the state] available for the resolution of significant media issues in the twenty-first century, unless we are prepared to believe that the 'free' market is the best regulator."

Globalized and globalizing free-market practices are sweeping the world. Yet even in media systems ruled by free-market principles, governments continue to license broadcast frequencies, impose limitations on media and telecommunications ownership and operations, and enforce existing laws—in other words, to set up and monitor the basic legal system supporting market policies that underpin media systems.

However, in the tug-of-war over media and telecommunications, states are not equally powerful in terms of their ability to negotiate with global corporations concerning the conditions of establishing media businesses in their countries. But for every example of state powerlessness when confronted by the market juggernaut, there is a counterexample of how states matter. Consolidation and concentration of ownership in media and communications are penetrating deeply into areas that were formerly highly regulated. A growing body of literature indicates how liberalization and privatization policies have opened up previously closed markets to omnivorous media companies (Bustamante 2000; McChesney 1999). India is a case in point, as Nikhil Sinha discusses in chapter 4. At the same time, large states with promising market potential are able to exert influence over global media conglomerates. China, for example, has gotten concessions from Rupert Murdoch in exchange for allowing his media companies to enter the largely untapped market of the most populous country in the world (Gittings 1998). Emerging supranational organizations can command sufficient political power to counter conglomerate economic power as illustrated, for example, by the conditions imposed by the European Union on the AOL/Time Warner merger.

For states, retaining control over communication is in part a matter of economics. Just like any other product or service, anything legally produced and sold within a country generates jobs and tax revenues and contributes to GNP, anything exported additionally generates foreign earnings, anything imported drains national coffers. Media policies regarding taxes and tariffs aim to achieve economic results.

Further, economic tools may be used for political ends. The protection of

internal markets for a country's own media and telecommunications companies can be used by ruling parties or dictatorial regimes wanting to gain or
maintain the cooperation of the domestic media. Notwithstanding globalization, governments retain the capacity to control the media to reinforce legitimacy or fortify a regime's hold on power. This use of the media goes directly
to the fundamental role of media as carriers of messages. (This is not to deny
that goods, too, carry messages, but without accompanying media to provide possible interpretations, the messages conveyed by goods are not transparent in the way that those conveyed by media are.) Considering that power
building today generally takes place in highly mediated societies, authorities
resort to a variety of media mechanisms simply for instrumental purposes.
Governments attempt to manipulate news and intervene in various media
and cultural matters. Covertly or openly, they court and cajole, control and
caress media organizations and orchestrate news management strategies to
gain political advantage and fealty from different constituencies. Authoritarian governments in Latin America and in the former Communist bloc exerted direct control over media through employing censorship, licensing of
journalists, or simply shutting down dissident media outlets (see Fox 1988;
Fox and Waisbord 2001; Downing 1996). Despite the demise of authoritarianism and totalitarianism in many regions of the world, these sorts of practices have not completely disappeared. Although they rarely advocate formal
censorship to domesticate public opinion, democratic administrations frequently resort to more subtle methods, such as libel suits to muffle critical
reporting or withholding official advertising to keep the news media at arm's
length.

Political and Cultural Citizenship

Certain areas of governmental control have been less susceptible than others
to globalizing forces. States continue to cordon off spaces for political debates. Within a country, the media are crucial to political participation.
Democratic theories, whatever their conceptual or normative differences,
consistently assign the media the role of providing information necessary
for democratic governance and citizen participation. This premise underlies
much of the analysis and criticism of media performance in contemporary
politics (McQuail 1992). Insofar as authorities wish to encourage democratic
participation, they may enact communication policies to that end. Government-mandated community access channels on U.S. cable TV systems are
one example of such a policy. Another is found in Germany, where broadcast regulations explicitly favor a strong community orientation (McQuail
1992: 59–60). Robert B. Horwitz describes the democratization of South Africa's broadcasting sector in chapter 3.
    States also still control the processes and mechanisms of formal citizenship

and the movement of people across borders. Mobility of capital and goods, ideas and images, does characterize the current global era, but citizenship, contingent on the lottery of birth, continues to be tied to states. Unprecedented numbers of migrants, refugees, and tourists daily cross political boundaries but states still monopolize the privilege of citizenship rights. Laws concerning the citizenship of media company owners are one manifestation of this control. Many countries, the United States and Canada being conspicuous examples, require owners of broadcast media licenses to hold national citizenship (United States 1998; McQuail 1992: 54). Europe's historic pattern of public monopolies of broadcast media is yielding to private ownership of new outlets, with citizenship requirements. The maintenance of provisions that establish that citizens should control the majority of media ownership was an important issue during the NAFTA (North American Free Trade Agreement) debates (McAnany and Wilkinson 1996). Rupert Murdoch took the exceptional step of becoming a U.S. citizen in order to further his media empire in the world's wealthiest media market—a glaring illustration of the power of the citizenship requirement.

On the other hand, transnational forms of political participation in a global public sphere together with growing numbers of diasporas, cyber-communities, and other cultural groupings that cut across state boundaries invite the reevaluation of national-based models of citizenship. The availability of transnational media may facilitate the creation of transnational collective identities. Electronic mail groups and global news networks provide the communication backbone for global political activities. Constant flows of media materials between home countries and diasporic communities feed long-distance nationalisms. Observing these phenomena, some analysts have taken the notion of belonging that accompanies citizenship and applied it in metaphorical ways, coining such phrases as "cultural citizenship" (García Canclini 1995) or "cosmopolitan citizenship" (Hutchings and Dannreuther 1999) to describe postnational forms of participation that supersede territorially based citizenship. Cosmopolitan citizenship is not only considered real but also has been posited by some as a desirable, democratic alternative to the limited, exclusionary, and biased nature of national citizenship (see Nussbaum 1996; Hutchings and Dannreuther 1999).

Media issues are of paramount importance for the prospects of "information citizenship" (Murdock and Golding 1989). Nation-based media continue to be important not only for propagandizing state ideals but, contrarily, for expanding the opportunities for citizens to produce and consume information that is relevant to them as members of political and cultural communities as well.

Information citizenship has an equivocal relationship with information sovereignty. Pursuing different goals and driven by different intentions, governments have invoked "information sovereignty" to justify various communications policies. Some governments have enacted statist cultural policies to protect indigenous media producers and fend off Hollywood interests. Mexico and Brazil, for example, have comprehensive and protectionist policies that have contributed to the development of relatively strong media industries (de Santis 1998; Sinclair 1999). Some governments have attempted to close off flows of information: Islamic governments in Iran, Afghanistan, Malasyia, and Pakistan have expressed concern about the effects of global media flows on cultural mores and gender images. To keep out foreign television programming, Iran's Islamic Council Assembly banned satellite dishes in 1994 (Mohammadi 1997b: 88). Germany has tried to curb Internet traffic in pornographic and Nazi material by targeting Internet Service Providers (Vick 1998: 420). The Chinese government has blocked satellite TV broadcasts of BBC news. But in the information realm, governments are finding it increasingly difficult to restrict access to external sources. Motivated, well-resourced, and technologically savvy citizens find ways to evade restrictions in order to connect to the Internet and to receive other globalized communications. Activist groups can now reach constituencies that were previously inaccessible. From the outside in, human rights groups such as Amnesty International communicate directly with affected publics, and from the inside out, opposition groups such as the Zapatistas in Mexico bypass traditional means and disseminate their statements worldwide on the Internet.

The political and cultural realms intersect in the formation of collective identities, a less tangible aspect of the relationship among globalizing forces, the state, and the media. Living in a country and holding formal citizenship have long been seen to engender a sense of belonging and identification with that country and its residents—one's fellow citizens. Several authors have stressed the relevance of print and broadcast media in articulating national communities and shaping real or imaginary cultural borders (Deutsch 1966; Anderson 1983; McQuail 1992). Issues of media and collective identity are discussed by Philip Schlesinger, Peter B. White, Stephen D. McDowell, and Joseph Straubhaar in their contributions to this volume.

The promotion and maintenance of national and cultural identities is a prominent reason why governments regulate certain aspects of the media. Nationally produced media can be used to promote local values and identities. Local identities may also be encouraged by language policies such as the Irish government's support of Gaelic media (Hall 1993) or Ecuador's bilingual education program for indigenous peoples (Rival 1997). Some policymakers feel that the complement to encouraging national media production is limiting foreign values or identity messages carried by communications originating from outside a country. This desire is based on the notion that imported media material damages national and cultural identities. Philip Schlesinger discusses problematic assumptions behind this notion in chapter 6.

The tools that governments use that go beyond economic inducements and sanctions include limiting foreign material by imposing "domestic content" quotas requiring that a certain percentage of the content on cinema screens, television, and radio be of national origin. The European Union, attempting to engender a "European identity," requires that broadcasters in member states devote 51 percent of their airtime to European works. This directive has significant loopholes and there have been conflicts about its implementation but it remains on the books. A number of countries throughout the world have also instituted domestic content requirements. Direct state support for film industries is widespread throughout the developing world (Armes 1987) and elsewhere. In Europe, for example, the U.K. allows tax write-offs of production costs of lower-budget films, and France subsidizes its filmmakers (Hamilton 1998). Stephen D. McDowell describes Canadian cultural policies in chapter 7.

Although factors such as language barriers and the size and wealth of domestic markets are responsible for different balances of domestic and imported media content (Hoskins, McFadyen, and Finn 1997), government policies are also crucial in understanding why communications systems are not equally permeable to media globalization. Many media systems worldwide feature a great deal of domestically produced content supplemented with imported content. Others, in contrast, consistently depend on imported media fare and have difficulties producing a steady flow of local audiovisual content. The cases of Canada, France, Japan, and Korea, among other countries where the proportion of foreign content on terrestrial television remains low, attest to the fact that government policies continue to make a difference. Daeho Kim and Seok-Kyeong Hong detail the Korean situation in chapter 5.

The flip side of controlling imported media is exporting media with the aim of disseminating certain messages internationally. Economic and cultural concerns overlap when exported media are deliberately used as carriers of positive messages about a country. The desire of some governments to keep foreign markets open for their media exports may stem from recognition not only of the direct economic payoffs of sales of media programming but also of the potential indirect economic benefits of creating an amenable environment for consumption of other products from the exporting country. This motivation is evident in U.S. film history (Guback 1969). Further, media can carry ideological messages that authorities wish to propagate internationally, a function that has also been noted in discussions of U.S. films (Izod 1988).

It would be premature to announce that states have become irrelevant either as sites for political activity or as hubs for cultural solidarity. Collective identity is still fundamentally tied to the state as both a power container and an identity container. State control over citizenship not only as the organization of persons within and crossing borders but also as a primary category of self-definition remains a powerful tool that has not succumbed to globalization (Waisbord 1998).

CONCLUSION

This introduction has identified several issues that need to be considered to understand state intervention in communications amid globalization. States maintain control over political tools, which are deployed differently in different parts of the world, depending on the type of regime, the level of media self-sufficiency, and the concerns of the day. Globalization has made it more difficult for all states to monopolize the information that citizens consume, but it has neither eliminated attempts to influence media content nor slowed governments' allocation of resources to make this possible.

States and global interests interact in complex ways. The tension between them is a defining force in contemporary media and telecommunications, and their overarching commercial and political environments. States remain important agents in shaping the global media order and the structure of media markets. They perform different functions that aren't equally threatened or obliterated by globalization, and they have tools for taming globalizing forces. States remain the locus for decision making on domestic policies, and they concentrate technical administrative capacities that are not currently replicated by any other institutional arrangement.

Not all states are equally important and effective in carrying out those functions, however. Power asymmetries among states in the international arena must be considered to understand how media globalization affects different societies. The U.S. government wields more influence in shaping international communications policies than any other state; members of the European Union (some more than others) speak louder than the majority of Third World countries in global communications matters.

These are some of the issues that form the multiple dimensions of the interaction between states and media globalization. This book seeks to reevaluate arguments about the decline of state power by suggesting that the interaction between the global and the national is more complex than is generally recognized in the globalization literature. An analysis of the various capabilities of states in regard to communications allows for nuanced and qualified conclusions that are not captured in broad-brush statements that announce the end of the state. Because the state will not disappear from international communications, it should not be absent from debates about the internationalization of communications.

I

STATES AND INTERNET REGULATION

1

Exporting the First Amendment to Cyberspace: The Internet and State Sovereignty

Douglas W. Vick

When democratic countries regulate media content, they engage in a precarious balancing act, attempting to accommodate a wide range of often conflicting interests and policy considerations. Policymakers are frequently required to weigh the interests of those who may be harmed by certain kinds of messages against the individual and societal interests in preserving freedom of speech. Because free speech is a recurring concern, policymakers constantly either explicitly or implicitly make judgments about what free speech means and what it requires. Yet, while most countries in the world profess a commitment to freedom of speech by giving it an exalted position in their constitutions (e.g., Fenwick 1998: 137), and while nearly all of the world's constitutions describe the right to free speech using broadly similar textual language (Schauer 1993: 868–872), the legal interpretation of this right varies greatly from nation to nation. (See Peter B. White, chapter 2 of this book, for a discussion of the Australian case.) Differences in the interpretation of what freedom of speech means are attributable primarily to differences in the history and cultural experiences of diverse societies. These experiences go a long way in determining whether a society will conceptualize or categorize certain social or political acts or events as relevant to free speech. That is to say, the understanding of an ostensibly "objective" legal principle like "freedom of speech" is culturally dependent; to a large extent, free speech is a social construction.

Global communications systems like the Internet bring into sharp focus conflicting interpretations of basic social and political values such as freedom of speech. Messages can be transmitted over the Internet directly and almost instantaneously to and from millions of computer users residing in over 220 countries (see Internet Software Consortium 2000). Any of these messages can contain information, ideas, or images that are lawful in some countries and unlawful in others. How such messages are perceived owes much to the cultural contexts of their reception by different people in different societies. A state's power to decide whether to allow or restrict the dissemination of messages perceived as harmful or "dangerous"—a perception informed by the political, social, and cultural history and circumstances within the state— has traditionally been seen as inherent to the state's "sovereignty," a fundamental if disputed legal concept at the heart of contemporary international law. Given the seemingly "borderless" nature of Internet communications, however, it is not easy for a government to regulate such communications internally without affecting communications externally. This has serious implications for the ability of a state to exercise its traditional sovereign prerogatives without offending the sovereign autonomy of other states.

Unilateral efforts to control Internet communications can "invade" the sovereignty of other states in at least two ways. On the one hand, if State *A* attempts to control the communicative activities of people residing in State *B*, it arguably encroaches on State *B*'s sovereignty. On the other hand, if State *A*'s laws permit individuals residing within its borders to disseminate messages into State *B* that violate State *B*'s laws, this too may be seen as an encroachment on State *B*'s sovereignty. While such "spillover" effects from a nation-state's internal regulatory decisions are not uncommon (see Goldsmith 2000), the very nature of the Internet increases the frequency of these effects.

Within the traditional framework of international law, the preferred non-coercive method for resolving the potential conflicts that can arise through the extraterritorial effects of regulatory decisions is through some form of international cooperation, whether formal treaties or informal regulatory objectives. Such cooperation implies negotiation, and a precondition of negotiation is the mutual recognition of and respect for the autonomy of the states that are negotiating (see Chalmers 2000). But cooperative solutions to potential conflicts presuppose that the states potentially in conflict are willing and legally capable (under their constitutions) to negotiate. In this regard, the international implications of the United States Supreme Court's landmark 1997 decision in *Reno v. American Civil Liberties Union* are particularly significant.

In the *Reno* decision, the Supreme Court determined that the First Amendment to the U.S. Constitution, which provides that "Congress shall make no law . . . abridging the freedom of speech, or of the press," prohibited governmental actions within the United States that would restrict an individual's freedom to disseminate messages over the Internet. Of course, the ruling only prohibits regulation that would restrict freedom of speech as that right is understood in the political and cultural context of U.S. society, expressed institutionally through court decisions. That is, government institutions within the United States will be allowed to regulate Internet communications if those regulations do not infringe on the "American understanding" of the meaning and scope of freedom of expression, but not if those regulations violate that culturally specific understanding. But while the *Reno* case ostensibly involved an issue of U.S. domestic law, it indirectly affects the entire international community, because it prevents U.S. authorities from regulating communications deemed protected by the First Amendment even if those communications would be considered unlawful in other countries. Moreover, since international agreements are inferior to the U.S. Constitution in the hierarchy of American law, the U.S. government lacks the power to enforce treaties and international accords that do not comport with the Supreme Court's interpretation of the First Amendment. This means that the particulars of U.S. free speech law will define the parameters of any international negotiations involving the United States over common rules for regulating Internet content, and because a disproportionate amount of Internet content originates from the United States, effective harmonization of regulatory rules probably requires the involvement of the U.S. government. In other words, effective harmonization requires the rest of the world to accept much of the American conception of free speech. In a way, the U.S. conceptualization of free speech has been foisted on the rest of the world by virtue of the formal structures of American constitutionalism.

This chapter explores the implications this has for policymakers outside the United States, and in particular how it affects the sovereign interests of the states indirectly affected by the *Reno* decision. The chapter first describes communication on the Internet and how this new medium of communication has been perceived as a threat to the regulatory autonomy of nation-states. It then examines the established legal conceptions of sovereignty in international law and how the problems posed by Internet communications affect national sovereignty. Finally, the chapter explores in greater detail the "cultural contingency" (Schauer 1993) of freedom of speech and considers the possible effects of the *Reno* decision internationally.

COMMUNICATIONS ON THE INTERNET

The Internet is, in essence, a "network of networks," interconnecting hundreds of thousands of computers throughout the world (see Manger 1995; Terrett 1997). Computer networks can vary greatly in terms of size and geographical dispersion, but however large or scattered they may be they are usually under the control of identifiable individuals or organizations. The Internet, on the other hand, is neither owned nor controlled by any single person or entity. While the basic structure of the Internet was erected through the efforts of the U.S. military in the 1960s and early 1970s, by the middle of the 1970s an "open-architecture" system was in place that allowed anyone operating a computer network and possessing sufficient technical expertise to connect with it (see Davies and Reed 1996: 416–419; Leiner et al. 2000). Today, any network operator wishing to gain access to the Internet need only comply with certain technical specifications ("protocols") for the transfer of data that allow the exchange of information between computers that otherwise would be unable to communicate with one another (Murray 1998: 287–288).

In its formative years, the Internet was not a "user-friendly" communications system, and this largely limited its appeal to computer hobbyists, the overwhelming majority of whom were Americans. In 1993 and 1994, however, major software innovations opened up cyberspace even to those who were barely computer literate, and the number of people using the Internet increased dramatically (Murray 1998: 286–289). Now, an individual can send and receive information over the Internet with relative ease so long as his or her computer is connected to one of the large computer terminals called "servers" through which computer networks link up to the Internet. Among others, universities, governmental entities, and commercial organizations like America Online (AOL) maintain servers and allow authorized users to connect with those servers and access the Internet. These institutions are commonly termed Internet Service Providers (ISPs).

An individual connected to the Internet can communicate with another individual on a one-to-one basis through electronic mail or with larger numbers of persons through various newsgroups and other distributed message systems. The World Wide Web allows users to store information on one computer server that can be located and retrieved by users connected to other servers located anywhere in the world. It is now estimated that 200 million people worldwide use the Internet (Lloyd 2000: 2), and every day hundreds of new World Wide Web sites are created.

The benefits the Internet brings, at least to those who have access to it, are immeasurable. Near-instantaneous global communication has accelerated the pace and enriched the content of scientific and academic discourse. The Internet has provided countless individuals and organizations with a historically unprecedented opportunity to communicate with a mass audience at relatively low cost. Moreover, the Internet has made it possible for computer users to form new relationships through various forms of interactive participation—relationships that are sometimes so strong that they engender a sense of "community" with other users sharing similar interests (Giordano 1998: para. 10). But the Internet is also an effective instrument for inflicting a wide range of societal harms. It makes possible the global dissemination of child pornography, fraudulent schemes, the messages of hate groups, and groundless defamatory allegations. National policymakers wishing to prevent these harms face unique problems caused by the technical characteristics of Internet communication.

In terms of infrastructure, the Internet is the first truly international medium of communication. The international dissemination of information, ideas, and entertainment is nothing new, of course. Companies from the United States and, to a lesser extent, other countries, have long sold, licensed, or distributed recorded music, television programming, and films to the rest of the world. Indeed, the dominant position of American companies in the international audiovisual market has given rise to fears that indigenous cultures throughout the world are being destroyed (actively or passively) by an onslaught of the sounds and images of American culture (e.g., Hirsch and Petersen 1992: 50). But while the distribution of the products of these older media has an international dimension, the infrastructures of such media are largely confined within national borders (Price 1994: 673). Borders have never been hermetically sealed, and broadcast and satellite transmissions have never fully respected national borders. But governments have been able to maintain a large degree of regulatory control over the distribution of media products within their borders, although some countries have felt compelled to resort to a greater degree of transnational regulation in recent years (e.g., European Commission 1989). With the Internet, however, the physical infrastructure of the medium itself is transnational. Material published on the Internet is immediately disseminated globally, traveling unpredictable routes through computer networks located throughout the world. This gives rise to daunting jurisdictional problems in the event that transborder disputes over Internet communications arise (see e.g., Johnson and Post 1996; Lessig 1996; Wilske and Schiller 1997).

Moreover, the Internet poses significant enforcement problems for national governments. Direct control over established forms of mass media is centralized in large public or private corporations, entities whose behavior can be effectively disciplined by actual or threatened civil or criminal sanctions, the traditional mechanisms of regulatory control available to national legal systems. In contrast, there is no central entity controlling the Internet that can be subjected to legal and extralegal pressures with the same effectiveness. Sometimes a message that violates the law of a country in which it has been disseminated is perfectly lawful in the country where the person who posted the message resides. Sometimes it is difficult to identify who is responsible for posting material that violates the laws of a country within which the material is distributed (Gringras 1997: 92). Sometimes, the person responsible for a harmful or unlawful use of the Internet lacks the resources to satisfy a civil judgment or criminal fine, limiting the effectiveness of the sanctions ordinarily used in democratic countries to discourage the misuse of communications systems. Often, even if the responsible party is identified and solvent, he or she resides outside the state and beyond the state's power to enforce its laws (Goldsmith 2000: 139).

Notwithstanding these jurisdictional and enforcement problems, however, there have been attempts by national governments to control the Internet. Some countries have applied preexisting legal principles to the new medium. In the United Kingdom, for instance, a university employee who used his employer's computers to disseminate images of child pornography was successfully prosecuted under child protection and antipornography statutes (*R. v. Fellows* 1997); the United States government ordered a public college to discontinue gender-specific discussion groups it sponsored because they violated federal antidiscrimination laws (Giordano 1998: paras. 41–46); Canadian authorities closed down a World Wide Web site containing anti-Semitic hate speech that violated Canada's human rights laws (Benzie 1997); the general manager of CompuServe Deutschland was prosecuted under Germany's antipornography laws for failing to block access to Internet sites containing pornographic images (Delacourt 1997: 212–215); and derogatory statements made on the Internet have given rise to defamation actions in Australia, the United Kingdom, and the United States (Vick, Macpherson, and Cooper 1999: 58).

In addition, national and local legislatures have debated and occasionally adopted new laws specifically directed at Internet communications. The best-known example is the Communications Decency Act (CDA) (1996), the first significant effort by the U.S. Congress to regulate the Internet. Among other things, the CDA criminalized the dissemination of obscene and indecent material on the Internet (47 U.S.C. section 223); outlawed the use of telecommunication devices to induce minors to engage in prostitution or other illegal sexual acts (amending 18 U.S.C. section 2422(b)); and encouraged private Internet Service Providers to restrict access to obscene, excessively violent, or "otherwise objectionable material" (47 U.S.C. section 230(c)).

Yet many commentators have concluded that such regulatory efforts at the national level can have only limited effect in deterring the misuse of the Internet. Internet communications are transnational and "borderless," they argue, and territorially bound governments cannot unilaterally control those who post and disseminate messages on the Internet if they are beyond the geographical limits of governmental jurisdiction. Nor can states indirectly control cross-border information flows, it is argued, without also blocking access to beneficial information that would otherwise be available to their citizens.

Various alternatives to a reliance on national regulation have been suggested. Johnson and Post propose that, for legal purposes, cyberspace should be considered a "place" distinct from geographically bound jurisdictions, and that an independent "law of cyberspace" should be developed and enforced by the "community of online users" and Internet Service Providers (1996: 1387). Most countries would resist this proposal, however, perhaps fearing that a "self-governance system" would be dominated by the United States, and in any event would regard such a system as exceptionally threatening to the sovereignty of national governments. A more traditional approach would be an international accord establishing a foundation of rules that could be enforced in all countries that agree to its terms. Commentators (e.g., Gigante 1996; Selin 1997; Soma et al. 1997; Zekos 1999) and official bodies such as the European Union's Council of Ministers (1997) have endorsed this approach. While not necessarily the most palatable option to strong nationalists, at least the states that are parties to such agreements have input into their content. Perhaps more importantly, the process of negotiating such an accord can be reconciled with traditional notions of national sovereignty. To see why this is, it is useful to examine the concept of "sovereignty" as it has been used in international law.

LEGAL CONCEPTIONS OF SOVEREIGNTY

International law regulates the relations of states, and the state lies at the foundation of legal conceptions of "sovereignty" (Zekos 1999). This is a fundamental reason why the state matters in discussions of globalization. The "first criterion" of statehood is a defined territory (Viotti and Kauppi 1993: 723–724); state boundaries are the primary means through which the extent of state power is circumscribed. It is impossible to talk about traditional conceptions of sovereignty without reference to physical territories bounded by defined borders, and it is unsurprising therefore that a "borderless" communications system like the Internet could be seen as a threat to sovereignty.

"Sovereignty," as that term is used legally, has both an internal and external dimension. Internally, sovereignty expresses the notion that the state and its institutions possess supreme authority within the state's borders. It is an axiom of classical international law that a sovereign state has exclusive authority over its territory and those who reside in it, and the basic functions of the state are to provide security, regulate economic activities, and "protect" civic and moral values (e.g., Hinsley 1966: 26). The principle that a state possesses exclusive authority within its boundaries is supplemented by the auxiliary principle of respect for the territorial integrity of states, which requires at a minimum that other states will not interfere with a sovereign state's internal affairs. In other words, the external dimension of sovereignty dictates that once a state's sovereignty has been recognized by other states in the international community, its ability to function as sovereign should not be undermined by the operation of another state's laws.

Some international relations theorists view the internal and external dimensions of sovereignty instrumentally, as a means of describing and rationalizing the allocation of power territorially. For example, the "realists" assume that states are the primary actors in the international system, that they act to maximize their power, and that the state's boundaries serve to confine state power (Viotti and Kauppi 1993: 35). A variation of this view is that states are vessels through which dominant social groups can legitimize their favored position internally and pursue their interests externally. Sovereignty is a mechanism through which elites within one territory maintain their power (internal) and negotiate with mutually recognized elites in other territories (external).

If this were all there is to the concept of sovereignty, the fact that certain cultural and economic forces (such as the Internet) are perceived to threaten it probably would not concern us greatly, except to the extent that such perceived threats might lead to political instability or political violence. But another conception of sovereignty might provide reasons other than the fear of intranational and international hostilities for considering sovereignty something worthy of respect and protection. A representational conception of sovereignty holds that the state is a "stand-in" for the autonomy and self-determinism of the individuals (collectively) who are citizens of the state. Put another way, "[t]he sovereignty of the state is derived from its utility to express the sovereignty of the individual" (Zekos 1999). In this view, the state exists through the "consent" of its citizens; the state represents the general will of its populace; and state sovereignty really represents the notion that the people of the state have the right to decide their internal political, economic, cultural, and moral policies (e.g., Viotti and Kauppi 1993; *Harvard Law Review* 1999: 1686–1687). Sovereignty, viewed this way, carries responsibilities along with power, including the responsibility of the state's institutions to be representative of and accountable to the state's citizens (*Harvard Law Review* 1999: 1687).

While the principle of noninterference requires that one state will not directly interfere with the internal affairs of another state—say, by imposing its culturally specific values on those residing in other states—it is well established that a state's unilateral actions pursuing its internal interests may indirectly affect other states without violating fundamental precepts of international law. A state's power to make laws that apply to matters that affect it subsumes the power to regulate "conduct outside its territory that has or is intended to have substantial effect within its territory" (Restatement 1987: section 402(1)(b)), a power subject to the territorial limits of the state's ability to compel compliance with its laws. Unilateral national regulations can have "spillover effects" on the regulatory efforts of other nations (Goldsmith 2000: 142). For example, when a prosecutor in Bavaria threatened to prosecute CompuServe Deutschland officials for allowing its German customers access to postings in discussion groups that violated German antipornography laws, CompuServe's immediate reaction was to block access to the discussion groups in Germany, which effectively blocked access to those discussion groups for CompuServe's customers throughout the world. But this nonetheless was a legitimate exercise of state power under international law: "There is no legal principle that requires Germany to yield local control over its territory in order to accommodate the users of the Internet in other countries" (Goldsmith 2000: 145). Absent some international agreement harmonizing relevant law, spillover effects are always a potential consequence of a state's unilateral actions.

Nonetheless, when activities within one sovereign state affect the internal affairs of others, tensions invariably arise. Sometimes these activities are perceived as threats to the sovereignty of the state affected by them. There have always been such perceived threats, resulting from cross-border trade, cross-border capital flows, and cross-border flows of cultural products, among other things (e.g., Chalmers 2000: 196–197; Ohmae 1995). These perceived threats can give rise to disputes that can, in extreme cases, boil over into military conflict or a trade war. The preferred method for easing tensions caused by spillover effects is negotiation between states, which can yield formal treaties and international accords, or informal understandings, regulatory targets, agreements to share information, and the like. In theory, the process of negotiating affirms the notion that states are "equals"—equal participants in the negotiating process—and act autonomously in deciding whether to sign on to particular proposed agreements. To negotiate implies mutual "recognition" among the negotiating states, and "[a] decision to recognize something carries with it an implicit duty of respect, as an autonomy, capacity, and responsibility for action is accorded to the person or body recognized" (Chalmers 2000: 213). In light of this, it is unsurprising that the French Conseil d'Etat recently urged an international debate about the regulation of the Internet as a necessary means of preserving European ideals of cultural diversity and human rights (see Mayer 2000: 150).

From the perspective of most governments outside the United States, the primary impediment to meaningful international negotiation on Internet regulation could be the First Amendment to the United States Constitution. The Constitution is paramount in the hierarchy of the U.S. legal system, and U.S. officials lack the power to enter into international agreements that would violate the First Amendment. To most Americans (and many others), this may not seem such a bad thing. Virtually all of the countries of the world formally recognize freedom of speech as a fundamental principle of their legal regimes; if the terms of a treaty must comply with this principle, this hardly seems an unreasonable or particularly onerous burden. But this argument ignores the socially constructed nature of "freedom of speech."

THE CULTURAL CONTINGENCY OF FREEDOM OF SPEECH

There are good "first-order" reasons (that is, reasons that at first blush seem compelling) that officials in open, democratic countries might wish to control what is communicated on the Internet. Policymakers could reasonably conclude that serious societal harms are caused by the electronic dissemination of pornographic images, hate speech, deceptive claims, and the like. But, as Frederick Schauer has said, there are often "second-order reasons for refraining from doing what we have good first-order reasons to do." Some policy choices that are otherwise desirable may threaten "larger or more enduring structural, moral, or political values" that are elevated to a preferred status within particular legal systems (Schauer 1993: 865–866). These values are frequently found imbedded in the state's constitutional law.

The modern constitution is among the institutions that legitimize, and thus are most closely associated with, the notion of a state's sovereignty (Chalmers 2000: 179). The constitution is foundational law that sets out the fundamental principles and objectives of the political community, distributes the administrative power for achieving these objectives, and constrains this administrative power within defined boundaries. In many legal systems, constitutional rules have the immediate effect of invalidating the actions of the legislative or administrative branches of government, and at first may seem inconsistent with traditional conceptions of sovereignty. But constitutional rules can be seen as mechanisms for the assertion of a society's more fundamental second-order values, and at least within the representational conception of sovereignty, this can be seen to reaffirm and strengthen the state's sovereign power.

A constitutional rule has effect, however, only if events occur that are perceived to fall within a larger set of hypothetical factual scenarios that require invocation of the rule. In this way, Schauer argues, constitutional decision making turns on a "process of descriptive generalization" whereby certain acts or events fall inside or outside of the set of hypothetical situations that define the relevant "constitutional categories" in particular legal systems (1993: 867).

Schauer illustrates the point by reference to the free speech clause of the U.S. Constitution. Despite the First Amendment's seemingly unequivocal language prohibiting governmental interference with speech, civil and criminal sanctions are often imposed on Americans who say what the government has found to be the wrong thing to say, or refuse to say what the government has required them to say. The Securities Act of 1933, which Schauer describes as "an elaborate system of communication control" (1993: 872, n.41), requires the disclosure and registration of a wide range of sensitive information; the Sherman Antitrust Act outlaws certain forms of "pure" speech (Schauer 1989: 563); perjury, conspiracy, solicitation, and misrepresentation laws directly punish speech (Greenawalt 1990: 132, 239–280, 315–321); the language used on package labels can be the basis for a successful product liability suit (Schauer 1997: 700); and the Federal Trade Commission frequently restricts speech in order to prevent misleading advertising or other deceptive practices (e.g., 15 U.S.C. section 45 et seq.). Such provisions offend neither the First Amendment doctrine developed by the Supreme Court nor the less formal appreciation held by most U.S. citizens of what freedom of speech means. In sum, even in countries like the United States where a broadly libertarian understanding of free speech is embraced there remains "a wide range of communicative activities [that] are generally considered to have, quite simply, nothing whatsoever to do with the constitutionally relevant category of freedom of speech" (Schauer 1993: 872).

Moreover, whether a set of facts triggers application of a constitutional rule is not always determined simply by reference to the "plain meaning" of the relevant constitutional text. For example, freedom of speech is a constitutional category "set out with more or less equivalent [linguistic] indeterminacy in all of the world's constitutional documents" (Schauer 1993: 868). No country has adopted constitutional provisions that define the specific contours of free speech and how it is to be interpreted in the context of specific factual scenarios (Schauer 1993: 871). Certainly, the textual language of constitutional provisions protecting free speech varies from country to country. Some constitutions use unqualified language prohibiting governmental interference with speech; the constitutions of Algeria, Syria, Tanzania, and the United States articulate the right in similarly unequivocal language (see Blaustein and Flanz 1999: Binders I and XVIII). Other constitutions couch the right in broad language but carve out specific exceptions. For example, the Canadian Charter of Rights and Freedoms guarantees "freedom of thought, belief, opinion and expression, including freedom of the press and other media of communication," but this freedom is subject to "such reasonable limits prescribed by law as can be demonstrably justified in a free and democratic society" (Blaustein and Flanz 1999: Binder IV). Similarly, the constitution of Denmark provides that "any person shall be entitled to publish his thoughts in printing, in writing, and in speech," but that anyone so doing might be "held answerable (after publication) in a court of justice" (Blaustein and Flanz 1999: Binder V). The Irish Constitution protects "the right of the citizens to express freely their convictions and opinions," but subject to the state's power "to ensure that organs of public opinion, such as the radio, the press, the cinema . . . shall not be used to undermine public order or morality or authority of the state" and to punish "blasphemous, seditious, or indecent matter" (Blaustein and Flanz 1999: Binder IX). But these textual differences do not explain differences in how freedom of speech is interpreted in various countries: There is little reason to suppose that the degree of freedom of speech under the equivocally worded constitutions of

Canada and Denmark is any less extensive than under the unqualified provisions of the constitutions of Syria or Algeria. Indeed, the First Amendment has never been interpreted by a majority of the Justices of the Supreme Court as an absolute bar to regulation, even when the Court recognizes that a particular action implicates free speech concerns. Thus, "the detailed explication of the categories 'free speech' or 'free expression' or 'freedom of opinion' or 'freedom of the press' must come from other than even the closest reading of constitutional text" (Schauer 1993: 871).

This textual indeterminacy contributes to fundamental differences within and among nations as to what protecting free speech requires in specific factual situations. This is starkly illustrated by comparing the application of the free speech principle in the United States with how the principle is applied elsewhere. When the private interests of speakers come into conflict with the interests of the state, the United States is the most speech-protective country in the world (Schauer 1992: 857). The Supreme Court interpreted the First Amendment to bar government efforts to prevent the wartime publication of the confidential Pentagon Papers, even though the documents may have been obtained illegally and arguably threatened national security (*New York Times v. United States* 1971). Even in an open democracy like the United Kingdom, the Official Secrets Acts of 1911 and 1989 would permit suppression in circumstances paralleling the Pentagon Papers case, and the approach taken in the United Kingdom is the rule, not the exception. Most countries also prohibit the publication of information potentially prejudicial to judicial proceedings until after those proceedings have ended; the Supreme Court has found such sub judice rules unconstitutional in the United States (*Nebraska Press Ass'n v. Stuart* 1976). Laws prohibiting disclosure of the identity of rape victims or juvenile offenders—which are commonplace in Europe and elsewhere—raise serious constitutional concerns in the United States (e.g., *Florida Star v. B.J.F.* 1989; *Smith v. Daily Mail Publishing Co.* 1979). The First Amendment prohibits the state from punishing the dissemination of obscene material unless a court finds that the material is wholly lacking "serious literary, artistic, political, or scientific value" (*Miller v. California* 1973: 24); many countries use a much broader definition for obscene material, which can be proscribed by the state (e.g., Obscene Publications Act 1959 [U.K.]). Many democratic countries prohibit the publication of material inciting ethnic, racial, or religious hatred (e.g., Stein 1986), and indeed such laws may be required by the terms of the Universal Declaration of Human Rights (United Nations 1948) and the Convention on the Elimination of All Forms of Racial Discrimination (United Nations 1965); in the United States, however, "hate speech" laws would be difficult to reconcile with established Supreme Court precedents (e.g., *R.A.V. v. City of St. Paul* 1992; *National Socialist Party v. Village of Skokie* 1977). Peter B. White's chapter in this book provides other examples of differences between and within Western countries about what communications are considered offensive.

The different interpretations of what free speech means in different contexts may reflect, at least in part, different views on why states should protect free speech in the first place. As Cole Durham (1993: 898) observed, "[f]or every explicit norm in a legal culture there are countless unstated and buried norms that help explicate and qualify its meaning." With regard to the free speech principle, various justifications have been proffered for placing constitutional limits on the power of governmental institutions. Some arguments focus on the benefits free speech brings to society at large: It is said to advance the search for truth (e.g., Marshall 1995; Greenawalt 1989: 130–141; Schauer 1982: 15–34); promote effective participatory democracy (e.g., Meiklejohn 1948; Schauer 1982: 35–46); provide checks on the power of the governing classes (e.g., Blasi 1977; Greenawalt 1989: 142); and encourage tolerance (Bollinger 1986) and the use of nonviolent means to achieve political or social change (e.g., Emerson 1970: 7; Greenawalt 1989: 141–42; Schauer 1982: 75–80). Other arguments focus more directly on the interests of individuals in society, emphasizing that free speech is a necessary precondition for individual autonomy and self-realization (e.g., Wells 1997; Strauss 1991; Wellington 1979; Scanlon 1972). These arguments presuppose that the state "has no dominion over our minds: what we believe, what we are persuaded to believe, and (derivatively) what others may try to persuade us to believe" (Fried 1992: 233). Differing views about which arguments are more important in various factual scenarios can yield different conclusions about whether a particular action violates or does not violate the free speech principle.

But this merely begs the question of how these differences come about. Schauer suggests that each society's relevant constitutional categories are defined in large part by "cultural constructs that determine what events will be considered members of what class" (1993: 867). These cultural constructs vary from time to time and place to place, and "cultural differences in the categorization of social and political acts may produce large differences in the shape of the constitutional constraints that are dependent on the products of that categorization" (1993: 867).

To illustrate this point, Schauer compares the legal treatment of hate speech by neo-Nazis in the United States and Germany. In the United States, the First Amendment forbids the government from stopping Nazis from marching through neighborhoods inhabited by Holocaust survivors (*National Socialist Party v. Village of Skokie* 1977). In Germany, such "expressive activities" are unlawful; indeed, it is a crime to deny that the Holocaust happened (Stein 1986). The U.S. Supreme Court resists restrictions on extremist groups like the Nazis or the KKK because the history of government efforts to suppress speech links these groups with other marginalized members of society who may be more sympathetic (socialist union leaders, radical pamphleteers, and the like) (see Durham 1993: 894). Suppress the rights of Nazis, an American might argue, and it could be the thin edge of the wedge leading to the suppression of all dissenting voices. In Germany, naturally, Nazis hold a different position in the collective consciousness. The possibility that "restricting Nazis will lead to restricting, say, Greens, is too remote to worry about" (Schauer 1993: 878). Schauer observes that "for Germans it appears that the likelihood that restricting Nazis will lead to restricting Greens is equivalent to the possibility in the United States that requiring the pre-registration of securities sales documents under the Securities Act of 1933 will lead to the precensorship of the utterances of fundamentalist Christians like Jerry Falwell or left-wing social critics like Noam Chomsky" (Schauer 1993: 879).

If differences in the scope of free speech protection in different societies reflect variations in the political, social, and cultural experiences of those societies, there are likely to be powerful pressures resisting a cross-cultural "assimilation" of the U.S. conception of free speech. In connection with transnational communications over the Internet, this is of profound importance. To the extent that American constitutionalism thrusts the values underlying U.S. free speech doctrines onto the Internet community, the sovereignty of other nations is arguably threatened.

EXPORTING THE FIRST AMENDMENT?

The U.S. Supreme Court addressed the free speech rights of Americans using the Internet in *Reno v. American Civil Liberties Union* (1997). *Reno* involved a legal challenge to the validity of two provisions of the controversial Communications Decency Act (1996). The first provision imposed criminal penalties on persons who transmit indecent material over the Internet with the knowledge that the material could be viewed by minors (47 U.S.C. section223(a)). The second provision made it a criminal offense to use "an interactive computer service" to expose minors to depictions of "sexual or excretory activities or organs" that are "patently offensive as measured by contemporary community standards" (47 U.S.C. section 223(d)). A person who allowed others to use a "telecommunications facility under his control" to transmit material in violation of these provisions could also be prosecuted.

The Supreme Court determined that these provisions violated the First Amendment because they were too vague and worded too broadly, effectively suppressing categories of speech that were beyond the regulatory power of the government (*Reno* 1997: 870–879). The terms "indecent" and "patently offensive," for example, were deemed too imprecise, and thus could deter expression that did not fall within the class of material the act was designed to restrict, such as "non-pornographic material with serious educational or other value" (*Reno* 1997: 877). More important than the specific holding of the case, however, was the Supreme Court's indication that its strictest constitutional test would be applied to future government efforts to regulate the content of Internet communications. While the Court has permitted the government a greater degree of latitude in regulating broadcasting than it has in regulating other media, ostensibly for technical reasons (e.g., *Red Lion Broadcasting Co. v. FCC* 1969), it clearly stated in *Reno* that a similarly lenient approach would not be taken with regard to the Internet (*Reno* 1997: 868–870). This means that it is likely that the Supreme Court's most libertarian First Amendment precedents invalidating government regulation of speech will be extended to the Internet.

The problem for policymakers outside the United States is that material that offends the laws of other countries can be (and often is) posted on the Internet from the United States and immediately disseminated internationally. One proposal for addressing the problems caused by this international transmission of harmful material is an international treaty establishing a comprehensive body of common rules for regulating Internet content. For such an agreement to be effective, the United States must be a signatory, because the United States remains the source of most of the material available on the Internet. In the hierarchy of American law, however, the Constitution is supreme law and a treaty provision is inferior to it; thus, a treaty would be unenforceable within the United States if it fails to conform with the requirements of the First Amendment (Henkin 1996; Vazquez 1999: 2177).

This does not foreclose altogether the negotiation of international agreements concerning Internet content regulations: Some areas of the law—intellectual property law, for example, and the laws prohibiting misleading advertising and child pornography—are largely unaffected by First Amendment doctrine because they involve factual situations that do not implicate important free speech issues in U.S. legal culture. But a wide range of communicative activity that does implicate the U.S. conception of freedom of speech would be beyond the reach of an effective international agreement simply by virtue of the unenforceability of such an agreement within the United States. Yet, it is unlikely that an international agreement that merely memorializes the doctrines of U.S. free speech law will satisfy many nations seeking more far-reaching measures against the misuses of the Internet (see Vick 1998).

Practically, this means that governments outside the United States that wish to exercise greater control over the Internet cannot simply rely on the most obvious method of deterring abuses—regulating such communications at their source by making those who create and post harmful messages legally responsible for the harms they cause. Those persons often reside in the United States and have been largely immunized by the *Reno* decision. But this does not mean that states are powerless to devise other strategies for controlling Internet content. As Goldsmith (2000: 135–137) observed, those who thought otherwise underestimated the resiliency of territorial sovereignty. As noted above, international law permits a state to regulate the harmful local effects of conduct occurring outside its territory, and most states have opted to regulate content transmitted from abroad indirectly.

Several strategies have been pursued. One option has been to impose greater legal obligations on the locally based companies and institutions that provide Internet access to users. These obligations have ranged from merely requiring access providers to warn users that access to certain material available on the Internet is unlawful in certain countries to making access providers civilly or criminally responsible for harms caused by the material passing through their computer systems unless they take steps to screen out offensive material. Another option, which has been advocated by the European Union's Council of Ministers (1997), has been to attempt to "empower" individual users to avoid exposure to unwanted messages and images through the use of computer software that can block access to Internet sites that have been identified as sources of pornographic or other pernicious material. A closely related strategy is to encourage some "neutral" arbiter—for instance, service providers or parents' associations—to "rate" Internet sites based on the level of profanity, sexual content, or other potentially offensive content available at those sites, leaving it to consumers to choose whether they want access to sites given particular ratings. Specific examples of these strategies—and their practical limitations—are discussed in Peter B. White's chapter in this volume concerning Australia's efforts to regulate Internet content.

There are more restrictive options available, of course. States can regulate the "in-state hardware and software" that make Internet communications possible (Goldsmith 2000: 137). Some states, such as North Korea, Iraq, and Libya, have not allowed their citizens access to the Internet at all; some, such as Belarus and Sudan, maintain a government monopoly over computer servers; and some, like China, require all users of computers linked to the Internet to register with the government (Mayer 2000: 161). More ominously, governments that for political or religious reasons do not want to allow exposure to certain material may make it a crime for citizens to access such material, perhaps enforcing such laws by encouraging snooping or snitching.

In short, states can do many things that "make the domestic side of Internet transactions more expensive," in economic or noneconomic terms, and "thereby indirectly regulat[e] the extraterritorial source of the offending content" (Goldsmith 2000: 137–138). But this approach is an incomplete, and in many respects unsatisfactory, substitute for international cooperation. The process of negotiation forces nations to take into account how their unilateral actions affect other states, as well as the values within those states that may be compromised by such unilateral actions (see Mayer 2000: 168–169). Moreover, as one European observer noted, "international Internet governance—multilateralism—is the only way for Europeans to effectively reduce the indirect unilateral US dominance of Internet regulation" (Mayer 2000: 169).

From the perspective of the United States, the issues implicated in First Amendment cases like *Reno* are primarily issues of domestic law concerning the constitutional limits on the power of the U.S. government to control the content of Internet communications. Yet the resolution of these issues within the United States has unintended but nonetheless potentially profound political and cultural consequences for other countries linked to the Internet. If a law is justifiable only if it conforms to the sensibilities of the majority of those who must live under it, the "exportation" of the U.S. conception of free speech through the Internet gives rise to serious questions of legitimacy. Yochai Benkler (2000: 174) has observed that the "incorporation of the values of one nation into the technology of communication shared by many displaces those of other nations, while a nation that refrains from such incorporation is exposed to communications that implement the values of another." Other countries have no say in what free speech means in the United States, and to the extent that that meaning is imposed on them, their ability to control what goes on within their own borders, an essential attribute of sovereignty, is diminished.

2

Where the National Meets the Global: Australia's Internet Censorship Policies

Peter B. White

In August 1999, Professor Nadine Strossen, the president of the American Civil Liberties Union, described Australia's Internet censorship laws as "draconian and repressive" and portrayed Australia as the "the global village idiot." She argued that Australia's Internet censorship laws were vague, relied on the values of those enforcing them, and that the laws should be reversed. She said that there was no way of drawing a distinction between what should and shouldn't be banned that was meaningful and coherent. Rather the government should allow each individual to decide exactly what it is that he or she doesn't want to see. According to Strossen the argument that children had to be protected from some Internet material—one heavily depended on by the Australian government to support its laws—had been rejected by the U.S. Supreme Court. She said that Internet censorship technology is such that you cannot censor the Internet for children without censoring it for everybody (Colson 1999).

This chapter examines how a liberal democratic nation such as Australia could develop an Internet censorship regime that can be described in this way, and why the state matters in terms of Australia's Internet censorship policies. The chapter reviews the background to Australia's Internet censorship regime, describes the regulatory framework itself, places the emergence of that regime in its domestic sociopolitical context, and considers its relationship to current debates about globalization of the media and the changing role of the state.

THE REGULATORY REGIME

Before I describe Australia's Internet censorship regime, it is important to note that Australians do not have a constitutional guarantee of freedom of speech. While censorship in Australia has been liberalized in the last thirty years, a federal government agency, the Office of Film and Literature Classification (OFLC), plays an active role in censorship of films, computer games, and publications. The bulk of censorship activity involves classifying films, video, and television programs to determine the allowable ages of audiences for cinema release and the times when television programs can be broadcast. The outright banning of materials usually relates to films and video programs containing sexually explicit materials or dealing with violence or minors. So Australia's Internet censorship regime emerges from a context of general acceptance of government involvement in censorship.

The Australian regulation of online content requires that Internet Service Providers (ISPs) provide users with tools to enable Internet filtering and with information about the ways that individuals can take control over the content of online services that are accessible in their homes. According to the Internet Industry Association (IIA) this strategy is designed to provide "industry facilitated user empowerment" that gives users choice and control over the way that they deal with the content of online services. The other component of the regulatory regime requires that ISPs and Internet Content Hosts (ICHs) provide access to approved PC-based and network-based filtering systems. Of the sixteen filtering products and services listed in the ABA-approved IIA Code of Practice, only one originates from Australia. In addition ICHs must "take down" any material that has been the subject of a complaint to the Australian Broadcasting Authority (ABA) and that the ABA has ruled to be in breach of Australian law (Internet Industry Association 2000, 1999b). Essentially the regulatory regime deals with the access to, the provision of, and the distribution of online content.

To deal with controlling access to online content, the regulatory regime requires that ISPs and ICHs take reasonable steps to ensure that Internet access accounts are not provided to children under the age of eighteen without the consent of a parent or a responsible adult. In practice this means that ISPs must rely on the use of credit cards for opening accounts, require that applications for Internet access accounts be accompanied by identification attesting to the age of the applicant, and place prominent notices on packaging of Internet accounts that advise that accounts are not to be accessed by persons under the age of eighteen without the permission of parents or teachers or responsible adults (Internet Industry Association 1999a). In addition, ISPs must provide users with information about the desirability of supervising children's Internet access, the nature of Internet labeling systems and how Internet content–filtering software can be used to control children's access to certain kinds of content. ISPs also provide users with lists of approved filtering software that will filter material deemed to be illegal by the ABA (Internet Industry Association 1999b).

The provision and distribution of Internet content by Australian individuals and organizations using Australian ISPs is controlled by a requirement that ISPs inform their subscribers that the publication of material on the Internet could have legal consequences in Australia. ISPs are also required to encourage content providers to use appropriate labeling systems when content is likely to be unsuitable for children. If the ABA classifies content as "prohibited," the ICH must take down that material and inform the customers who placed that material on the system that their material has been defined as prohibited content or potential prohibited content and, as a consequence, is in breach of the law and their customer service conditions (Internet Industry Association 1999b).

Further, ISPs must advise subscribers that they have the right to complain to the ABA if they believe that an ISP is providing access to materials that could be defined as either prohibited content or potentially prohibited content. Subscribers must be advised how such a complaint can be made. The complaints procedure covers materials hosted by Australian-based ICHs as well as materials that are located internationally but which are accessible through an Australian ISP. ISPs must make approved filtering software or a network-based filtering service available to their subscribers. The providers of approved filtering software or network-based services must comply with directives of the ABA when it identifies prohibited content material. That material must be blocked by the filtering software or service. ISPs are not obliged to provide access to a network-based filtering service to schools, educational, or other institutions if they advise their ISPs that they have created an arrangement that will provide a reasonably effective means of preventing access to prohibited content (Internet Industry Association 1999b).

ORIGINS OF THE LEGISLATION

In 1995 the Minister for Communications and the Arts directed the ABA to conduct an investigation into the nature of online information and entertainment services and to consider an appropriate regulatory regime for online services (Australian Broadcasting Authority n.d.). The ABA presented its report to the minister in July 1997 and the key recommendations were that online service providers should develop substantially self-regulatory regimes for the regulation of the contents of online services, complaints-handling procedures, a content-labeling scheme compatible with the Platform of Internet Content Selection, and community education projects that emphasize the benefits of online services. Subsequently the Minister for Communications and the Arts and the Australian Attorney General announced a set of principles that were to underpin the regulation of online services. The key principle was that "material access through online services should not be subject to a more onerous regulatory framework than 'off-line' material such as books, videos, films and computer games" (Australian Broadcasting Authority n.d.).

In August 1997 the minister asked the ABA to extend its previous work and the ABA convened a Children and Content On-Line Task Force. Key recommendations made by the task force in its June 1998 report were that children should be encouraged to use the Internet and their exposure to unsuitable material online should be minimized, parents should be responsible for determining the appropriateness of content for children though direct supervision in the home, and the use of filtering and rating systems should be encouraged when adult supervision of children was not possible. Also, the task force proposed that filtering software and content-labeling and rating systems should not create a significant barrier to the expression of opinions and content and their use should be voluntary for users and content providers (Australian Broadcasting Authority n.d.).

These recommendations formed the basis of the Broadcasting Services Amendment (Online Services) Bill (1999), which was first referred to and approved by the Senate Select Committee on Information Technologies in May 1999. The passage of this legislation has been attributed to the position of an independent and conservative senator, Brian Harradine, who was also a member of the Senate Select Committee. Senator Harradine's religious and moral stance had resulted in him championing family issues and opposing abortion and any form of birth control (Grubel 1999). His conservative views of the Internet were apparent when he said:

> Never before in history have the purveyors of a debased culture had direct access to the minds of young people online. . . . The public and parents in particular will not accept the lame excuse that cleaning up the Internet is technically too difficult. . . . Information technologists and the Internet industry would quickly come up with technological ways to efficiently remove offensive material if given a regulatory incentive for doing so. (Mathieson and Hamilton 1998)

So in May 1999, when the government needed Senator Harradine's support for the partial privatization of Telstra, the government-owned telecommunications carrier, Senator Harradine held the balance of power in the Senate. While the communications minister denied any link, following discussions between the minister and Senator Harradine, the government announced that it would introduce legislation to regulate Internet content as well as regulate telephone-based sex lines (Mathieson and Hamilton 1998). Subsequently Senator Harradine supported the partial privatization of Telstra. Following the passage of the Internet censorship legislation, Senator Harradine said that while the Internet legislation was not without fault, it was a step in the right direction. He stated that the government should be absolutely congratulated for trying to do something about the Internet and that the communications minister had done a sterling job (AAP Newsfeed 1999).

RESPONSES

The Internet censorship legislation was condemned by Senator Mark Bishop from the opposition Labor Party and Senator Natasha Stott Despoja, the information technology spokeswoman for the Australian Democrats Party. They argued that the legislation was unworkable because it was unable to control material that was hosted offshore. Senator Stott Despoja said the legislation was drawn up in haste to satisfy the conservative Senator Harradine and to secure his vote on other bills (AAP Newsfeed 1999).

Electronic Frontiers Australia, which is a member organization of the Global Internet Liberty Campaign (GILC), argued that it was an error to involve the Australian Broadcasting Authority—the national broadcasting authority—in Internet censorship, and that the use of censorship classifications applicable to film and video were major weaknesses in the legislation. EFA board member Danny Yee stated, "An underlying assumption of the Bill is that the Internet is a form of television. The vast bulk of online content will continue to be text and graphics, and rating this as if it were video will result in publications sold without restriction in book shops being illegal online" (Creed 1999). He argued that using the Internet was more like visiting a library or using a telephone and that Australia could not hope to take advantage of the opportunities afforded by the Internet while it had a government that insisted on forcing it into a totally inappropriate mold.

GILC supported the EFA position and argued, "The filtering and blocking regime that has been announced by the Australian government will restrict freedom of expression and limit access to information. Government-mandated use of blocking and filtering systems violates basic international human rights protections" (Creed 1999).

Australia's new Internet censorship regime was universally condemned by libertarian groups prior to its implementation. But what were some of the practical consequences of the new legislation?

CONSEQUENCES OF THE LEGISLATION

The most obvious response of a content provider whose material has been targeted by a take-down order issued by the ABA would be to move offshore. In fact within eighteen days of the legislation taking effect, a Web site containing pornographic images relocated to the United States after it had been served an order (Creed 2000a). The operators of a Web site at http://

www.teenager.com.au posted notices on the site that said, "The Australian Broadcasting Authority (ABA) is satisfied that Internet content hosted at http://www.teenager.com.au/pics.html, being a page containing depictions of female nudity and actual sexual activity . . . is Prohibited Content" (Creed 2000a).

The company was given until the end of the next business day to take down the site. But taking down the site involved the owners relocating the entire Web site to a hosting service located in the United States, where it was accessible under the same domain name and URL. This meant that for an Internet user, there was no noticeable change (Creed 2000a). Given that the Web site was now outside the jurisdiction of the ABA there was no longer anything that the ABA could do apart from notifying the manufacturers of approved filters that this site should be blocked in their filtering software. Since Australian Internet users who were not using a filtering service would still have direct access to the site and would not notice any difference when it was relocated to the United States it is interesting to consider the ultimate significance of ABA take-down orders.

One way of explaining the policy is to see it as an example of the "not in my backyard" syndrome. Normally this refers to attempts by citizens and governments to ensure that activities that they consider to be offensive are not allowed to operate in their immediate environment. While toxic waste and other potential environmental pollutants are often a necessary by-product of manufacturing activities, political energies are frequently directed toward ensuring that the nuisance is located elsewhere. Is the Australian legislative regime an example of this approach?

If users still have access to targeted Web sites that have been found by the ABA to have prohibited content, does relocating Web sites that are believed to be offensive do anything more than express moral outrage or distaste? Unless there is international agreement on appropriate action against offensive Web sites the relocation option will be used by content providers. And, as is detailed in Douglas Vick's chapter in this volume, given the diversity of legal structures and views on censorship internationally, there is little chance that any coordinated international action will occur. Apart from some minor irritation to content providers, the Australian legislation merely moves content hosting out of the country and beyond legislative reach.

THE COMPLAINTS SCHEME EXPERIENCE

The Australian Internet content complaints scheme commenced operation on January 1, 2000, and the ABA reported that in the first three months it received 124 complaints (Australian Broadcasting Authority 2000). Three were deemed to be frivolous, and in ninety-nine cases the investigations had been completed. Thirty-five of the investigations dealt with items that contained prohibited or potentially prohibited content. With prohibited or potentially prohibited content hosted in Australia the ABA issued take-down notices to the ICH; for material hosted outside Australia the ABA sent details to the manufacturers of approved software-filtering products and in some instances to law enforcement agencies.

In February 2000, using the provisions of the Freedom of Information Act (FOI) Electronic Frontiers Australia (EFA) requested that the ABA provide details of the Internet sites that had been the subject of complaints and the outcomes of the ABA's investigations. As the FOI legislation allows government agencies to charge for the time and resources required in responding to a request, the ABA advised that providing that information would cost A\$4,600 (U.S.\$2,816), because it involved 220 hours of agency time to examine and decide which documents could be made public (Creed 2000b).

The EFA objected to the estimate of costs and requested they be reassessed or waived. They argued that "[t]he process of assessing complaints about Internet content should be open and accountable. . . . With other forms of media censorship, in relation to films, videos, publications and computer games, the outcomes of classification decisions are openly available to the public at no cost in the online database of the Office of Film and Literature Classification." The EFA also said, "The public interest is not served when decisions about Internet content are made in secret, and the process will be greeted with even greater suspicion if our attempt to obtain details of these decisions is stymied by exorbitant charges" (Creed 2000b).

The ABA rejected the EFA request to waive the fees, the EFA modified its request, and the ABA commenced processing the application. In its response the ABA advised that it would need to consult with "third parties" before releasing the details of the take-down notices because release of that information could have an adverse effect on those persons (Electronic Frontiers Australia 2000). Given that the ABA was operating with the protection of the law it seems unusual that the "publishers" of material subject to take-down orders had to be consulted before the details of the take-down order were made public. If the take-down order process was to have any educational value, publicizing take-down orders could have the dual benefit of confirming that the regulator was active and sensitizing parents to the potential risks associated with children's unsupervised access to the Internet.

But given the relative novelty of the complaints scheme it is not possible to make a definitive judgment about its effects. The initial level of complaints does not seem to be very great given the penetration of the Internet in Australia, but this could be attributable to the novelty of the scheme and a lack of knowledge about it. When Internet users become more familiar with the complaints procedures there could be an increase in the number of complaints. An ongoing low level of complaints could be used to support a number of quite different positions about the desirability of the Australian scheme. One argument could be that this is evidence that there is little public concern about the content of the Internet and that the elaborate regulatory framework and enforcement regimes are unnecessary.

Other issues arise from the implementation of the Internet censorship policy. The OFLC, which classifies films, computer games, and published materials, operates in the public domain. As the EFA noted in objecting to the cost estimates for fulfilling its FOI request, details of OFLC decisions are open to public scrutiny without the need for FOI requests. In contrast, the ABA-run Internet censorship scheme operates largely in private and access to its operation relies on the use of the FOI process. The Internet regulator appears to be less accountable than the censor of Australian films, computer games, and publications.

INTERNATIONALIZATION OF AUSTRALIAN CENSORSHIP

By mandating that the use of filtering systems be promoted, the Australian government has shifted control of filtering functions to the largely U.S. providers of those services. While the approved services adhere to the ABA's decisions on particular Internet sites, their filtering processes deal with a far wider range of content. In effect the Australian government has delegated its censorship processes to private-sector organizations located outside Australia. But a recent study has revealed that there are quite significant differences about what is considered offensive in developed Western countries (Bertelsmann Foundation 1999). For example in a study by the Bertelsmann Foundation, the identification of content that was offensive and might create a danger for children differed in Germany, the United States, and Australia.

According to the study's authors the definitions of what was seen to be offensive were influenced by national culture, religious beliefs, political ideas, and the individual's socialization and sensitivity. While there was a reasonable consensus on the need to block racist messages and pornographic messages, the definition of what would count as pornographic differed. For example, nudity was not considered to be offensive by many Germans (13 percent) but 43 percent of Americans considered it to be offensive. On the other hand, the German population is more offended by obscene language, which is considered to be less disturbing by some, particularly Americans. Understandably Germans were especially sensitive to the presentation of radical right-wing or left-wing content on the Internet. Approximately 58 percent of Germans found politically radical material offensive but only 26 percent of Americans saw that material as offensive. The depiction of violence is also considered much more problematic in Germany than in the other two countries. Sixty-one percent of the German, 39 percent of the American, and 41 percent of the Australian populations consider violence to be such a problem that they would block it from the Internet (Bertelsmann Foundation 1999: 19).

These figures show that there are differences among Western democratic countries. And while those differences have been identifiable geographically in the past, technologies such as the Internet make it possible to assemble audiences of like-minded people regardless of their geographical location. So in a country such as the United States where access to the Internet is relatively widespread, it is possible to assemble audiences and services for groups with distinct constellations of views. It is highly likely that filtering services oriented to specific constellations of values will be established. It is possible to imagine the emergence of filtering services designed to meet the needs of all varieties of extremist groups.

Encouraging Australian Internet users to rely on filtering services provided by U.S. corporations without adequate consumer information that describes the nature of the filtering rules being applied raises a number of problems. How are Internet users able to discover what is being filtered beyond the sites mandated by the ABA? For example, ifilter/N2H2, one of the approved Internet-filtering services, provides "teachers, parents and employers the ability to turn on and off more than 40 Internet categories (e.g. pornography, auction sites) to fit the objectives, beliefs or comfort zones of users and [a search engine that] effectively weeds out harmful or distracting search results" (N2H2 n.d.).

While the N2H2 service explains that it utilizes search bots, artificial intelligence, panels of viewers, and user nomination of problematic sites to identify and filter objectionable sites, the company provides only general statements about how "pornography" and "harmful" or "distracting" materials are defined. An Australian ISP that offers an N2H2-filtering option provides some additional details.[1] But if the ABA is attempting to encourage informed consumer choices, more needs to be done to articulate the nature of each filtering service that it approves. Public access to the filtering criteria that are applied should be assessed when filtering services are approved by the ABA.

SYMBOLIC USES OF REGULATION

One way of characterizing the Australian policy is to see it as "symbolic" (Edelman 1964). Australia's Internet content regulation signals official support for a moral position but could be seen to have no practical import. Edelman argues that by taking the roles of interest groups whose support they need, public officials achieve and maintain their positions of leadership. The official who correctly gauges the response of the publics to his acts, speeches and gestures makes those behaviors significant symbols, evoking common meanings for his audience and for himself and so shaping his further actions as to reassure his public. (1964: 188)

Edelman suggests that this occurs when large groups view the political scene as spectators and lack direct bargaining power. They feel threatened by developments in a world that they perceive they cannot control and that relate directly to their own inner tensions. Potent inner tensions would surround issues such as pornography and sexuality and these tensions would be promoted through membership of organizations that have firm positions on these issues. Edelman suggests that as these inner tensions are exacerbated, the need for symbolic reassurance through politics becomes even greater (1964: 191). For groups of people watching the Internet expanding around them and providing ready access to contents that conflict with their innermost values, Australia's Internet content regulation can provide reassurance.

CONCLUSION

Australian governments have a long history of controlling the content of the broadcast media. Government regulation of television has focused on the enrichment and protection of children, the development of Australian culture, and support for the Australian film and television industries. Australian cultural values, and the creators of Australian film and television, were nurtured by the requirement that licensees transmit Australian-produced programs. Regulators have attempted to enhance children's television experience by requiring that television licensees produce and transmit programs designed for children. In addition, programs that were deemed to be unsuitable for children were screened when children were assumed to be sleeping.

While the regulation of the content of Australian television rested on the two pillars of Australian cultural identity and the protection and enrichment of children, the new Internet content regulation focuses squarely on the perceived needs and interests of children. But is there a way of locating Australia's interventionist approach within a more enduring set of social practices? Could Australia's approach to the regulation of the Internet be seen as an extension of social practices specific to Australia, that see Australia as a remote and isolated nation, which is self-reliant and independent of the outside world?

In his influential socioeconomic history of Australia, *The Tyranny of Distance,* Geoffrey Blainey developed the idea that Australia's distance from the major population centers of the European world could be used to explain its social and economic development. He documented how the European exploration of Australia from the sixteenth century onward and its subsequent occupation by European settlers in the eighteenth century was profoundly influenced by Australia's geographical isolation. And, for example, he showed how British settlement was driven by the desire to guarantee reliable sources of timber for masts and flax for sailcloth that would not be threatened by Europe's maritime powers and its rebellious American colonies (Blainey 1982: 33). According to Blainey this isolation had profound implications for Australia's agricultural and economic development and the way that Australians thought of themselves as inhabiting an outpost far removed from the center of European culture and civilization.

Blainey makes the point that while distance might have been tamed since the end of World War II it has not been conquered. He states that "those who have been brought up in a more isolated era . . . believe much more than the young that the isolation persists" (Blainey 1982: 341). He notes that while Australia's isolation has been dramatically reduced as a result of improved communications and transport, many Australian attitudes belong to a more isolated era and that they need to be reexamined in the light of what Blainey calls the " 'new geography' . . . where no place can be an island and the world cannot provide a hideaway" (1982: 342).

If Blainey is correct and many Australians persist with the view that Australia can isolate itself from events elsewhere, the emergence of global communications systems where connectivity and content is at the discretion of individuals places great strains on these views. In the past, national governments were able to regulate the mass media because they had ultimate control over the allocation of broadcasting frequencies. But with telecommunications-based communications systems such as the Internet where the users create the contents of communications and control connectivity that can go beyond national boundaries, government regulators are less able to take control. While governments can monitor the outputs of the broadcast media, control of the content of the Internet is impossible. By introducing a complaints-based regulatory regime, the Australian government has enlisted citizens in the campaign to regulate the Internet. In the new Australian Internet regulatory regime, citizens have become the agents of government regulation.

To provide a response to the question of where Australia's Internet regulatory regime fits into the debate about globalization of the media and the changing role of the state, it is useful to consider the various components of this regulatory regime. The complaints scheme and the take-down policies assert that material found to be objectionable by the ABA must be taken down and not hosted in Australia. The Australian policy makes an assertion about what is acceptable and what is not acceptable in an Australian context. (Whether there would be universal support for the decisions about particular subject matter is another matter.) So at a primitive level there is a claim to control of Internet content by the Australian state. But given that content providers are mobile and can move their content to a non-Australian host almost instantaneously, this aspect of the regulatory policy is more symbolic than practical.

The requirement that filtering systems be made available to those Internet users who choose to use them can be seen as the state partnering with the private sector to provide filtering services. By approving a limited number of filtering services, the state is giving its imprimatur to and endorsement of those services. But the criteria used for the selection of filtering products and services do not acknowledge the potential normative implications of selecting a particular filter or filtering service. The formal criteria are ease of installation, ease of use, configurability, ability for updates in respect to content to be filtered with regard to the requirements of the designated notification scheme provided for in the IIA Code, and availability of support (Internet Industry Association 1999b). The focus on operational characteristics of these services and the complete absence of any normative criteria implies that filters and filtering services do not differ in any substantial ways.

While acknowledging that the use of those services is entirely voluntary, the state could be seen as privatizing a censorship function that has been its exclusive domain in other media in the past. Of particular importance is the fact that filtering organizations are under no obligation to perform in any specific manner. They could choose to filter out content based on rules that are not publicly revealed and that cannot be easily deduced by users. In other words, filtering organizations are not publicly accountable. If they are responsive to external forces it is to the needs of their targeted market. These organizations could be driven by conservative forces whose values might be rejected by many Australians. And given the current distribution of Internet users, that market would be dominated by users in the United States. In effect the Australian government has devolved some of its censorship powers to global U.S. corporations oriented to the U.S. market.

So while much of the debate about the cultural and economic effects of globalized media focuses on the unwanted incursion of market-driven, globalized media operators into national cultures, the Australian Internet policy can be seen as a conscious handing over of its powers to privately controlled global Internet-filtering service providers. Given the "leaky" nature of the Australian Internet policy, in that there is no compulsion to actually use a filtering service, this handing over of censorship powers might be seen as benign. All that the government is invoking is a free-market principle where its citizens are able to ignore censorship altogether or choose an Internet censorship regime from a range of censorship offerings. If nudity or blasphemy offends, choose one censorship option. If another constellation of values is preferred, choose another. The major constraint is that if individuals choose to have their Internet service filtered, their filtering options must be selected from a menu of offerings that have been developed for a global media market and according to parameters that are not necessarily defined.

The Australian government's attitude to the regulation of Internet content harks back to that earlier era when distances were real and travel was slow. At the heart of Australia's Internet regulatory system is the view that Australia can create a walled garden, maintaining the barrier between Australia and the European world that had previously existed due to physical distance.

Through its regulatory actions, the Australian state has attempted to affect the workings of Australian online services. But the global nature of the Internet and global forces renders the Australian take-down policy practically ineffective, and with filtering requirements, the only thing that the government is mandating is that Internet users be given a choice. Because of the technical features and consequent cross-border nature of Internet communication, Australian Internet censorship regulation could be seen as essentially symbolic and having little real force. But in a perverse way it is possible to argue that to a large extent Professor Nadine Strossen's exhortation has actually come to pass. Perhaps the Australian government has indeed developed a system that "allow(s) each individual to decide exactly what it is that he or she doesn't want to see" (Colson 1999). But can Australia maintain even this Internet censorship regime in an ever-shrinking world, or will it just remain as a token policy and a monument to an increasingly distant memory of Australia's past?

NOTE

1. These are available from the iPrimus Web site, an Australian ISP that offers an ifilter/N2H2 network-based filtering option to its subscribers. The categories blocked for subscribers who elect to take the filtering service provided by this ISP are:

Adults Only: Material labeled by its author or publisher as being strictly for adults. (Examples: "Adults only," "You must be 18 to visit this site," "Registration is allowed only for people 18 or older," "You must be of legal drinking age to visit this site.")

Hate/Discrimination: Advocating discrimination against others based on race, religion, gender, nationality, or sexual orientation.

Illegal: Advocating, promoting, or giving advice on carrying out acts widely considered illegal. This includes lock picking, bomb making, fraud, breaching computer security ("hacking"), phone service theft ("phreaking"), pirated software archives, or evading law enforcement.

Pornography Site Material: Material intended to be sexually arousing or erotic.

Sex: Images or descriptions of sexual activity. Any sexual merchandise. Sexual fetishism.

Violence: Graphic images or written descriptions of wanton violence or grave injury (mutilation, maiming, dismemberment, etc.). Includes graphically violent games.

The categories that are not currently filtered or blocked are:

Education Material: Material under another category (such as sex, nudity, violence) that has educational value (such as classic literature, sex education, etc.).

"For Kids" Sites: Sites that are designed specifically for kids.

Medical Material: Material under another category (such as nudity or tasteless/gross) that relates to the study or practice of medicine. (iPrimus n.d.)

II

STATES AND COMMUNICATIONS REFORM
IN SOCIETIES IN TRANSITION

3

"Negotiated Liberalization": The Politics of Communications Sector Reform in South Africa

Robert B. Horwitz

Much has been written about the seeming inexorable march of globalization and the power of global capitalism to mold state policies according to its requirements. Yet the state remains the center of political action and social solidarity. Notwithstanding the transformational power accorded to globalization, any given country's public institutions remain tied more to the specific political architecture of states than they are directly determined by the forces of globalization. This can be seen in the communications realm. Old monopoly structures in telecommunications and broadcasting have been giving way to new models of liberalization, competition, and privatization. Such models are pushed by transnational corporations, multilateral organizations, and trade regimes. But though globalization creates pressures, opportunities, and constraints, communications reforms are shaped largely by domestic actors through domestic political institutions. This chapter deals not only with the pressures on the state from globalizing forces, but it also examines another source of pressure on the state—from within and below. The case under examination is post-apartheid South Africa.

The end of apartheid in South Africa entailed not just a political transformation from racial authoritarianism to one person–one vote democracy, it encompassed the widespread reform of a great many national institutions—social, political, economic, cultural. How could various government functions, economic sectors, cultural organizations, and the like be stripped of their apartheid pedigree and be converted into democratic and accountable institutions capable of serving the needs and reflecting the aspirations of the previously disadvantaged black majority? The economy was and remains the key terrain of struggle in this regard, inasmuch as the economy, more than any other post-apartheid institution, determines the life chances of now politically enfranchised South African citizens. But accountability in economic institutions is not just accountability to the newly democratic polity; it also now encompasses accountability and adaptation to the "rules" and constraints of the new global economy. Indeed, South Africa's transition to democracy, like many other grand political transitions of the last couple of decades, was a *double* transition: from authoritarianism to democracy, and from a controlled or command economy to a market system more or less in line with the exigencies of globalization.

I argue that the reform of the South African communications sector is an example of a "negotiated liberalization," in which a retrograde sector was transformed into a set of accountable institutions—in both of the senses described above—through participatory and deliberative democratic stakeholder politics (see Adler and Webster 1995, 2000; Webster and Adler 1999). Such negotiated liberalization shows that there is some room for progressive maneuvering in reforming institutions to meet the exigencies of the global economy, and, moreover, that participatory democratic policymaking can make both liberalization and the state more progressive and more legitimate. The latter is of no small importance given the threat that globally prescribed liberalization poses to new democracies, where, frequently, the process of institutional reform is fenced off from politics and the cost of reforming the economy falls on the backs of the poor and the working class (see Przeworski et al. 1995).

In a nutshell, the reform of the communications sector in South Africa accomplished the following:

Broadcasting

In the apartheid era, the South African Broadcasting Corporation (SABC) more or less monopolized radio and television broadcasting. A putative public broadcaster but in reality an arm of the apartheid state, the SABC reflected the National Party's (NP's) political agenda and vigorously promoted apartheid ideology in its programming, editorial practices, and hiring. The SABC was remade in 1993 into a nonpartisan public broadcaster with responsibility to program for all the people in all eleven now-official languages. A new SABC Board of Control, reflective of the diversity of South Africa's population, was appointed to direct the transformation of the SABC toward a democratic and inclusive orientation. Constitutional negotiators created an independent regulatory body to direct the changes and to oversee the broadcast sector as a whole. The Independent Broadcasting Authority, or IBA, licensed scores of new, low-power community radio operators. Some of the SABC radio stations were sold to private bidders and the IBA authorized a new commercial television service. All have public service and local content requirements, in different percentages.

The South African broadcast system is now a mixed system of commercial, community, and public service broadcasting.

Telecommunications

In the old days the South African Post Office operated the state telephone monopoly as an economic infrastructure for apartheid, servicing, for the most part, whites and business exclusively. Exhibiting the kinds of budgetary, efficiency, and monopoly boundary-operating problems that state-owned telecommunications companies experienced worldwide in the 1980s, the white minority government initiated a process to modernize the structure of South African telecommunications in 1991 when it created Telkom as a state-owned telecommunications enterprise separated from ministerial control. The ANC (African National Congress)-led democratic government revamped and completed the process, creating a regulatory body, the South African Telecommunications Regulatory Authority (SATRA), to oversee the sector. The legislation that established SATRA also plotted a phased liberalization of the sector, opening its various service markets gradually over a period of several years. Resisting both big-bang privatization and retention of full state monopoly, the new policy permitted a foreign telecommunications consortium (a partnership of Telekom Malaysia and U.S.-based SBC Communications) to take a 30 percent minority stake in Telkom to bring an infusion of capital and expertise. Telkom now has extensive universal service obligations as a condition of its license.

I want to suggest that, while the reform of the South African communications sector brings its institutions well into line with liberal democratic international trends and models, in fact, South African communications institutions are more progressive than the models they apparently ape. This is due largely to the distinctive internal political processes that established the new communications policies and to the unusually open nature of the South African state during the transition period. The South African reforms, contrary to current conventional wisdom of top-down, state-directed liberalization, were built via participatory democratic practice that engaged civil society and the state in policymaking (see Horwitz 2001).

THE CONVENTIONAL WISDOM OF POLITICAL "TRANSITIONS"

The new conventional wisdom among scholars of political transitions is that a successful transition from authoritarianism requires a pact, a set of compromises between hitherto bitterly contending elites that essentially leaves the fundamental structures of capitalist society in place. Largely because of the control that the old regime elite exercises over the machinery of state—particularly the military—the prodemocratic forces in the opposition most often must offer concessions in exchange for democracy. The fear of a coup limits prodemocracy options. Hence most successful transitions produce a dispensation that is economically and socially conservative, and that ensures the loyalty of the propertied classes (see e.g., O'Donnell & Schmitter 1986; Przeworski 1991).

As if this axiom of political constraint were not enough, the economic forces and institutions of an increasingly globalized capitalism create strong pressures to reform import-substitution industrialization policies—now considered to be largely archaic—to comport with the new market. These pressures are, of course, particularly strong since the fall of the Soviet Union and the disappearance of a counterhegemonic power and model to global capitalism. The economies of new democracies are usually not just out of step with contemporary global economic practice, they are frequently in serious decline and disorder at the moment of political transition (Haggard & Kaufman 1995). But securing economic reforms is not easy in developing countries, as they breach the basic social compromise inherent in historically state-directed corporatist development, to wit, the class coalition of industrial and export interests that paid the price of social peace with concessions to the urban masses (Walton & Seddon 1994). Indeed, as democracy takes hold and becomes consolidated in these transitions from authoritarianism, economic policy is often sealed off from politics. Only by insulating economic reform from the chaos of distributional claims, so the logic goes, can coherent and necessary economic policies be successfully undertaken. This axiom is a key component of the so-called Washington consensus on political and institutional reform.

The Washington consensus, a term coined by the political economist John Williamson (1994), emphasizes fiscal and monetary discipline, outward (export) economic orientation, tax reform, liberalization of product and financial markets, deregulation and privatization, and marketization of state activity. This set of policy prescriptions has become a talisman, a mantra, for virtually all key players in international economics, including the U.S. government, the IMF and World Bank, the big consulting agencies, and the World Trade Organization (WTO) (Waterbury 1992; World Bank 1995). Global organizations try to impose these policies on developing nations as a condition of granting a loan or negotiating a trade agreement or a promise of foreign direct investment. As suggested above, the policy prescriptions implicate a politics. Essential reforms can only be secured if the reform process is protected from "special interest groups." Organized labor is usually understood as the special interest group par excellence. Labor's key role in democratic transitions seems to be to stabilize them by binding its constituency to democracy at the cost of surrendering the pursuit of social and economic gains. And while labor is excluded from the politics of policy reform through its demonization as a disruptive special interest group, even legislatures are sometimes kept out of the policy-making process. In this reckoning, economic reform requires what amounts to the quiet suspension of democracy. The state fabricates top-down reforms that revamp the economy consonant with current "best practices," that is, in ways that also align it with the interests of global capital. While intensely critical of the Washington consensus, some scholars on the left in effect admit its power under the analytic rubric of the tyranny of globalization. This, after all, is what TINA— the acronym for "there is no alternative"—comes down to.

There are problems with both the political elite-pacting axiom and the axiom of globalization's imposition of economic reform when applied to South Africa. To be sure, crucial elements of elite-pacting were at play in the compromises struck between the National Party and the ANC, in ways that approximate the conventional wisdom of political transitions. The ANC felt compelled to guarantee both existing property rights and the security of tenure (including the payment of pensions) in posts for civil servants, as well as the near-complete independence of the central bank (Republic of South Africa 1993a: sections 28, 236, 245). The problem with the conventional elite-pacting analysis is that, at least in the case of South Africa, its focus is too narrow. It neglects the role of the trade unions and civil society organizations in the anti-apartheid struggle and slights the other constituent parties in the "tripartite alliance" of the ANC, the Congress of South African Trade Unions (COSATU) and the South African Communist Party (SACP). While the ANC was in exile, the democratic transition in South Africa was fundamentally the product of a general internal mass movement, whose actions and internal participatory political practices set the transition's political agenda. The unions, fighting with the white regime on behalf of labor rights for blacks, were a central player in the anti-apartheid democratic movement. Black civic organizations campaigned for improved living conditions in the townships and opposed municipal authorities foisted on them by the apartheid state. Though clearly linked to the ANC in spirit and general ideology, the unions and the "civics" were autonomous manifestations of self-organized activity. The internal anti-apartheid movement of the 1980s, under the umbrella of the United Democratic Front (UDF), not only engaged in mass insurrection, it also provided the kinds of alternative structures and mechanisms that shaped the transition and continue to affect the public debate and the process of consolidating democracy.

While the problem with an analysis focused on elite-pacting is that it does not explain enough, the economic globalization argument explains too much. It would be absurd to deny or belittle the pressures on a developing country by powerful international institutions like the IMF or the WTO, not to mention the "invisible hand" of currency speculation and investment strikes, now more easily abetted by ubiquitous finance and communications networks. But constraints and pressures do not dictate policy outcomes. Globalization is not an omnipotent force utterly depriving states of maneuvering room in their choice of development policy. Opening a formerly closed economy or a state-owned enterprise to the global market does not necessarily mean whole-hog liberalization and the blood sacrifice of national companies to more efficient and rapacious foreign corporations. Liberalization can be negotiated, in ways that aim to open up closed and often inefficient institutions while minimizing huge price hikes and their attendant social disruption, or without causing widespread labor retrenchments—that is to say, without the cost of reform falling, as it so often does, inordinately on the backs of the poor and the working class. Privatization, a key feature in the economic reform toolkit, is often simply a means to improve a government's balance of payments, or, worse, a political tool to hollow out the state sector. But privatization, depending on its intent and implementation, can also be a way to revitalize a stagnant, even corrupt, state-owned enterprise.

Against the conventional wisdom of the Washington consensus, the reform of the South African communications sector was an example of a kind of negotiated liberalization. Reform succeeded in the communications sector not because technocrats were insulated from politics, but because reform efforts proceeded by way of participatory and deliberative democratic mechanisms. Those democratic mechanisms came not so much from the political elites—even the ANC—but from the labor movement and the civic organizations in the black townships that made the popular struggle and internal insurrection of the 1980s. The specific politics of the transition period—the weakened apartheid state between 1990 and 1994 and the not-yet-consolidated democratic state dominated by the ANC between 1994 and 1996—made the state unusually open to participatory politics from below even as it was pressured by international forces from above.

SOUTH AFRICAN CIVIC POLITICS

COSATU's role in helping bring down apartheid has been documented by many scholars (Friedman 1987; Baskin 1991; Waterman 1991; Seidman 1994). The labor federation's disciplined militance in the 1980s was an important factor in convincing National Party stalwarts and leading businessmen that whites alone could no longer dictate South Africa's future. Labor engaged in a series of national strikes in the 1980s. It refused to participate directly in government institutions and hence contributed to the strategy of the internal insurrection to make apartheid South Africa "ungovernable." COSATU's strong organizational mechanisms of internal democracy, of reporting back, and accountability between the leadership and the rank-and-file also influenced the participatory democratic tenor of the latter stages of the anti-apartheid struggle (see Baskin 1994). Together with the township civic associations, the labor movement sparked the spread of "stakeholder forums" in the initial transition period after the ANC was legalized in 1990. COSATU demanded a macroeconomic negotiation on economic and social issues parallel to the political negotiations that had commenced under the Convention for a Democratic South Africa (CODESA). This was the origin of the National Economic Forum (NEF). Following its formation, the Mass Democratic Movement (as the internal anti-apartheid movement was called after the banning of the United Democratic Front) established hundreds of stakeholder forums under the political slogan of "a culture of consultation and transparency." Constituted outside of government, in effect forced upon government by anti-apartheid civil society organizations oriented around particular issues, the forums functioned as broadly consultative bodies where stakeholders, from business leaders to township dwellers to NGO representatives to old apartheid government bureaucrats, met to discuss how to transform a particular government function or industrial sector and bring services to the people in keeping with emerging democratic principles. The legitimacy of the forums rested precisely in the fact that they took place outside the regular channels of the old government. The anti-apartheid movement championed the forums largely as a means to prevent the apartheid government from taking decisions unilaterally during the transition period. At the same time, the government felt compelled to participate in the forums because any policy government might undertake risked being vetted by the anti-apartheid alliance through strikes and street action if it proceeded without agreement from the forums.

The forums functioned both to institutionalize the tripartite alliance's efforts to thwart the apartheid government's policy options in a great many areas of economic and social life, and to instill the principles of participatory democracy in all aspects of political life. Representing the direct antithesis to apartheid authoritarianism, the forums embodied a post-1990 manifestation of the UDF/labor/civics program of multiracial participatory democracy and served as a crucible for the emergence of more focused civil society organizations attentive to particular issue domains. This was a bit of a mixed bag for the ANC, whose exiles and prisoners returned to take up most of the leadership positions in the newly legalized organization, and who believed that the internal anti-apartheid organizations, perceived as ANC proxies, should now move aside. The forums were clearly of great political benefit to the ANC in the early 1990s when it was making the arduous transition from an exiled liberation movement to a political party and needed every edge in sparring with a clearly better prepared National Party/South African government. But participatory democracy and the culture of transparency and consultation were almost as out of step with the political inclinations of the ANC exiles, who tended toward statism and a leaders-know-best style, as they were with the apartheid government. The civil society activist groups that energized the stakeholder forums, though intimately allied with the ANC and often a source of expertise for it, in many instances also served as a brake on the discretionary power of the ANC leadership.

BROADCAST REFORM

These dynamics were initially seen in the reform of broadcasting, the first major state-owned enterprise and state-dominated sector to undergo structural transformation. At a concrete level, the content of apartheid authoritarianism and racism was directly visible in broadcasting, and this made the South African Broadcasting Corporation an early candidate for institutional transformation. The future of South African broadcasting was a major focus of anti-apartheid civil society groups, in part because the SABC was such a hated institution, but also because of the homologous relationships among a free, open, and accessible mass media; the culture of consultation and transparency; and the practice of participatory democracy.

Civil society–based campaigns mobilized public debate on broadcasting through various conferences, seminars, and protest actions, and succeeded in driving the debate toward the acceptance of the idea of a transformed SABC as a nonpartisan, independent public broadcaster. The activism of civil society media organizations such as the Film and Allied Workers Organisation, the Community Radio Working Group, and the umbrella Campaign for Open Media propelled broadcasting policy directly into the CODESA negotiations. The apartheid government earlier had initiated a reform effort in broadcasting through a government commission (see Republic of South Africa 1991b). Fearing unilateral government action to "marketize" broadcasting in the guise of reforming the SABC along the lines of global best practices, and watching the apartheid government surreptitiously commence the privatization of broadcasting through quiet radio license grants to favored white constituencies, the ANC-aligned civil society media groups pushed the ANC leadership to demand that broadcasting be taken up by CODESA directly (see Louw 1993). Because both the National Party and the ANC saw the question of the control of broadcasting as crucial in the election to come and in the political dispensation to follow, both parties assented. In the ensuing compromise at CODESA, both the National Party and the ANC agreed to an impartial public broadcaster overseen by an independent regulatory authority as the most viable, if a second best, policy option. Here, as in the constitutional negotiations generally, bargaining worked because there were a small number of strong political parties—essentially two—at the center of negotiations. The ANC was anxious about continued NP control of broadcasting before the 1994 election; the NP feared the possibility of ANC control of broadcasting after the election. Thus it was essential to both parties that the SABC be reconstituted as an independent, nonpartisan, if still state-owned, broadcaster.

The drafting of the Independent Broadcasting Authority Act was then in effect handed over to the "experts" attached to the major political parties. The principal political players had many more immediate questions of political structure to settle at CODESA. This gave a remarkable leeway to some of the activists in the ANC-aligned civil society media groups in the writing of the draft broadcast legislation. Rejecting international market liberal broadcast practices and borrowing progressive features of communications law from several countries, they wrote draft legislation establishing the public broadcaster as the anchor of a mixed system of public, commercial, and community broadcasting. Public service obligations were to be shared by all broadcasters, with substantial local content requirements and tough cross-media limitations to ensure the diversity of ownership and voices. The draft legislation and subsequent law, the Independent Broadcasting Authority Act (Republic of South Africa 1993b), stipulated that applicants for new commercial broadcast licenses demonstrate substantial evidence of the inclusion of the black majority in the ownership and operation of those enterprises. The future domain of commercial broadcasting could not be exclusively white.

I call these principles post-social democratic, in that they endeavored to create a mixed public-private broadcast system with a substantial nonstate and noncommodified presence built into the system's structure. Both state broadcasting and commercial broadcasting, for all their differences, were understood by the civil society media groups to render citizens passive and uninformed. Even traditional public service broadcasting often displays a tendency toward cultural and big-city hegemony, a tendency that was felt to be inappropriate for a new South Africa. The model of broadcasting embodied in the IBA Act sought to avoid the worst aspects of both market and state controls in broadcasting, while pragmatically placing market forces and public forms in a hoped-for creative tension. The triumph of the model rested in no small measure on the fortuitous fact of the deadlocked negotiated struggle between the ANC and the National Party, representing, in caricature, state versus market. This created a space for the effective intervention of civil society media groups and their post-social democratic vision. This is not to oversimplify the ANC's position on broadcasting and media policy. Like the tripartite alliance itself, there were many tendencies. The official ANC Media Charter (African National Congress 1992: 67–71) clearly was consonant with the general aims of the civil society media groups (though the charter was a general manifesto and not a concrete policy blueprint). Moreover, the civil society media groups did not stand apart from the ANC, but were constituents internal to the alliance. But there was also an important faction in the ANC supportive of the idea of state broadcasting, notwithstanding the Media Charter.

With the general structure set, the political battles in broadcast policy shifted somewhat after the 1994 election from one that pitted the ANC against the National Party to a struggle within the ANC alliance over the size of the SABC station portfolio—a complicated question not reducible to the conflict between statist versus post-social democratic visions, but nonetheless with clear elements thereof. Many supported a large SABC because of the need to deliver broadcast programming to all South Africans and in the eleven official languages. But others supported a large SABC because they still at bottom conceived the public broadcaster as, essentially, a state broadcaster. And now that the leadership of the SABC was in principle in the hands of trusted ANC comrades, the purview of the public broadcaster should remain expansive. At the very least, many proponents of the large SABC portfolio flirted with the "developmental" theory of the media, in which the media are to augment and assist, not criticize and disparage, governmental efforts at reconstruction and nation building (McQuail 2000). The SABC was conceived as a cardinal ally in the nation-building project.

The SABC itself lobbied heavily for a large portfolio but envisioned the broadcast system, particularly in television, as essentially market driven. Anticipating—correctly—that little money would come from government, the SABC planned for two of its television channels to become commercial, and would cross-subsidize the third public service channel with their proceeds. In contrast, those who argued for a smaller SABC portfolio, including the Independent Broadcasting Authority and several of the civil society media groups, fought for a leaner SABC better able to concentrate on its public service mission, and for more opportunities for new broadcast innovators—including private commercial broadcasters—particularly at the regional or provincial level. But, they argued, public service obligations and local content requirements would be imposed on *all* broadcasters so as to establish an overall public service broadcast *system*, rather than to ghettoize public broadcasting as the sole responsibility of the SABC.

Party politics did not disappear from the debate over the size of SABC's portfolio, and their dynamics played a major factor in the debate's resolution. Because the National Party had consistently strived to diminish the power of the SABC after 1994 (which included a constant and malignant public denigration of the new SABC as the ANC's mouthpiece) and to create more space for private broadcasters, the ANC's instinctual political response was to protect the public broadcaster and bolster its portfolio. The civil society media groups had almost nothing in common with the National Party's market-based broadcast policy vision, but they found themselves on the same side of the SABC portfolio fight. This would prove to be a factor in the distancing of the ANC leadership from the civil society media organizations. With the ANC leading the way, Parliament rejected the Independent Broadcasting Authority's Triple Inquiry recommendation that the SABC portfolio be trimmed from three television channels to two (Republic of South Africa 1995a). Parliament restored some of the radio stations to the portfolio as well. A large SABC was seen as necessary to do its part in the tasks of reconstruction and nation building. Here, however, the dismal budget situation inherited from the last white government doomed even the positive feature of this vision. With housing, education, and health care desperately in need of public monies, and with a sizeable portion of the budget precommitted to honoring state pensions as per the transition agreements, the government declined to allocate funds to an institution that *had* a proven source of funding. Advertising for decades had constituted the primary source of SABC's funding, and under the new ANC-led government it would continue to do so. But the reliance on advertising to fund SABC's three television channels and numerous radio stations could only pit the SABC's public service mission against its desperate need for revenue, thus reinforcing the commercializing dynamic in broadcasting found worldwide (see, among others, Dyson and Humphreys 1990). Paradoxically, the combination of the transition agreements and the ANC's statist tendency served to reinforce the power of the market in South African broadcasting. Still, the basic structure of the post-apartheid broadcast system embodied a post-social democratic cast.

TELECOMMUNICATIONS REFORM

In telecommunications a slightly different set of forces came to bear on the process of reform, though the overall political dynamic closely resembled that of broadcasting. Like broadcasting, telecommunications were targeted for liberalization and privatization by the last white government (see Republic of South Africa, 1989). The apartheid government's hope to privatize South Africa's telecommunications parastatal (the term for state-owned enterprises) was widely interpreted as a gambit to maintain white control in the event of a future black majority government. The effort was defeated by labor opposition and the ANC's threat to renationalize, but the government did manage to pass a more limited reform bill in 1991, whose provisions generally comported with the worldwide trend in telecommunications policy. Telecommunications were separated from posts and the ministry would no longer operate the telecommunications parastatal. Parliament created a new telecommunications company, Telkom, that, though state owned, was expected to behave like a normal, private corporation (Republic of South Africa 1991a). But the legislation did not, and, given the overall politics of the transition period, could not, create a comprehensive policy for the sector. A stakeholder forum failed to coalesce in telecommunications until 1994, and this meant that there was no arena in which the major players could engage in debate and negotiate new policy during the transition years. The upshot was that the environment within which Telkom was to operate was left undefined. As a consequence, telecommunications policy served as a flashpoint between the ANC alliance and the government between 1990 and the 1994 election. Amid great controversy, the government licensed two cellular telephone providers in 1993. But to gain the ANC alliance's acquiescence, one of the licensees had to include a substantial percentage of black shareholding. The cellular deal initiated an important pattern in black economic empowerment and the deracialization of the economy, where state tenders and contracts are used to foster private black capital. Another consequence of the cellular story was that the rapid introduction and success of cellular telephony provided real-world evidence—especially to ANC leaders—that competition could be beneficial.

Following the 1994 election and the formation of a stakeholder forum in telecommunications, Pallo Jordan, the new (ANC) minister of Posts, Telecommunications and Broadcasting in the Government of National Unity, initiated a Green Paper/White Paper policy process. Jordan's initiative institutionalized and gave government blessing to the broad consultative policy-making processes that had been the hallmark of the United Democratic Front/Mass Democratic Movement and were reinscribed in the stakeholder forums. The National Telecommunications Policy Project (NTPP), the mechanism created to carry out Jordan's policy initiative, clearly represented some version of corporatism, but it departed from classic corporatism in that participation was general and open, not restricted to large, powerful institutional stakeholders. Another distinguishing feature was that for much of the process government played a rather circumspect role. Government was there, in the personage of Minister Jordan, initiating the process, selecting (in consultation with the newly formed telecommunications stakeholder forum, the National Telecommunications Forum) the persons to facilitate it, and providing very general policy guidelines. The broad policy guidelines essentially followed the election results (a 62.6 percent ANC victory) and the compromises of the political transition: commit the sector fundamentally toward the provision of telecommunications service to the previously disadvantaged while providing the kinds of sophisticated services to business that are essential to economic growth and job creation. But for the most part government was not directly active in the telecommunications reform process, in part because Minister Jordan did not trust his own bureaucracy (another instance where the political transition agreements protecting the apartheid civil service had consequences), and in part because he was committed to deliberative democracy. Jordan evidently believed a better policy result would come from the structured interaction of public and open negotiations among stakeholders.

In this regard the telecommunications reform process followed the Reconstruction and Development Programme (RDP), the tripartite alliance's post-apartheid political-economic policy framework, in both spirit and in deed. The RDP document, pressed on a somewhat reluctant ANC by its COSATU and South African Communist Party alliance partners and other civil society organizations, called for the direct inclusion of civil society in policymaking, and conceived the new democratic state as a social power that would facilitate, at the minimum, Keynesian-based economic development directed toward the previously disadvantaged. The RDP document explicitly directed the new government to work with the stakeholder forums (African National Congress 1994: 120–121). Reflecting the political and economic orientation of the RDP, Minister Jordan's National Telecommunications Policy Project consisted of an open, consultative set of discussions and negotiations conducted largely within the realm of civil society, and wherein the principle of universal service stood at the core.

In the struggle to reform South African telecommunications a homology could be identified between the goal to equalize access to information and communications embodied in the commitment to universal service, and the understanding of democracy as, in part, expanding the number of active participants in the process of public deliberation and expanding the social basis of communications generally. The expansion of communications was manifested both in the ends (the goal of universal service) and in the means (citizen participation in policy determination). Like the broadcasting struggle, the post-social democratic effort to reform telecommunications displayed a kind of Deweyan pragmatism, where democracy was both a goal and a means.

The first phase of the stakeholder reform process in telecommunications resulted in a set of politically and technically viable compromises embodied in the White Paper on Telecommunications Policy, in which Telkom was given a limited period of exclusivity to meet extensive network expansion obligations. The White Paper plotted a sectoral liberalization in which various service markets would be gradually opened to competition at explicit time intervals over a period of six years. A strong independent regulatory body, SATRA, was to oversee the sector generally, license new entrants and administer the liberalization timetable, and settle the inevitable disputes that would result from bold policy reform. As in broadcasting, new business entrants in telecommunications would be expected to include the previously disadvantaged in ownership and operation as a condition of licensing (Republic of South Africa 1996b). The telecommunications White Paper thus envisioned another mixed system in which state and market forces were balanced against each other in a hoped-for creative tension to expand service, and in which a timed liberalization would abet black entrepreneurship. Telkom, the large and dominant state-owned telecommunications provider, was reaffirmed as the sector's main actor, but conditions for contestability and accountability were established at several junctures and explicit provisions for competition were written into the policy document. The liberalization timetable was to be fixed in legislation so as to build certainty into transformation and elicit "buy-in" from the sector's players. SATRA's independence was to guard against improper ministerial interference. The establishment of a Universal Service Agency represented an additional institutional check to keep SATRA's attention focused on the universal service goal. Universal service, of course, meant the obligatory expansion of telecommunications service to blacks and to historically black geographic areas (see Horwitz 1997).

It was the stakeholders who essentially hammered out the telecommunications White Paper, but they did so within a tightly prestructured political framework established by the electoral victory of the ANC and the policy environment fabricated by the RDP. This was why even the white business interests had to embrace universal service as the fundamental orientation of the reform effort. The central sticking point was whether Telkom should remain entirely state owned or whether some portion of its equity could be sold to an international telecommunications operator. This issue highlighted tensions within the tripartite alliance, as labor had proclaimed an antiprivatization stance and insisted on separate discussions with government regarding the disposition of state assets as a general policy. Yet without some large infusion of capital and new management skills, Telkom would not be able to succeed in the fundamental mission to expand telecommunications service to blacks.

Government reentered the politics of telecommunications reform in a direct fashion when the Cabinet considered the White Paper. Here, like the space created by the stalemated negotiations between the ANC and National Party in the broadcast arena earlier, the divided nature of the Government of National Unity Cabinet actually eased the acceptance of the telecommunications White Paper. The ANC alliance could support the White Paper because it retained the state-owned Telkom as the key player in a sector reoriented toward the delivery of universal service; the National Party could support the White Paper because it plotted the opening of the sector to competition. Indeed, the fact that the National Party strongly backed competition made it politically difficult for those market-oriented ANC cabinet ministers to side with the NP against the central thrust of the White Paper. The fact that the White Paper came to Cabinet under the general imprimatur of the RDP meant that its civil society–stakeholder consultation pedigree had to command respect from the ANC, even from those who quietly wished for more extensive privatization and a quicker path to competition.

And that was important, as was soon to be underscored when telecommunications reform entered into a second phase.

Soon after the publication of the telecommunications White Paper, general political dynamics shifted. In short succession, the government closed the RDP ministry and Pallo Jordan was removed as minister of Posts, Telecommunications and Broadcasting to be replaced by Jay Naidoo. Parliament passed the final version of the Constitution and the National Party announced its withdrawal from the Government of National Unity. Economic performance had been generally disappointing, and in 1996 the currency fell in value. The ANC replaced the RDP with the more orthodox Growth, Employment and Redistribution (GEAR) macroeconomic policy, and the ANC turned away from the politics of consultation. The turn away from consultation manifested itself in the telecommunications arena with the reassertion of ministerial authority. The minister substantially altered the language of the draft legislation on telecommunications policy. The bill Minister Naidoo brought to Parliament removed the White Paper's liberalization timetable in favor of ministerial discretion and diminished the functions and independence of SATRA. The new draft elevated the role of the ministry in the substantive regulation of the sector.

Just as the White Paper had been written under the political imprimatur of the RDP, the telecommunications bill was written under the political imprimatur of the GEAR policy. GEAR comprised a largely orthodox macroeconomic policy of deficit reduction and fiscal and monetary discipline. With GEAR, strict attention would be paid to the budgetary implications of government-delivered services. Parastatals should not lose money; indeed, they could be a new source of revenue through privatization (Republic of South Africa 1996a). GEAR was predicated on the assumption, following the Washington consensus on economic policy, that if the government demonstrated its credibility to such discipline, private investment, particularly direct foreign investment, would materialize. To pull GEAR off, the ANC leadership, again following the Washington consensus script, insulated the politics of GEAR's adoption from participatory democratic structures.

The changes to the telecommunications White Paper were consonant with the spirit and timing of the government's adoption of GEAR and reflected the move toward centralizing power in the now ANC-identified government. The telecommunications bill's reassertion of ministerial control gave Minister Naidoo more flexibility in the search for a partner for Telkom (an ability to trade a higher sale price for greater concessions on exclusivity) and more leeway to bring labor and black economic empowerment groups into an overall settlement. This had its desired effect. With the muted acquiescence of the trade union organization COSATU, the government was able to sell a 30 percent stake of Telkom to an international telecommunications consortium of SBC Communications and Telekom Malaysia. Government held out another 10 percent of Telkom for black economic empowerment. Of the U.S.$1.2 billion the consortium paid for the 30 percent stake, $1 billion was to stay in the telecommunications sector.

The contest over the independence of SATRA assumed outsized importance because it represented a fight over the power of the state in the new South Africa. At this stage in South Africa's evolution, so went the argument, there was a need for the government to direct the telecommunications sector toward addressing "the imbalances of the past." The position had some salience, particularly given the long fear that SATRA might be captured by the old white business interests. But the alignment of the ministry and black economic empowerment groups in the effort to weaken SATRA pointed to something more: the general ANC political strategy represented by GEAR, which was to increase the power of the state and use the state for development by way of establishing patronage for a politically loyal black bourgeoisie through selected privatizations, tenders, and contracts.

In the end, this gambit in telecommunications was turned back to some degree. The final legislation reinscribed many of the elements of the White Paper, including the restoration of some independence to SATRA. Among the reasons for this development was the interplay of deal making that is part of coalition party politics. With the Democratic Party and National Party in acrimonious opposition, the partial restoration of SATRA's independence may have been the price for bringing the Inkatha Freedom Party on board with the ANC for the final vote. Whatever the combination of reasons, the appearance, if not the reality, of a stronger, more independent SATRA served to resuscitate the post-social democratic vision that was attached to the telecommunications White Paper.

The telecommunications reform process was full of small paradoxes. It was the ANC that, after both consolidating power and finding government relatively helpless before the decline in the value of the currency in early 1996, moved to embrace significant features of the Washington consensus and the "TINA" discourse. It was labor and the civil society media groups that effectively modified the government's position in the telecommunications policy arena. Labor's unyielding demand for universal service essentially succeeded in framing the discourse in the telecommunications reform process. No one could articulate a policy option without addressing and embracing the goal of universal service as fundamental. This was very important in a society where service had been provided to whites and business only. Labor's seemingly retrogressive stance demanding the maintenance of the state monopoly in telecommunications had a paradoxically progressive effect. In the context of business' call for immediate privatization, liberalization, and competition (a position promoted endlessly by the EU, the United States, and the WTO), labor's position created a dynamic of necessary compromise not unlike the broader political compromises.

The ensuing stakeholder bargain maintained a strong Telkom as an interim exclusive service provider and established a timetable for liberalization—all within the discourse of universal service. Telkom was to utilize its unionized workforce to expand the infrastructure to the previously disadvantaged. Yet it was COSATU's membership in the tripartite alliance that allowed the ANC government the political purchase to secure labor's acquiescence on the privatization question and to put forward an offer on telecommunications to the World Trade Organization. To complete the series of compromises, labor and civil society pressure undoubtedly played a role in keeping the proceeds of privatization connected to social needs. One billion U.S. dollars were pumped into the sector to contribute to universal service, not diverted for general deficit reduction as had been explicitly envisioned in an early planning document on the disposition of state assets and was implicit in the GEAR macroeconomic strategy (see Cameron 1995; Republic of South Africa 1995b).

CONCLUSION

I have characterized the reform of broadcasting and telecommunications in South Africa as an example of negotiated liberalization. The reform of South African communications proceeded by way of a complex set of compromises among the state, political parties, labor, and civil society groups through remarkably open forms of participation in policymaking. The outcome was the establishment of new communications institutions largely accountable both to the new democratic polity and to the norms of global markets, embodying what I have called a post-social democratic vision. What perhaps marks the South African example as unique is that such policy-making exercises took place in the context of a strong labor movement (with union density at about 50 percent, far greater than most labor movements in countries transitioning to democracy), an energized and intellectually acute set of civil society organizations, and a strong culture of consultation and transparency that derived from the internal mass democratic anti-apartheid movement.

Although I have highlighted the importance of civil society in this exercise in policymaking, it was not a matter of civil society activism alone. Successful civil society struggle depends on a state open to such interventions. Participatory politics works when the state is hospitable to such politics. In the 1990–1994 period the state was open because it was in fundamental transition and was being continually contested; in the 1994–1996 period the state was open because of the way that the RDP embodied the sometimes politically conflicted, but in the larger sense politically complementary, aims of the tripartite alliance, in particular the accommodation of the stakeholder forums and other forms of participatory democracy. In other words, effective civil society participation needs both a strong state and viable, hospitable points of political entry (see Evans 1997b).

The success of the South African communications sector reforms, while notable, should not be taken to mean that such negotiated or bargained liberalization is easy. The constraints and development paths established by globalization are, if not ironclad, nonetheless indisputable and powerful. As has been suggested, the ANC-led government has moved toward rather orthodox macroeconomic policies to accommodate these constraints, much to the dismay of its labor and communist party alliance partners (see, e.g., Marais 1998). Labor has not been particularly successful in its interventions in macroeconomic issues such as exchange controls and tariff reforms in recent South African policy. The point, as Webster and Adler (1999) suggest and that the communications reform process illustrates, is that movements resisting liberalization may be able to create new institutions through which they process their demands. In turn, these institutions may be able to create new rules of the game, allowing a kind of bargained liberalization in which prominent groups renegotiate the terms on which a country engages with the global economy, establishing a new balance between market and society, and even, perhaps, a new class compromise.

4

State Transformation and India's Telecommunications Reform

Nikhil Sinha

Developing countries are currently in the midst of a widespread restructuring of their economies. After decades of state control over the economy, import-substitution-led industrialization, and the proliferation of state-owned enterprises, many governments are now privatizing their state-owned enterprises, increasing the operation of market forces, and opening their economies to global economic forces. The reforms have raised serious questions about the nature and role of the state in guiding national economies. Paradoxically, Third World states seem to be moving aggressively to reduce their own dominance in society. Understanding the role of the state in this transformation of national economies is crucial to understanding the trajectory of the political economy of developing countries.

Studies of the state and state transformations have generally been conducted at three major analytical levels: at the level of the international system, at the level of the state itself, and at the level of civil society. What has been missing from most accounts is an analysis of the mutual interaction between society, states, and the international system. This chapter seeks to develop a synthetic account of state actions by analyzing the influence of the global political economy and the changing structures of India's state and civil society on the country's attempt to restructure its telecommunications system. Building on what Ronen Palan (1992) has called the "second structuralist" trend in scholarship, the article identifies the political and economic imperatives that influenced the Narasimha Rao–led Congress Party government to formulate a new telecommunications policy, and the role and influence of forces operating at the level of the state and that of the international system in the process.

Indian telecommunications provides a particularly revealing sector on which to conduct such an analysis. Telecommunications has emerged as a pivotal sector in ensuring the success of many economic restructuring programs in the developing world. In the past, telecommunications were considered a good example of a natural monopoly, an essential public good that governments should provide in a noncommercial mode. Consequently, telecommunications services were provided by public enterprises under monopoly conditions. The declining role of the state and the technological pressures to rapidly modernize and expand telecommunications sectors are forcing developing countries to engage in widespread policy reform. In most countries, this has involved the liberalization of telecommunications policies through the introduction of privatization and competition to replace the traditional public monopoly structure.

In India, this transformation of telecommunications is taking place as part of an economic restructuring program that is transforming one of the world's most tightly controlled economies. The new economic program signals a radical break from decades of insular, even autarchic, economic policies, and the socialist ideology that governed economic planning between 1950 and 1991. The Narasimha Rao government's new telecommunications policies reveal why the state matters in the complex interplay of political and economic forces, both international and domestic, that have shaped and constrained the country's overall economic restructuring.

SOCIETY, STATE, AND THE INTERNATIONAL SYSTEM

Scholars of state actions, policies, and transformation have generally presumed the existence of separate and analytically distinct "levels of analysis" (Waltz 1979; Singer 1961; Keohane 1980; Krasner 1976, 1991). These levels are differentiated in terms of the assumptions about the influence of factors operating at the domestic and/or international level on state behavior. For "internationalist" approaches, the state is considered to act more or less independently of domestic social forces, and explanation is sought primarily at the international systemic level and in terms of the imperatives of a given configuration of the international system (Cafruny 1995). Most efforts to understand state actions from this level of analysis have focused on either the international political structure, from what has been termed as the realist or neorealist perspective (e.g., Morgenthau 1956; Krasner 1976; Gilpin 1981), or on the logic of world capitalism, from a world systems theory perspective (e.g., Wallerstein 1980; Bousquet 1980; Chase-Dunn 1989), with much less attention devoted to the national arena.

Traditional realist approaches viewed the state as a unified and autonomous actor making rational calculations with a view to maximizing power and security in a world characterized by the absence of overarching authority structures (Underhill 1994). International relations were seen as largely a political struggle for power with nations acting to maximize their national interest while attempting to maintain systemic stability. Economic issues were subordinate to the security interests of the state, and international politics were largely independent of the influence of domestic socioeconomic groups and politics.

Neorealist approaches have sought to rectify traditional realism's neglect of economic variables by incorporating elements of neoclassical economic theory into their analytical frameworks, building on the groundwork done by Kindleberger (1973) and Waltz (1979). Neorealists maintain that an international market economy, institutionalized in international economic "regimes" characterized by liberal norms and rules, would constitute a public good for all nations in the system because it ensured the greatest economic benefit for the greatest number. But the existence of a liberal economic order is dependent on the distribution of power among states in the system. A hegemonic system, in which a dominant power or "hegemon" is able and willing to bear the "cost" of providing stability, is seen to be the most propitious for the emergence of a liberal market system (Gilpin 1987; Krasner 1991). Hence, these approaches are sometimes referred to as hegemonic stability theory.

A growing number of critics have questioned the underlying epistemological assumptions of realist and neorealist theory (Smith 1988; Lapid 1989). An exclusive or primary focus on the international system appeals to the desire for methodological rigor and parsimony. But it paints a stylized, one dimensional, and ultimately unconvincing portrait of continuity across time and space. It offers no means of identifying dynamic social, technological, and economic factors that produce historical change (Ruggie 1989). The debate between advocates of a systems approach and those who seek more inclusive accounts of domestic and international factors turns not only on empirical claims, but also on methodological assumptions and, more generally, conceptions of social science itself (Cafruny 1995).

Realists and neorealists have sought to "uncover" invariant laws relating to systemic properties that transcend particular historical periods, cultures, and levels of economic development (Waltz 1979; Gilpin 1981). Appealing to the canon of "parsimony," they have incorporated economic models of rational choice to buttress their claims for the superiority of systemic explanations (Keohane 1980; Snidal 1985; Grieco 1988; Krasner 1991). Central to much criticism of realism and neorealism is a rejection of the traditional distinction between levels of analysis—and the priority given to the international system—not only because this type of approach ignores variables that are decisive to historical change, but also because it offers an idealized and static account of the state itself (Wendt 1987, 1991; Palan 1992).

One formidable challenge to the realist conception came from world systems and dependency theory. Scholars from within these perspectives have taken issue with the assertion that states can be considered as autonomous entities or that there is a purely power-political logic of the behavior of states (e.g., Wallerstein 1908; Chase-Dunn 1989; Frank 1994). According to world systems theorists, the imperatives of global capital accumulation shape the basic contours of the international system and determine the possibilities for social and economic development of the states within it.

One of the distinctive accomplishments of world systems theory is its emphasis on the evolutionary, dynamic character of the global political economy. Yet, world systems theory has also neglected the importance of national politics, including class conflicts and domestic political and economic struggles that often decisively influence national and international outcomes (Skocpol 1977; Evans et al. 1985). The emphasis on a more or less self-regulating global economy has meant that the state remains largely untheorized and derivative, although now the logic is one of adaptation to the structure of the world market, rather than that of global power.

Recently, attempts have been made from within the "internationalist" perspective to develop more comprehensive empirical analyses by including domestic and international variables (e.g., Katzenstein 1978, 1985; Gourevitch 1986; Haggard & Simmons 1987) and to redefine the terms of the debate over the level of analysis (Yurdusev 1993). Nevertheless, for the most part "domestic structures" have been granted a status of second-order or supplementary explanatory forces. This neglect of domestic structures and conflicts is overcome by two very different bodies of theory: Marxist and statist conceptions of the state.

The resurgence of interest in Marxist state theory, which began in the late sixties, produced a wide variety of theoretical and methodological approaches to the analysis of the structure and character of the state. These include the initial structuralist position of Poulantzas (1969, 1973); the instrumentalism of Miliband (1968); the class forces perspective of Block (1977); and the relational approach eventually adopted by Poulantzas (1976, 1978). Much of this theorizing has greatly advanced our knowledge of the logic of capital accumulation; the complexities of class struggle in different societies; the state's various forms—ranging from abstract features such as the rule of law or the bourgeois tax form to more concrete types of state and regime; and the tensions, dilemmas, and contradictions involved in different modes of policy production. In particular, Nicos Poulantzas made a crucial contribution to Marxist theory in developing the twin arguments that (1) the state apparatus, considered as an institutional ensemble, constitutes a strategic terrain with a distinct structural bias and (2) state power should be understood as the complex result of political class struggles occurring both on this strategic terrain and at a distance from it (Poulantzas 1978; see also Jessop 1985, 1989).

Poulantzas and other theorists also explored the nature and limits of state autonomy both in general terms and in relation to specific regimes and conjunctures. But despite some of the sophisticated and complex arguments presented, in the ultimate analysis the state is conceptualized in this body of work as subservient to the class composition of societies, and this class struggle is the primary causal variable that explains state actions and behavior.

Reaction to the subordination of the state to the forces of global politics (as in the realist and neorealist school), the global economic system (as in world systems theory), and class conflict (as in Marxist theories of the state) has contributed to something of a renaissance of the concept of state autonomy (Skocpol 1977; Evans et al. 1985; Nordlinger 1981; Krasner 1978). State-centered theorists have argued that there are sui generis political pressures and processes that shape the form and functions of the state and that endow it with a real and important autonomy vis-à-vis all pressures and forces in civil society (Jessop 1989). They argue that the state is a collection of institutions with a unique centrality in both national and international formations. While different theorists have emphasized different factors, the conclusion remains the same: The state is a force in its own right and does not simply reflect the dynamics of the economy, civil society, or the international system.

The question of state autonomy is a crucial plank on which the state-centered approaches rest. Two dimensions of autonomy are particularly important within these approaches. First, state autonomy is understood as the ability of state managers to exercise power independently of social forces located in civil society. This power is rooted in the state's own specialized capacities and in the room for maneuver that state managers enjoy with respect to an environment of pluralistic social forces. Second, state autonomy stems from the state's "infrastructural power," for example, its ability to penetrate, control, supervise, police, and discipline modern societies through its specialized capacities, which include its authority to manage and allocate economic resources, in addition to its coercive powers (Block 1977; Mann 1983; Nordlinger 1981; Skocpol 1985).

Despite the proliferation of state-centered literature, it remains exceedingly uncertain as to what exactly is meant by the concept of the state. The state has been defined in a variety of ways in the literature, most of which take it to be not just distinguishable from society, but partially or wholly autonomous from it. But rather than addressing the difficulty of distinguishing between state and civil society, the state-centered literature has largely evaded the problem. It has done so by reducing the state to a subjective system of decision making, a conception that Mitchell (1991) argues is exceedingly narrow:

> The narrower focus locates the essence of the state not in the monopolistic organization of coercion, nor, for example, in the structures of a legal and ideologi-

cal order, nor in the mechanisms by which social interests find political representation, nor in the arrangements that maintain a given relationship between the producers of capital and its owners, but in the formation and expression of authoritative intentions. Construed as a machinery of intentions—usually termed "rule making," "decision making," or "policy making"—the state becomes essentially a subjective realm of plans, programs, or ideas. (82)

But this approach tells us little about how to establish a clear boundary between state and civil society. Decision making is a complex process that involves a number of parastatal and extrastatal political and economic institutions such as parties, interests groups, trade unions, business associations, and the like that are located on the uncertain boundary between state and society (Almond 1988). Robert Horwitz, in the previous chapter, illustrates a particular version of the interaction of these forces in recent South African history. The customary Weberian definition of the state, as an organization that claims a monopoly within a fixed territory over the legitimate use of violence, is only a residual characterization. It does not tell us how the actual contours of this indistinct organization are to be drawn (Mitchell 1991).

More recently, a number of scholars have offered theoretical and empirical accounts of state-society linkages that identify, in Robert Cox's words, "the continuities between social forces, the changing nature of the state and global relations" (1986: 206). These theoretical traditions have rejected the assumption of the causal primacy of the international structure and the corollary assumption of the analytical separation of state and society. Recognizing that the modern state is, in Schmitter's words, "an amorphous complex of agencies with ill-defined boundaries, performing a great variety of not very distinctive functions" (1985: 33), they argue that there are powerful continuities between society and the state and the state and the international system. An emphasis on continuities, rather than discrete levels of analysis might retain the important insights of world systems theorists while avoiding the definitional pitfalls of statism.

Ronen Palan (1992) has cited the emergence of a "second structuralist" trend in scholarship, which focuses on the mutual interaction of processes operating at the level of the nation-state and that of the international system. "A common feature of this approach is the rejection of the Weberian conception of the state as a directly given, atomized actor operating within the framework of anarchy in favor of an approach which considers the state to be constituted by a combination of domestic and international social forces" (Cafruny 1995: 288).

Like world systems theorists, scholars who have favored this approach have identified structural relations at the level of the world political economy that, within certain limits, shape the choices and constraints of any given state (Strange 1988). However, they also emphasize the causal role played by societies and states together in the formation and transformations of these structures. The state is thus conceptualized not as a "transmission belt" through which global forces—either political or economic—generate domestic changes, nor as an autonomous actor acting independently of societal forces, nor as a mere instrument of domestic class coalitions, but rather as a "framework of social and political activities" (Palan 1992: 23) that involve both global and domestic forces.

This study of telecommunications reform in India begins from the assertion that if we are to understand how states manage the constraints of the domestic and international domains, we must understand the political economy of the state itself, situated as it is between domestic and international society. What is needed is an explanation of how structure—domestic and international—sets the parameters of state decision making. This requires some notion of how the economic interests involved in the transnational and domestic economy become articulated in the politics of the state. At the same time we need to disaggregate the state to understand its politics, focusing on the preferences and political resources of political and social groups to understand how particular material interests are articulated politically.

The liberalization of telecommunications in India provides an exceptionally good case for such an analytical project. India is in the midst of an economic transformation that may have far-reaching consequences for the future of the Indian state. Telecommunications reform has become one of the most visible symbols of that transformation. Using the perspective of the "state as decision maker" as an entry point, this chapter analyzes the process by which the government of Prime Minister Narasimha Rao formulated the new telecommunications policy and identifies the global and domestic forces that shaped the new policy. It discusses the changing role of the Indian state in the country's economy, the politics of telecommunications reform, and the economic imperatives underlying the liberalization process.

STATE AND ECONOMY IN INDIA

Nandy argues that the Indian state emerged as a compromise between two political impulses. The first is the traditional Indian notion of the state as a "*post facto* justification of a slowing emerging political order built on existing political practices . . . a projection of, and a means of dealing with, a chaotic political reality" (1989: 3). That is, an overarching construction that retrospectively coped with the heterogeneity and contradictions of the Indian political process. And the second is the relatively new idea of an Indian state to be modeled along the lines of the modern European nation-state. To the early architects of the Indian state, Jawaharlal Nehru, Vallabhai Patel, and Babasaheb Ambedkar, the compromise was to be temporary, and in time

India would develop a modern nation-state as the country's chaotic political diversity and heterogeneity disappeared. This expectation was not only part of the formal ideology of the new Indian state but was also written into the institutions of political socialization that evolved in the postindependence era (Nandy 1989).

The Indian Constitution, adopted in 1950, mandated a strong role for the state in the economic development of the country. Alongside a bill of rights it lays down a set of principles directing the Indian state to actively engage in the process of economic development. There was a firm conviction that the problems of underdevelopment in India required an activist state and could not be left to the markets to solve. The role of the state and the need for planning and deliberate public action seemed stronger in underdeveloped countries than in the more mature market economies of the industrialized countries, and in India it took on a strong socialist flavor. The arrangement of the Planning Commission and the adoption of a five-year planning mechanism institutionalized the government's control over the economy.

Nandy has argued that the most prominent feature of modern India has been the emergence of the state as the principal "hegemonic actor in the public realm" (1989: 1). The Indian state has taken upon itself the task of setting the ideological agenda of the nation, rather than implementing the will of its citizens. As long as the state was identified as the only viable mechanism for ensuring political stability, economic growth, and social modernization, it was relatively easy to identify the development of the state with development in general. The emergence of state-led development within a socialistic agenda provided the rationale for the control over the economy, at least until the economic reforms of 1991. Along with controlling the economy domestically, the India state also attempted to insulate the economy from international economic forces. Import substitution, self-reliance, and limits on foreign direct investment characterized the country's external sector orientation.

However, over time the state's autonomy from forces in civil society became progressively constrained. Bardhan (1984) has argued that the political economy of India can be understood as a coalition of the three proprietary classes in the economy: industrial capitalists, rich farmers, and professionals (particularly those in the state bureaucracy). The conflicts within this "dominant coalition" framed the degree of autonomy possessed by the state. At the time of Independence, the governing elite that inherited power "enjoyed enormous prestige and a sufficiently unified sense of purpose" to redirect and restructure the economy (Bardhan 1984: 38). In time, the dominant classes became better mobilized and continually forced the state to grant them budgetary subsidies. For the industrialists it took the form of protectionist and oligopolistic markets; for the agriculturists it took the form of large farm subsidies and exemption from income tax on agricultural income;

for the state bureaucrats it took the form of greater control over the economic, social, and cultural life of the country. As industrial capitalists, rich farmers, and members of the bureaucracy competed for ever-larger shares of a slowly growing pie, resources needed for public investment were whittled down by current consumption. At the same time, to ensure their electoral survival successive governments were forced to resort to deficit financing to fund populist economic measures.

Four characteristics of this post-1991 period are important to note. First, the Indian state was only partially successful in protecting the country's economy from the global economy. The policies of self-reliant industrialization, import substitution, and relative economic autarchy resulted in a fairly closed economy, though not one that was completely immune to global events like increases in oil prices. These policies were maintained despite opposition from multilateral development agencies like the IMF and the World Bank, which continually pressured India to open its economy. Clearly, the socialistic and nationalistic ideology of the postcolonial Indian state was largely responsible for this partial closure of the Indian economy. But part of it was also the result of pressures exerted by the domestic private industry, which wanted protection from global competition.

Second, the interests of the bureaucracy were not necessarily coterminus with the interests of the state. The bureaucracy competed for political power with other state institutions like political parties and the judiciary, and an expansionist state became the instrument through which it strove to extend its influence. Third, despite the influence of the "dominant coalition" successive governments continued to implement populist antipoverty measures and used their political control over the state's coffers to finance these measures. Fourth, despite the socialistic rhetoric, the country's economy always has been, in principle, a market economy subject to forces of capital accumulation and capitalistic development.

The picture that emerges is not that of a state that is an autonomous actor in its environment, or one that is subservient to the interests of global or domestic capital, or one that is merely an instrument or reflection of the dominant forces in civil society. The postliberalization Indian state was often rife with internal dissension, struggling to pursue its ideological agenda while suspended in a complex web of global and domestic forces.

ECONOMIC LIBERALIZATION AND THE STATE

It took the economic crisis of 1990–1991 to force the state to recede from the forefront of the economy and change the political-economic landscape of the country. The years 1990–1991 were among the most difficult in India's recent history. After a decade of Congress Party rule, the opposition

National Front Party came to power in 1990 with high expectations of setting the country on a new path of social and economic development. But the National Front government collapsed within a year and the stopgap government that formed in its wake fell within a few months. Two successive governments in one year not only caused considerable political uncertainty but also pushed the economy into a downward spiral. The Gulf War further aggravated the country's economic crisis. Foreign exchange reserves dipped to levels below one month of imports, imports exceeded exports by over 50 percent, and the government's budget deficits soared (Sinha 1996).

When the Congress government under Narasimha Rao was elected in 1991, it faced one of the country's most severe economic crises. Spearheaded by Finance Minister Manmohan Singh, the new government's response to the crisis was twofold. It initiated steps to deal with the immediate crisis, avert the danger of defaulting on its debt repayments, raise the level of foreign exchange reserves, and restore overall confidence in the economy. A massive loan from the IMF took care of the immediate fiscal crisis. But it also initiated a widespread new economic policy to restructure the economy and eliminate its basic problems. The government's New Economic Policy (NEP) had five main components:

1. Devaluation: Devaluation of the rupee was aimed at increasing exports, narrowing the trade gap, and preventing capital flight.
2. Deregulation: Deregulation or, more accurately delicensing, was aimed at dismantling controls on domestic private industry by abolishing licensing requirements, lifting restrictions on capacity and permitting it to operate in areas previously reserved for the public sector, in effect sweeping away the so-called *license raj*.
3. Privatization: Privatization involved a number of different measures including the outright sale of public-sector enterprises, offering shares to the public and joint public-private ownership of enterprises.
4. Liberalization: Liberalization involved the opening up of monopoly or oligopoly markets in both the public and private sector to increased competition.
5. Globalization: Globalization in the Indian context involved the opening up of one of the most closed economies in the world to international trade and foreign investment. First, trade polices were revamped to lower or eliminate restrictions, quotas, and tariffs on imported goods while providing significant incentives for exports. Second, the terms and conditions of foreign investment were restructured to attract greater volumes of investment into the country and to encourage foreign companies to relocate productive activities in India.

What was missing from the NEP were explicit goals or policies aimed at reducing income inequalities, fostering balanced economic growth, reducing concentration of the means of production, or fostering the development of the public sector, which had been the cornerstone of the socialistic policies of the previous four decades. Gone also was the goal of economic self-reliance, at least in terms of manufacturing locally most, if not all, the critical goods and services required by the economy. Self-reliance was recast as the ability to generate the foreign exchange required to pay for imports. The protections offered to domestic industry were also rolled back and the Indian private sector was opened to significant global competition for the first time since Independence. But perhaps the most dramatic change in the country's economic orientation was the move away from the import substitution policies of previous regimes and the opening up of the country's economy to direct foreign investment (Sinha 1996).

The government's decision to radically restructure the country's economy, and in doing so to dramatically redefine the role of the state in India, was the result of a complex interplay of global and domestic forces and the changing nature of India's civil society. These conditions were not new and some of these pressures had existed for past governments, but it was the coming together of these forces at a single historical moment that made the reforms not only possible, but also imperative.

The economic crisis forced the country to approach the IMF to rescue it from its immediate problems, and it did so from its weakest bargaining position in decades. This move also took place in a transformed international political economy, one in which states' role in managing and guiding national economies had been severely undermined. From the dissolution of the planned economies of the members of the erstwhile Soviet Union and Eastern Europe to the loosening of state control over economic activity in China, Vietnam, and Cuba; from deregulation and liberalization in the Western industrialized countries to the sale of public enterprises to private interests in developing countries as diverse as Chile, Malaysia, and the Ivory Coast, the lessons appeared to be the same: that the competitive market system was a better mechanism for organizing economic activity than state intervention, regulation, or ownership. Forced to resort to IMF lending in this changed international ideological environment, the Indian state finally succumbed to the structural reforms required by the IMF–World Bank stabilization package that have been applied across the developing world. (See chapter 5 for a discussion of the South Korean case.)

The package has four main components: (1) stabilization, which basically implies the reduction of fiscal deficits and cutting the rate of growth of the money supply; (2) domestic liberalization, which consists of relaxing restrictions on production, investments, and prices, and increasing the role of market signals in guiding resource allocation; (3) external sector liberalization or relaxing restrictions on international flows of goods, service, technology, and capital; and (4) reduction in government subsidies and support mechanisms. While all of these measures were seen in India's New Economic Policy, the government was much more responsive in pursuing the first three but was (and successive governments continue to be) reluctant to take steps to reduce subsidies, particularly to agriculture. Clearly, the power of agriculture remains significant and the government could not afford the political backlash of removing fiscal supports from the sector that still maintains over 65 percent of the country's population.

At the same time, the fact that the government could institute such a sweeping reform program with little domestic opposition also provides evidence of the rise of new groups in India's civil society who are competing with the dominant coalition for a piece of the economic pie. These new "demand groups" (Rudolph and Rudolph 1987: 50), like the rising middle class or the new agrarian movements, put increasing pressure on the state's ability to manage the economy through its traditional process of patronage and subsidies. A primary task of any state is the processing of social claims. As the number of claims rises, the ability of the state to internally arbitrate and manage the process is strained and the very survival of the state could be threatened. Liberalization provides an instrument to cope with this threat. By shifting the burden of managing the increasing claims arising out of civil society from itself to the more invisible hand of the market the state relieves itself of the demands for resources that it can no longer satisfy.

However, the ease with which the Rao government could institute the reforms should not suggest that there was no opposition to the liberalization program. But groups that expressed opposition to the reforms were less concerned about the principle of the reforms and more concerned with their own position in a liberalized national economy. This was a very different form of opposition than that documented by Kohli (1989), which scuttled the liberalization efforts of the Rajiv Gandhi government between 1985 and 1990.

Opposition to the reforms came from four main sources. Politically, the government was attacked from the Right by the Bharatiya Janata Party, which argued that the easier entry of multinationals would hurt domestic industry, and from the Left by the National Front parties (Janata Party and the two Communist parties), who accused the government of forsaking the country's antipoverty and income redistribution goals. But in both cases, there was little direct opposition to the principle that radical reforms of the economy were both necessary and desirable. The government also encountered resistance from within the Congress Party, with some prominent party members breaking away to form a splinter party on the ostensible grounds of opposition to the reforms. But unlike the situation faced by the Rajiv Gandhi government in the 1980s, there was no sustained opposition to the reforms from the rank and file of the Congress Party (Kohli 1989).

The third important source of opposition came from some parts of Indian industry that, while welcoming the dismantling of the *license raj*, felt threatened by the anticipated competition from multinationals. Finally, government faced opposition from the trade unions and the lower echelons of the bureaucracy. Trade unions had played an important role in scuttling many of Rajiv Gandhi's liberalization initiatives (Kohli 1989) and slowed a number of the Narasimha Rao government's plans as well. The particulars of the government's reform measures, and specifically the scope of the reforms in telecommunications, are a direct outcome of the struggle between the government's drive to restructure the economy and the specific direction or opposition to the reforms emanating from international and domestic forces.

THE STATE AND TELECOMMUNICATIONS REFORM

The government's onslaught on the traditional structure of telecommunications in the country was launched after the recognition that a modern telecommunications system was essential to the success of the entire economic reform program (Sinha 1996). The critical role of telecommunications in the economic reforms was acknowledged in the government's annual survey of the country's economy in 1994.

> Telecommunication is important not only because of its role in bringing the benefits of communication to every corner of India but also in serving the new policy objectives of improving the global competitiveness of the Indian economy and stimulating and attracting foreign direct investment. (*Economic Survey of India* 1993–1994: 32)

This realization was clearly articulated in the National Telecommunications Policy Statement released in May 1994.

> The new economic policy adopted by the Government aims at improving India's competitiveness in the global market and rapid growth of exports. Another element of the new economic policy is attracting foreign direct investment and stimulating domestic investment. Telecommunication services of world class quality are necessary for the success of this policy. It is, therefore, necessary to give the highest priority to the development of telecom services in the country. (*National Telecommunications Policy* 1994: 2)

The new Indian telecommunications policy had a number of characteristics that made it one of the most interesting telecom reform programs in the developing world. It began the restructuring process by introducing competition in the local loop, breaking from the normal process that begins with the liberalization of long-distance services. It forced Indian and foreign companies to form joint ventures in order to enter the bidding to provide basic services. Instead of licensing one or two companies to provide services nationally, the government planned to grant separate licenses for about twenty telecom "circles," holding out the potential for a number of different providers to enter the market. Finally, it avoided the privatization of the government PTT, which continues to provide services in head-to-head competition with the private telecommunications companies (telcos).

Four decisions taken in the process of formulating the National Telecommunications Policy were critical to shaping the overall structure of the telecommunications reforms. The first dealt with the extent of liberalization, the second with ownership of telecommunications companies, the third with the selection of the sectors to be liberalized, and the fourth with the service obligations to be imposed on the newly licensed private telecommunications companies.

PRIVATIZATION VERSUS LIBERALIZATION

The May 1994 policy statement began with the recognition that the ambitious targets set for development of telecommunications could not be achieved by "government funding and internal generation of resources. Private investment and association of the private sector would be needed in a big way to bridge the resource gap" (*National Telecommunications Policy* 1994: 4). But the policy document also made very clear that "private initiative would be used to complement the efforts" of the Department of Telecommunications (DoT) to raise additional resources and provide services, not to supplant it (*National Telecommunications Policy* 1994: 4). In short, the policy ruled out the privatization, either full or partial, of the DoT.

Privatization, as commonly used, refers to the "transfer of ownership and control from the public to the private sector, with particular reference to asset sales" (Hemming and Mansoor 1988: 2). Faced with a mushrooming budget deficit, the government was committed to divesting a number of state-owned enterprises as part of the privatization component of the NEP. Privatization of the state-owned telecommunications monopoly (either full or partial) had been carried out in a number of other countries (e.g., Mexico, Argentina, Chile, Jamaica, and Venezuela) and it was also the recommended course of action to the Rao government by the World Bank. Multinational corporations like AT&T and British Telecom had expressed a strong interest in acquiring controlling interest in a potentially privatized DoT. After seriously examining this option, the Indian government eventually chose to stay away from privatization of the DoT for two main reasons.

First, the Rao government had to ensure that the telecom reform process was politically acceptable and did not threaten the viability of the government itself. This was not easy. By the time the new telecommunications policy was devised, the government had already experienced electoral defeats in key states and the opposition parties had made the government's economic reforms a major electoral issue. Ideologically, the government was faced with the long-standing suspicion of private industry, particularly multinational corporations, bred during the forty years of socialistic policies. While privatization may have been easier to push through for loss-making Public Sector Enterprises (PSEs) operating in the consumer goods sector, to do so in a highly visible infrastructure sector like telecommunications was fraught with political consequences that the government could not ignore.

Second, the government was not prepared to deal with the fallout of selling one of the country's largest employers. The DoT employs 450,000 unionized workers and its employees are represented by some of the strongest trade unions in the country. Even without privatization the unions had been a major stumbling block in the government's efforts to restructure the sector. A nationwide strike in June 1995, coupled with an appeal to the country's courts, almost prevented the government from opening the tenders that had been submitted by private telephone companies for cellular and basic service licenses. The government took pains to placate the trade unions. Communications Minister Sukh Ram publicly announced that a substantial part of the one trillion rupees (approximately U.S.$27 billion) the DoT hoped to generate through license fees and revenue sharing over the next fifteen years would be used to upgrade skills and undertake welfare programs for its employees.

In choosing to reject the option of privatization, the state withstood pressures from the World Bank, multinational corporations, a section of the political and bureaucratic establishment, and the imperatives of its own economic restructuring program. Instead, it chose to attract private investment into telecommunications by opening up various parts of the sector to private industry. The liberalization of telecommunications equipment had already begun in the 1980s and early 1990s with the licensing of equipment providers in the customer premises and switching and transmission segments. In 1992, the government initiated the gradual liberalization of value-added services like electronic mail, voice mail, information services, audio- and videotext services, video conferencing, and paging. The government also licensed two private cellular companies in each of the four metropolitan cities of Delhi, Bombay, Calcutta, and Madras.

But the most significant step in the liberalization of Indian telecommunications came in the 1994 policy statement in which the government announced the opening up of cellular services in the rest of the country, and, more dramatically, the entry of private companies to provide fixed basic telephony. The policy statement and the guidelines that were issued to implement the policy stipulated that private companies would be allowed to provide basic services in competition with the DoT. Only companies registered in India were permitted to apply for licenses. By stipulating that potential bidders were required to have a track record of having run a system of at least 50,000 lines for five years, the government virtually forced Indian companies to enter into partnership with foreign telephone companies. But the government also limited foreign participation to 49 percent of the equity holding of the joint-venture company. The government initially divided the country into 20 "circles," each more or less corresponding to a state boundary, and invited separate bids for each of the circles. By stipulating that only one private company would be licensed to provide fixed basic services in each "circle," the government set up a duopolistic market structure in each of the circles with the private telco competing head to head with the DoT. The particulars of the liberalization policy reflect the diverse economic and political objectives the government seeks to achieve as it struggles to balance the competing demands of domestic and foreign forces.

FOREIGN VERSUS DOMESTIC OWNERSHIP

The government's decision to allow foreign telephone companies to participate in the licenses was motivated by three main considerations. First, it was evident that domestic companies would have considerable difficulty in raising the huge investment needed to build infrastructure by themselves. Nor would domestic or foreign capital markets be very interested in investing in these projects without some foreign participation, because no private company in India had any expertise in the area. This lack of experience also made the government uncertain of the ability of domestic industry alone to deploy the technology and provide advanced services. Second, forcing domestic companies to join forces with foreign telcos contributed to the government's overall design of encouraging Foreign Direct Investment (FDI) into the country. By current estimates, the twenty or so foreign telcos that have partnered with Indian companies to bid for cellular and basic service licenses will bring about US$5 billion into the country over the next ten years. Finally, foreign participation was encouraged to achieve the technological leapfrog that would be needed to build a world-class telecommunications network.

Having decided that foreign participation was critical to the modernization and development of the sector, the government had to decide the extent to which foreign companies would be allowed to participate in the ownership structure of the new telecom companies. Powerful bureaucrats like N. Vittal, the then chairman of the Telecom Commission, and A. N. Verma, head of the Foreign Investment Promotion Board, strongly favored allowing foreign companies to own 51 percent or more of the new companies (Petrazzini 1996). This position was supported by the foreign bidders, their governments, and the World Bank. But this option had little support from Prime Minster Rao or the communications minister, Sukh Ram (Petrazzini 1996).

While encouraging foreign participation was important, the government also had to involve domestic industry in the reform process. Politically, the government had sold liberalization to the public and to Indian industry by limiting the extent of the participation by foreign companies in Indian enterprises. Very few foreign companies were initially given permission to set up 100 percent–owned ventures in the country, and even 51 percent ownership was limited to a select list of high-priority areas. Not only has the government been faced with political objections to liberalization from the country's opposition parties, it has also had to deal with complaints from Indian capitalists that the reform program threatened the viability of Indian industry. Organized objections came in the form of the so-called Bombay Club, a group of industrialists who came together to oppose the government's opening up of the economy. By forcing the multinationals to partner with Indian companies, the government disarmed many of the objections of both the political and industrial opposition. In the end the political imperatives of being able to successfully push through reforms in a highly visible sector like telecommunications made limiting foreign companies to minority positions (49 percent or less) almost inevitable.

BASIC VERSUS LONG-DISTANCE SERVICES

The decision to liberalize local services rather than the more attractive long-distance services was one of the most controversial decisions of the reform process. Both within the government and in outside agencies like the World Bank, there was the conviction that opening up basic services would not attract the private investment necessary to jump-start the reforms. Indeed, many of the U.S. Regional Bell Operating Companies (RBOCs) stayed away from the bidding partly because the short-term profitability of the licenses for basic services was far from apparent.

By liberalizing local rather than long-distance services, the government disarmed potential criticism that it was selling out profitable services to private capital. By holding out the prospect that the private telcos might be allowed to provide long-distance services after five years, it held out the promise of significant rewards for the private telcos in the long term.

The government's decision to keep the private telcos out of the more lucrative long-distance market also dampened some of the initial enthusiasm among the potential bidders. In order to continue to attract significant private-sector interest in the bids, the government was compelled to give in to a number of demands from the private telcos. For instance, having maintained DoT's position as the monopoly long-distance provider, the government was faced with the difficult task of setting access charges—the amount DoT would charge from the private telcos—for carrying national and international calls. Initially the rates were set at about 50 percent of DoT's costs for a unit of national long-distance carriage and 62 percent of its costs for a unit of international carriage. Under protest from the potential bidders that the charges were too high, the government finally set them at 40 and 50 percent, respectively.

CIRCLES VERSUS NATIONAL LICENSES

The government sought to ensure that the expansion of telecommunications and the development of the national network took place in a uniform manner across the country and that the interests of more and less industrially advanced states and of rural and urban areas were evenly balanced. Because nationwide private providers could be tempted to cream-skim, investing only in urban areas or in states with high potential returns, the government decided not to license any national service providers, but rather created the twenty "circles," or service areas. The attempt was to ensure that poorer states like Uttar Pradesh or Bihar or the northeastern states like Manipur, Mizoram, or Arunachal Pradesh, which already suffered from very poor infrastructure, would not be neglected. The government hoped to protect itself from any political or electoral backlash against the Congress Party in these states.

Along with balanced regional development, the government also sought to ensure that the private telephone companies invested in the expansion of the rural network. It mandated that the private telcos install 10 percent of all new lines in rural areas and provide all villages with access to at least one Public Call Office (PCO) by the end of the first two years of the license. In addition, 15 percent of the weight for the evaluation of the bids for basic services would be based on the number of lines in rural areas a company committed to install in excess of the mandatory 10 percent. The government also announced that heavy penalties (Rs. 66 or U.S.$2 per day for each rural telephone line not installed) would be levied on companies that did not meet their rural installation commitments.

The emphasis on rural expansion clearly had a strong political component. It not only deflected the charge that the government's policies were pro-rich, it also provided a shield against accusations that the government was allowing the private telcos to engage in cream-skimming. It was also a signal to the rich farmers that the government would manage the reform process in a manner that protected the interests of the agricultural sector, and that the benefits of the reforms would not accrue to industry alone. At the same, the rural service component of the new policy signaled the government's continued commitment to the balanced development of the economy and the recognition that rural development constituted an important component of economic development, even in a market-oriented economy.

This analysis of the four crucial decisions the government made in developing its telecommunications policy provides evidence of the interplay among the various political, economic, and bureaucratic interests within the telecom arena. These include multinational corporations, domestic private-sector companies, local equipment manufacturers, DoT's 450,000 unionized workers, and the nearly five million current or anticipated consumers waiting for a phone connection. The Indian courts also played an important role in monitoring and correcting the course of telecommunications reform. They have not hesitated to force the government to reconsider policy decisions, strike down DoT policies, or, as in the cellular case, to redo a significant portion of the license allocation process. The analysis also reveals the compromises the government made to prevent opposition parties from making the reforms a political issue and ensure that the new policies do not hurt the government's electoral chances.

Based on the presumption that a world-class telecommunications system was critical in achieving the overall goals of the new economic policy, the government set a series of ambitious targets for the growth of the sector over a three- to five-year period. Liberalization of basic services and the decision to allow private companies, in partnership with foreign companies, to provide services in competition with the DoT were expected to provide the structural, fiscal, and technological engines required to arrive at those targets. The decision not to privatize, or even corporatize the DoT, maintaining DoT's monopoly over long-distance services and limiting the extent of foreign participation, provides evidence of the government's continued sensitivity to making the reforms politically palatable as well as its inability to fully free itself from the economic nationalism that had guided past policies. But while this analysis clearly reveals the compromises the government had to make to drive through the reforms, it also reveals the ability of the government to act in the face of both foreign and domestic opposition to all or parts of the reforms and the continuing importance of the state as an autonomous actor in the policy process.

CONCLUSION

This account of telecommunications restructuring in India has focused on the continuities among society, the state, and the international system. While recognizing that the international environment establishes the specific constraints and opportunities for states, it rejects a rigid distinction between "levels of analysis" in favor of an approach that situates state actions within a specific global situation while identifying the imperatives and objectives of the state as well as the domestic political and economic forces that shaped the particulars of the government's telecommunications reforms.

As the internationalists have shown, the global political economy influences the behavior of states in powerful ways. The Gulf War provided the immediate trigger for India's economic crisis, and faced with declining investor confidence in the global fiscal markets the country was forced to resort to a bailout from the IMF. The IMF and the World Bank ensured that any rescue plan for the economy would require the government to initiate a sweeping structural reform program. The collapse of communism and the Soviet Union as economic and ideological forces in international affairs left the government with little alternative. In its struggle to liberalize the economy, the government soon realized that a modern and efficient telecommunications system was vital to the success of the overall reform program. The government monopoly that had existed for forty-five years was no longer capable of delivering such a system. In the face of these difficulties, the government had little choice but to open up the sector to private capital and multinational corporations.

But it would be a mistake to view the Indian reform program as simply an outcome of the operation of powerful international forces. The state itself was a prime mover in restructuring the economy in general and telecommunications in particular. Over the past years of state-led economic development, the state itself had become hostage to the competing interests of the country's "dominant coalition" of rich farmers, industrial capitalists, and bureaucrats and professionals. With its ability to act in the economic realm increasingly constrained, the state chose to break this stranglehold by shifting the processing of economic claims from itself to the market. The economic reform program was also the result of a shift in ideology in a section of the political and bureaucratic apparatus that had come to realize that India must liberalize in order to ensure long-term development.

At the same time, the power of the state to act was constrained by powerful and often contradictory forces within civil society and within the state itself. The rise of new "demand groups" that wanted a piece of the country's economic pie put increasing pressure on the state to process their competing social claims. Liberalization was the safety valve resorted to by the state to relieve these pressures. But traditional forces within the state bureaucracy, the trade unions, and other political parties forced the government to continually change the telecommunications policy in order to counter opposition and ensure its own political survival. The courts played a watchdog role throughout the process and forced the government and the bureaucracy to be more transparent in the reform process.

The telecom reforms provide evidence of the difficult compromises the government had to cobble together as it sought to manage the overall institutional transition of the country's economy. These compromises and policies were an outcome of the confluence of a number of different domestic and international forces at a particular historical moment in India's economic development. This examination of that historical moment has provided some insight into the structural constraints on the autonomy of the Indian state to initiate and implement policy decisions.

The theoretical implications of this analysis might be summed up in a plea for greater attention to the multilevel character of the influences shaping state actions and the importance of grounding the study of the state in concrete historical research. By ignoring the interplay of domestic economic and political forces, the character and imperatives of states, and the operation of the global political economy, we may be unable to identify the dynamics within a given historical moment that are instrumental in producing changes in nation-states. Although the focus on the continuities between societies, states, and the international system limits generalizations about the historically contingent strategies of actors in the international and domestic political economy, it provides deeper and more comprehensive explanations for events like the restructuring of Indian telecommunications.

5

The IMF, Globalization, and the Changes in the Media Power Structure in South Korea

Daeho Kim and Seok-Kyeong Hong

In November 1997, the South Korean economy came under IMF control. As Korean economic difficulties unfolded, IMF officials insisted on opening Korea's capital market to foreign investors. This policy led to the deregulation of all media sectors, a condition that even the World Trade Organization (WTO) had not been able to impose on the Korean media industry. Heavily indebted *chaebol*s (conglomerates) could no longer protect their newspapers and cable TV companies. Broadcasting companies, which had been the beneficiaries of a highly protected market, now had to face up to foreign media magnates like Rupert Murdoch and Ted Turner. The 1999 Broadcasting Act finally adjusted the Korean regulatory scheme to this demand from the market.

This chapter's main objective is to describe the changes taking place in South Korean media under the IMF regime in order to analyze how these changes are mediated and transformed by the traditional media power structure in Korean society. In so doing, it considers why the state matters, even when it is subject to a strict externally imposed regime such as the one mandated by the IMF conditions. We try to explain these changes in globalization terms. We do so not to sustain the globalist discourse but to reappraise and question some of its hypotheses.

MEDIA, GLOBALIZATION, AND THE IMF IN KOREA

Globalization as a National Goal

In November 1994, then Korean president Kim Young Sam proclaimed the globalization of Korea during the APEC (Asian Pacific Economic Cooperation) summit held in Sydney. The Kim administration elaborated governing principles for its five-year term and proclaimed globalization as the country's new vision and development strategy. Since then, globalization has been a keyword in South Korean mass media and public opinion.

Traditionally, Korean society has maintained a passive and inward-looking view. Korean history is filled with invasion, dominance, and oppression by other countries, particularly China and Japan. In the early twentieth century, Korea spent thirty-six years as a colony of Japan. After gaining independence, the Korean peninsula was divided by overseas powers, which later resulted in the Korean War. More recently, a market opening was forced by foreign countries led by the United States. These events have made the Korean people hostile toward globalization. In this situation, the Kim administration's globalization drive was surprising. Seemingly the launchpad for a veritable cultural revolution, this reform had various implications for Korean development.

First, it meant that Korean society overtly assumed a neoliberal political view. During the last decade the neoliberal philosophy has been dominant worldwide, eclipsing, for instance, socialism and nationalism. Market principles, including the liberalization of trade and capital inflow, the deregulation of financial markets, and the flexibility of the labor force, have gained global primacy. This model is quite different from the government-led development policies that had been in force since the 1960s. The Kim administration tried to maintain economic growth and continue its reform programs by introducing neoliberalism into Korea. The government used the "globalization" concept to become an industrialized country by joining the WTO and the OECD. Since then, globalization has been accepted as the country's leading governing ideology.

Second, key figures of the Kim administration equated globalism with deregulatory policies. They discarded long-standing government-driven policies that had been deemed efficacious and were preferred in the early stages of industrialization. They felt that these policies no longer worked in an economy as large and complex as South Korea's. Market efficiency replaced the old government-driven development policies.

Third, the notion of "globalization" was based on constructing an information society based on computer networking. The government adopted the slogan "globalization through informatization." The government's rationale is that successful globalization requires computerization to effectively connect all the elements of the state.

Nevertheless, globalization in Korea was unpopular before the IMF bailout period. Nationalist discourse opposing the globalization policy was based on the concept of the "Korean way to development." However, in the IMF era, Korean people have realized in a dramatic way that they live in a "global village," whether they or not they want this, in which globalization and liberalization supersede national boundaries.

The Not-So-Globalized Media

It is interesting to observe how these globalizing tendencies are reflected in the media sector. Media theories, whether the leftist media imperialist approach or the more conservative or postmodernist globalization approach, estimate the degree of globalization of the media in terms of the following criteria: the ratio of imported programs to domestic programs, the quantity of program traffic, media market openness and the penetration of foreign media capital, the formation of an audience able to consume foreign media content (intellectually and economically), and the availability of foreign content (Cunningham 1996; Ferguson 1992; Mohammadi 1997a). (See also Joseph Straubhaar's chapter in this volume.)

According to these criteria, Korean media are not very open. Even though Kim Young Sam's government promoted globalization, the advancement of globalization in the media sector did not proceed at a rate comparable to other economic sectors. As in many Asian countries, Koreans traditionally prefer domestic television programming. For example, according to a 1994 survey, viewers in Indonesia, the Philippines, Singapore, Thailand, South Korea, and Malaysia prefer domestic programs; in these countries 90 percent of the top twenty programs were local. In Hong Kong, 100 percent of the top twenty programs were local (Cunningham and Jacka 1996: 622). Except for the film market, which has been largely dominated by Hollywood since the 1960s, the majority of South Korean media content and capital remain domestic. Contrary to worldwide globalizing tendencies, foreign programming has decreased on South Korean television, despite the fact that U.S. and Latin American programs are increasing their market share in the world (Cunningham and Jacka 1996: 622) (see table 5.1). Since the late 1980s, the popularity of domestic programs has caused imported programming—mostly American series—to be relegated to hours outside of prime time.

The Broadcasting Act limits foreign content to 20 percent for terrestrial channels and to 30 percent for cable channels, or up to 50 percent if the cable programs concern technology and science, culture, or sports. This is a stricter standard than is found elsewhere, such as in Australia, France, and the European Community, which protect domestic audiovisual products in "cultural exception" terms.

The rigidity of the Korean foreign programming quota doesn't actually restrict terrestrial broadcasters' activities: As seen in table 5.1, the ratio of foreign content remains far under the bar. Thus, it can be said that the quota is a normative line rather than a practical restraint. Cable TV is an exception.

Table 5.1   Transition of Foreign Programming in Korean Television

Year	KBS1	KBS2	MBC	SBS
1998	2.3%	8.6%	—	13.4%
1997	2.2%	9.3%	7.2%	10.7%
1996	3.6%	13.6%	8.8%	—
1995	3.6%	13.6%	8.2%	14.1%
1994	4.6%	12.8%	9.2%	13.1%
1993	3.8%	11.9%	8.9%	14.8%
1992	3.0%	13.5%	11.1%	13.3%
1991	3.0%	12.5%	8.7%	13.9%
1990	8.5%	18.6%	—	—

Key: KBS1, KBS2 (Korea Broadcasting System); MBC (Munwha Broadcasting Company); SBS (Seoul Broadcasting System).
Source: Internal Report, Korean Broadcasting Commission, June 1998.

Introduced in 1994 and motivated by the economic crisis, several cable TV channels, specializing in films and animation, are not adhering to the quota.

The Broadcasting Act completely bans foreign investment in terrestrial broadcasting channels and cable system operation. However, cable program providers are allowed to have foreign investment up to 33 percent.

The market in print media has traditionally been as closed as the broadcasting sector, but with globalization it has rapidly advanced; many multinational press companies are publishing weeklies and monthlies in Korean. They prefer publishing the local version to distributing the original version. These local versions are mainly computer magazines and beauty and fashion magazines targeted at women (see table 5.2).

As far as satellite broadcasting service is concerned, foreign broadcasts have already become widely available. Even though a legal framework for regulation has not yet been established, Japanese and Chinese satellite broadcasting channels and various channels of Rupert Murdoch's Star TV can be received via dish antenna. Japan's SkyPerfec TV programs and even the Playboy channel can be seen in Seoul with the installation of a 6-foot satellite dish antenna. An estimated 3 million households currently receive foreign satellite broadcasting services. Over 40 percent of them regularly watch satellite broadcasting programs. Japan's public service broadcaster NHK is received in more than 6 million households through relay wire broadcasting and cable TV. Another sign of increasingly open media is seen in the changing policy toward Japanese popular culture products. The Korean government formerly restricted the entry of Japanese media material such as pop music, films, and television programs, because they were thought to be "contrary to national sentiment." Recently, however, after considering the great influence of Japanese mass culture, the government has permitted the import of Japanese cultural products.

Table 5.2   Media Multinational Periodicals Published in Korean

Country	Periodicity	Title	Content	License Date
U.S.A.	monthly	Guidepost	religion	03/74
	monthly	Golf Life	sports	05/89
	monthly	WWD	fashion	12/92
	weekly	Newsweek	actuality	10/91
	monthly	Success	marketing	08/95
	monthly	LAN	computer	09/94
	monthly	Reader's Digest	cultural	11/77
	monthly	Lan Times	computer	12/95
	monthly	Byte	computer	03/94
	monthly	Becket	sports	03/97
	monthly	Upline	currency	04/94
	monthly	Esquire	masculine	04/95
	monthly	Working Women	feminine	08/95
	monthly	GEO	human life	09/92
	monthly	Computer Gaming World	computer	09/96
	monthly	PC Week	computer	06/95
	monthly	PC Computing	computer	04/96
	monthly	Hawaii Number One	computer	10/92
	monthly	Harper's Bazaar	feminine	04/95
France	monthly	Les Nouvelles Esthétiques	beauty	02/96
	monthly	Marie	feminine	03/92
	monthly	Votre beauté	beauty	06/96
	monthly	Enfants	child care	02/95
	monthly	Elle	fashion	05/92
	monthly	UNESCO Courier	actuality culture	04/95
	monthly	Cousteau Junior	nature education	07/96
	quarterly	Top Model	fashion	03/95
	monthly	Première	cinema	09/95
	monthly	Figaro	feminine	03/94
U.K.	monthly	Vogue	feminine	03/96
	weekly	Camera Wise	camera	10/95
Japan	quarterly	Stereo Sound	music	05/89
	monthly	Monthly Science Newton	general science	02/85
	monthly	With	feminine	06/96
	monthly	Quintess	dental science	07/96
Italy	biannual	MM Magasine	fashion	03/95
	quarterly	Colors	tourism	05/95
Australia	monthly	One on One	sports	05/95

Source: Korea Press Institute 1998.

Due to its cultural and geographical contiguity, and the Japanese colonial experience, Japanese culture has easily penetrated the Korean territory. American programs are also familiar to Koreans through the U.S. Army's television service, which established a terrestrial channel in 1957 before any Korean television began to broadcast. Learning English has been greatly stressed, as a result of government-promoted globalization, and English-language satellite programs are very appealing to Koreans. Rupert Murdoch's plan for satellite transmissions to the Korean market is thought to be based on careful analysis of Korean viewers' favorable attitude toward and familiarity with English-language programs.

IS THE IMF A GLOBALIZING FORCE?

Although the Korean government and conglomerates have promoted globalization, the extent to which the Korean media sector has globalized is still quite limited. How is globalization changing after the IMF bailout in Korea? What direction is the globalization of the media taking after the IMF plan? The economic crisis that forced Korea to adopt the IMF program grew out of the financial and foreign exchange crisis. Government measures intended to overcome the IMF era attracted foreign capital by opening the domestic market. IMF officials asked the government to accept the drastic economic restructuring that the organization requires. Such pressure for an open-door policy applies as well to the media sector.

It remains unclear whether the IMF restructuring will promote globalization and an opening up to the world. One year after the IMF bailout, there were indications that globalization was moving backward in most aspects, excluding the influx of capital. Travel abroad was dramatically reduced, while the number of foreign visitors to Korea did not increase as much as had been expected with the depreciation of the Korean currency. Cultural and scientific exchanges were nearly at a standstill. Broadcasters programmed shows designed to help the unemployed and struggling small firms, which appealed to nationalistic sentiments. There was popular opposition to Murdoch's intent to enter into Korean satellite broadcasting.

The Media Industry and the Media Power Structure in Korea

The powerful economic development of Korea's media scene has gone hand-in-hand with the evolution of the media industry. Since martial law was lifted in 1988, media companies have had genuine freedom. The traditional press cartel was demolished, and print media regulation was liberalized. These measures increased the competitiveness of the press, and the number of publications increased. In 1996, the number of newspapers published in South Korea was 113, while it had been only 28 a decade earlier. The broadcasting industry also expanded quickly. Between 1991 and 1997, one commercial quasi-nationwide TV network and eight terrestrial regional channels were launched. Moreover, in 1995 cable TV started service with twenty-nine program providers, indicating that Korea has entered into a genuine multichannel period. In 1998, seventy-seven cable stations were operating nationwide, with a total of 820,000 subscribers.

In the meantime, satellite broadcasting had begun its trial broadcasting service. Three broadcasting satellites, launched in 1995, 1996, and 1999 respectively, can carry more than 150 channels. Because the legal framework regulating satellite broadcasting was delayed in the National Assembly, only four satellite channels (two KBS channels and two EBS services) were transmitting their services on a trial basis.

The growth of the media industry is evident in Korea. But there have been serious problems. First, most media owners are large industrial companies or wealthy media families. In the former case, the media are often used as a means to protect parent companies, or as lobbyists or information-gathering agencies. Even though these media companies often operate at a deficit, they have survived thanks to reckless investment from the parent companies. In the latter case, however, Korea's leading papers, *Chosun Daily*, *Dong-A Daily*, and *Hankook Daily*, are all owned by old media families (see table 5.3). Generally, media companies have been operated with motives other than simply business success.

Second, the audience market has been functioning in an abnormal way. Most newspapers have not joined the ABC system, which calculates the audience market objectively. They do not want to make their subscription figures public. Moreover, in the cases of conglomerate-owned press and religious press, subscriptions are allocated to their employees or parishioners. In broadcasting, all advertising must be approved by the Korea Broadcasting Advertising Corporation (KOBACO), which is controlled by the government. So audience demand is not directly reflected in the market.

Table 5.3   Main National Press Ownership

Newspaper	Ownership
Chosun Daily	90.9% owned by Bang family
Dong-A Daily	76.7% owned by Kim family
Hankook Daily	99.0% owned by Jang family
Joongang Daily	67.9% owned by Samsung
Munwha Daily	99.6% owned by Hyundai
Kyunghyang Daily	98.9% owned by Hanwha Group

Source: Korea Press Institute 1997.

These features of the media environment have facilitated a peculiar form of power dominating the media power structure. In Korea, political power elites have always tried to control the media, and the media developed under their influence. This relationship is referred to as "adhesion." Since 1960, Korea has experienced radical political changes: two military coup d'états and four constitutional amendments. The rapid changes in the structure of political power have made political questions the essential issues in Korean society. Political elites have considered the media's potential capacity for social control extremely important in solving political problems and in legitimizing regimes.

In the 1970s, the military dictatorship used repressive media policies, but the new military dictators of the 1980s began to control the media with carrot-and-stick strategies. Forced media closures and mergers, the mass dismissal of journalists who were critical of the regime, and censorship of information guidelines were the stick. Fiscal favor for media enterprises and economic benefits to journalists were the carrot. These two different devices were not used consecutively as alternate means of control, but were employed simultaneously in an interrelated way. For example, because newspaper companies merged by implementing a "one newspaper per province" policy, only a few companies could be beneficiaries of the monopolistic position.

As for broadcasting companies, private broadcasters were forced to close in favor of government-mandated public service broadcasting. From 1980 to 1991, a duopoly of the KBS (Korea Broadcasting System) and MBC (Munhwa Broadcasting Company) was maintained. The result was that these two survivors found themselves in an advantageous position, even without direct governmental prerequisites: Having no competition, they divided the advertising market between themselves. Under this system, the media would not be seen as obviously assisting the power structure, but neither would they act against the interests of the existing power structure, which was providing them with exclusive benefits. Journalists who survived the dismissal of their colleagues were assured that they would earn high salaries and benefit in various ways. "Noblesse journalist" became the stairway to success and power through the 1980s. Many journalists were recruited to be secretaries in the presidential residence, high-ranking public officials, employees in the state apparatus, ministry spokespersons, and also as members of the National Assembly. The last case is noteworthy: In 1996, 12 percent of the entire National Assembly membership came from the media sector.

This power structure is maintained by a number of control systems and governmental regulations. However, the device that allows a specific power structure dominance in South Korea is not official control but unofficial control through traditional mechanisms: the Blood Tie, the Regional Tie, and the School Tie (Korean Society for Journalism and Communication Studies 1993). The Blood Tie is the most fundamental according to general domination logic (Seo 1988) but in the political sphere, Blood Ties and School Ties are mobilized for the sake of the Regional Tie. The Regional Tie has exercised crucial influence on the elections held over the last thirty years. Its effect is reflected in current political geographic disparities: Two provinces in the southeast part of the Korean peninsula vote for one party and two provinces in the southwest part vote for the other. Elites affiliated with the president's native province are often chosen as high-ranking public officials, cabinet members, and media representatives. The media constitute a lobbying network, capable of unofficial influence by assuring smooth communication with the power structure. Media organizations sometimes replace staff members with people who come from the same province as the president. Political power holders and the media cooperate with each other using regional ties.

This kind of premodern power game has worked not only in the political sphere, but also in many sectors, including the economic sector. The IMF regime requires social restructuring according to the universal criteria of a capitalist system: competition and efficiency. The South Korean case allows observation of whether the IMF regime will break this traditional media power structure relationship or whether the IMF's international power is mediated by the domestic media power structure to produce a specific effect distinguishable from other countries subject to the organization's regulations.

Another important factor to be considered in understanding the power balance around the media is civil society. The democratization movement in the 1980s bred the television monitoring movement and other significant activities. A campaign against paying the license fee was organized to contest the biased information of the leading public service broadcaster, KBS. There was also a "turn off the television" campaign and a "civil surveillance movement for impartial coverage of elections." The latter played a crucial role in establishing the equal time principle for political candidates on television. Civil society enlarged its ideological and practical influence with these movements. Television monitoring results and media criticism have been published regularly, occupying an important position in producing discourse about broadcasting policy. As a consequence, television monitoring professionals in civil society were invited to participate in the hearings and seminars for the amendment of the Broadcasting Act and for other important media issues.

The most important and visible result of the civil movement against the conservative media sector was the creation of *The Han-Gyoreh* daily, the symbol of an independent press, detached from political power and big capital. *Han-Gyoreh* means "one nation." This unique daily was born in 1988 after a dramatic national campaign to give birth to "our own press." Its capital is dispersed among 63,000 volunteer shareholders, and the maximum individual shareholding is set at 1 percent. (Kim 1993: 398). *The Han-Gyoreh* has contested the conservative press since its inception. After the last presidential election, which converted the longtime ruling party into the opposition, *The Han-Gyoreh* took on a more informative than critical tone. Nevertheless, it is a unique daily that is safe under the IMF regime.

THE IMF AND THE LOGIC OF STRUCTURAL CHANGES IN THE MEDIA

Media in Crisis under the IMF

Most Koreans consider the IMF situation to be a crisis comparable to the Korean War. The media industries share this view. The most important force for structural reform is the advertising market, which has been reduced considerably. The total amount of broadcast advertising (including radio, TV, and cable TV) decreased from U.S.$1.5 billion in 1997 to U.S.$1.01 billion in 1998, a 35 percent reduction. The number of people employed in media companies decreased from 42,368 to 37,969, a 10.4 percent reduction, from June 1997 to June 1998.

Because of the drastic rise of the foreign exchange rate and the interest rate under the IMF regime, the media companies that have to pay for imported equipment and whose loan proportions were extremely high have all been in danger of bankruptcy. Media companies owned by conglomerates suffered the side effects of the affiliated firms' deficits, or they went bankrupt simply because owners did not want to cover media company deficits.

The newborn cable TV business faced a critical situation. Since 1995, a total of about U.S.$970 million had been spent on the cable TV business alone. As of June 1998 the entire cable TV sector had enormous debts, five out of twenty-nine program providers had gone bankrupt, and only three had no deficits. To cut expenses, terrestrial broadcasting companies reduced the number of programs they commissioned. As a result, the independent production companies that no longer had production orders from broadcasters went through a major structural adjustment as well.

Moreover, a mortal shock came from Korea Telecom and Korea Electricity, which had been in charge of cable TV network installation: They decided to withdraw from the business. Several program providers gave up their licenses to the government while others tried to lure foreign capital for their survival. Others organized going-out-of-business sales of their remaining equipment. Considering that such equipment would need to be repurchased after the economic recovery, this meant a tremendous loss for the entire program industry. The cable TV companies begged the government not to subject the industry to the severe "exit policy" (bankruptcy program) that it had applied to other businesses. The cable companies had to ask for government recognition as key industries and for financial support.

A great change in the nature of the state's involvement took place. This was a result of the changes in both the international situation and in the domestic political regime occasioned by the IMF intervention. In the 1980s, Korea experienced a radical social movement and people's liberal campaigns, and in 1987 it achieved a peaceful revolution when the military party surrendered and a democratic government emerged. Furthermore, in 1989, newspapers acquired unprecedented freedom of speech as the dismantling of the Eastern European Communist countries weakened South Korea's nationalistic anti-Communist ideology, which had justified repression of the press.

The new president, Kim Dae Jung, elected in February 1998 after a long period of opposition leadership, advanced this liberalization. First, he got rid of the Ministry of Information, which had functioned as the formal actor in media control. The 1999 Broadcasting Act represented the liberalization of the government's media control. The act strengthened the Korean Broadcasting Commission's competence as an independent regulatory body in charge of all broadcasting business administration and policies. It also represented the ideology of viewer sovereignty, by requiring the constitution of a viewers' board of commission in every broadcasting company. The act weakened the state's control over media content, abolishing all pre-review (censorship) and introducing a self-regulation system for each broadcaster.

To attract foreign capital, the government planned overall market deregulation. However, it does not appear that the government will leave the media industry entirely to market logic. This is because the government can now intervene any time in a more active manner than ever before, by applying the "exit policy" bankruptcy program.

Changes in the Media Power Structure Relationships

Therefore, since the IMF bailout, the crisis in the media industry has changed the relationship among media, capital, and the state, which has resulted in changes of control over the media.

First, the relationship between the media and capital has changed, particularly in the realm of media ownership. Major conglomerates have given up press ownership. Restructuring programs have marginalized press companies. Hyundai, Korea's largest conglomerate, abandoned its equity in the *Munwha Daily*. Samsung, Korea's second largest conglomerate, decided to sell its stock in the *Joongang Daily* newspaper. The Hanwha Group, Korea's sixth largest conglomerate, pulled out from its participation in the *Kyunghyang Daily*. These changes have led employee groups to seek to manage the media on their own. *Munwha Daily* and the *Kyunghyang Daily* have taken the lead in this respect.

Second, transnational media groups are now allowed to enter the Korean market. Before joining the OECD, the government had banned the entry of foreign media or foreign investment into the Korean media market. But since the IMF crisis, the government has tried to attract foreign investment in all sectors, including the media. In an effort to encourage more overseas investments, the government revised the Foreign Investment Promotion Law.

Rupert Murdoch's interest in joining Dacom's satellite broadcasting project provoked a heated public discussion and growing concern about cultural dependency. The majority of the public felt that the deal would threaten Korean culture and the nation's developing broadcasting infrastructure. There was such a harsh debate on that matter that the new government has taken gradual steps to this point. Even the new Broadcasting Act, which extends the allowance of foreign capital, exhibits a very cautious approach.

Foreign investment in media industries would affect not only direct media dependency but also the big local media companies' future strategies. Considering that newspaper publishers are not permitted to enter the broadcasting market, the entry of foreign capital will affect local media cross-ownership policies, and local media companies will establish relationships with foreign capital.

Third, the nature of state intervention in the relationship between capital and media has changed. KOBACO, the public advertising agency established in 1981, collects public funds out of advertising fees in an attempt to return profits from broadcasters to society. Six to seven percent of advertising money has gone to the public fund, which is used to support various journalistic and cultural projects. But this system has been criticized for distorting market principles. The KOBACO is regarded as a barrier that prevents advertisers from doing business directly with broadcasters. In a global age, this monopoly system has been seen as an unfair business practice. Now the KOBACO is subject to the reform program affecting overall government enterprises.

Fourth, as media company managements fell into crisis, the relationship between the media and the state also changed. The level of media dependency on the state is growing. In late 1997, three newspaper companies would have gone bankrupt, but government intervention rescued them; the government forced banks to provide emergency loans. Among the national daily newspapers, six out of ten companies showed large deficits.

The situation of broadcasters was similar. The government has recently provided special funds to rescue cable TV companies from falling into the red. Most cable TV channels and system operators asked the government to provide financial support or to allow increased foreign investment in programming.

In this situation, it is difficult for media companies to remain independent from the government. The government's capacity for direct or indirect control over the media is growing. Since the onset of the IMF economic crisis, the government has taken a deregulatory policy direction based on market principles. This policy makes it easier to control the media in certain ways. The government's control over the financial market has made the media more dependent on its political power.

In sum, the relationships among power, capital, and media caused by the IMF regime are still in transition. Nevertheless, important changes are perceptible in the state's intervention logic. To meet the IMF's structural adjustment requirements, a deregulatory policy based on market principles is being applied. As a result, certain special benefits given to the media have been drastically reduced. Now that the general privileges in financing and the taxation system have disappeared, many media companies are on the verge of bankruptcy. Several media companies whose holding companies are conglomerates also face the possibility of going bankrupt in the process of managerial and financial restructuring programs.

A relationship between the media and the power structure constituted on economic principles is something new in South Korea. Previously, the media power structure relationship evolved from political factors such as power shifting between political classes and the civil movement for democratization. Since the IMF crisis, however, structural adjustment on the basis of economic principles has become the main factor of change in the media power structure relationship. This does not mean, however, that the political power elite has given up its controlling influence over the media. Without exercising direct control over the media, the government now holds the reins through its power to intervene in the overall process of financial decision making.

CONCLUSION

The IMF plan forced Korean society to accept market principles. There is now a strong consensus that the Korean media industries, which developed guided by political principles, should operate according to market principles. There are positive aspects of this shift in terms of the media, in the sense that market forces may weaken the traditional media power structure ties by reducing the privileges allocated to the media sector. Some observers have also noted that the crisis could improve the health of Korean media by increasing editorial independence and diversity of information. It may also provide an opportunity for publications to define their own niches and to differentiate themselves from one another editorially.

However, this conjuncture may also favor governmental intervention. To survive in the market, financially fragile media companies have greater dependence on the government. One typical example is the twenty-four-hour cable news channel YTN. YTN recorded a deficit of about U.S.$80 million in 1997. This channel tried to sell its equity, but, in complete contrast to the enthusiasm shown by many companies five years previously when the channel was launched, no company showed an interest. Having begged the government for financial support or state investment, the news channel could be directly influenced by the government.

Meanwhile, the IMF plan has become a mediator of deregulation. The government is willing to open the broadcasting market to press companies and conglomerates that had previously been banned. The 1999 Broadcasting Act allows them to enter into the cable TV and satellite broadcasting market, but not into the terrestrial broadcasting market.

However, the new government's attitude toward media deregulation is still ambiguous. On the one hand, it advocates deregulation and market principles, but on the other hand, it still emphasizes the public interest. The government has shown a hesitant attitude about foreign capital as well. Since the IMF era began, it has induced foreign investment in all industry sectors. However, it has been reluctant to do so in the media sector because media trade unions and citizen groups are negatively disposed toward foreign capital.

FURTHER DISCUSSION

The IMF program designed for developing countries is being severely criticized. Some critics, citing the example of India, even insist that the alternative is refusing to be integrated into the world system (Kolko 1998). (However, as Nikhil Sinha's chapter in this volume indicates, India is also undergoing economic liberalization.)

Considering the fact that the IMF's uniform and market-oriented structural adjustment does not respect differences of tradition, customs, values, and social systems of each beneficiary country, the IMF is clearly propelling a globalization process. The IMF program fits Ferguson's (1992) definition of globalization very well: massive privatization, deregulation, acceleration of international trade and capital transfer, the promotion of mergers and acquisitions, and finally the enhancement of economic interdependence around the world.

However, this economy-centered interpretation seems rather simplistic. This question should be addressed with a multidimensional and contextual approach. In a country like South Korea, with a long tradition and a peculiar media power structure relationship, the media globalization process brought about by the IMF plan is contradictory.

First, although the IMF reform brought foreign capital and a massive inflow of foreign programs into the Korean media industry, the economic and ideological attractions of the domestic market are decreasing. Reduced purchasing power has led to fewer and fewer sales of cultural products. Trips abroad have dramatically decreased. The economic crisis led to feelings of guilt among all Koreans. After the IMF bailout, the slogans "bear part of the pain" and "save foreign currency" were heard constantly. Even those with high incomes cut down on consumption, which in turn hurt the domestic market.

On the other hand, consistent with Joseph Straubhaar's discussion of cultural proximity in chapter 8, Koreans prefer domestic to imported television programming. In the case of cable and satellite television, it is not yet known how expensive the program services financed by foreign capital will be. However, considering that Korean viewers are accustomed to nearly free programs relayed by wired cable services and that the purchasing power of the middle class has weakened, securing a market share is thought to be very difficult. In sum, the IMF has opened the market, but it may not attract much capital.

Second, the role of the government in the globalization process needs to be further discussed in media imperialism accounts as well as in political economy terms. The coming of foreign capital in the form of association between the core of the core and the core of the periphery fits the traditional formula of media imperialism. However, the current government, conscious of the value of national culture, will not be looking on with folded arms before the unilateral advance of foreign capital and its influence. It is elaborating a protectionist policy of support for the national audiovisual and film industries. It is probable that other Asian countries under IMF constraints or under any type of globalization pressure are preparing comparable policies. Asian Pacific countries, invaded by Anglo-Saxon media multinationals, have shown a common interest in establishing a regulatory framework for satellite broadcasting. The Regulatory Roundtable for Asia & the Pacific, consisting of sixteen member countries, is not as homogeneous and unified as the European Union. However, the group agrees on the necessity of cooperation concerning the content of transborder satellite broadcasting. The third Regulatory Round Table, held in Seoul in September 1998 and hosted by the Korean Broadcasting Commission, adopted guidelines for transborder satellite broadcasting services in the Asia-Pacific region (Korean Broadcasting Commission 1998).

Furthermore, the hypothesis that globalizing forces can weaken economic and political sovereignty functions in two different ways. As a negotiator in the international capital market and as executor of the structural adjustment required by the IMF, the government finds its political sovereignty considerably limited. But for the same reason, the government's influence over the domestic economy under structural adjustment becomes even greater. The government can now decide whether a media company will survive by applying or not applying the general "exit policy."

This observation seems important considering that the majority of globalization theorists insist on the weakening of the state's influence as one of the major proofs of globalization. But the IMF situation in Korea contradicts this assumption: Even though the IMF has imposed an evident globalization process on South Korean society and changes in the economy bear out that process, the state's influence as decision maker in economic and political realms has not decreased. The globalization process propelled by the IMF intervention is largely mediated by the domestic power structure and cultural and political particulars. This argument invites the reflection that globalization is not a homogeneous process. Identical phenomena are not observed in different countries; the concrete aspects of globalization vary enough to challenge some assumptions concerning state power and globalization theory.

III

STATES, MEDIA, AND REGIONAL CULTURES

6

Tensions in the Construction of European Media Policies

Philip Schlesinger

The ongoing process of European political and economic integration presents challenges to conventional thinking about both political organization and communicative space. The relations between mass media, identity, and the states of the European Union (EU)—a regional grouping of fifteen member states—are becoming ever more pertinent theoretically. Looked at comparatively, the EU's drive toward the creation of common political institutions is quite distinctive and far-reaching when compared to other trading blocs around the world (Katzenstein 1996). Hirst and Thompson (1996: 153) consider the EU to be "the most ambitious project of multinational economic governance in the modern world." Since the sharing of economic decision making has impinged on national sovereignty, the union may be seen as "a complex polity made up of common institutions, member states, and peoples" (Hirst and Thompson 1996: 154) that combine their efforts in governance.

In the contemporary world, the key framework for the practice of democratic politics and the exercise of citizenship is the state. Customarily, in the international system of states, politico-communicative space is taken to be co-extensive with territorial space. But this rather tight functional fit is disrupted by the emergence of a supranational polity such as the EU. By introducing a new "higher" political level above that of the state, the shift to a supranational formation begins to transform the established communicative relations between national publics and state-centered systems of power.

Thus, European political developments are throwing up new questions about communication and identity. In the incipient process of Europeanization, the state matters, as it retains some regulatory power and remains the preeminent locus and focus of collective identity. Marked institutional differences, distinct "national" languages, and still-unsurmounted historical antipathies between, and indeed within, nation-states shape conceptions of public space at levels below the lofty aspiration for "Europeanness."

In this respect, cultural production, distribution, and consumption become a matter of importance. The processes of Europeanization are transnationalizing processes. Hence, a key emergent issue is how external forces affect the problem of constructing a cultural policy at the level of the state. Putting it differently, what, if anything, can the state do to ensure that it sovereignly pursues nationally determined media and cultural policies in a Europeanizing political and economic context? Is such a conception now out of date? Further, the putative "Europeanization" of media and culture cannot be thought of in isolation from wider processes of globalization.

These considerations invite analysis of whether or not Europeanization implies that a European common communicative space might be constructed via media, as some EU leaders are actively promoting, and if it does under what conditions. The interrelations between such a European space and communicative spaces at the level of the nation-state are also a key area. This chapter raises two questions: First, can the contemporary machinery of the state exercise sovereign control over national cultures, and, second, what conceptions of democratic communication exist at the regional European level and how might these articulate with the national levels.

Contemporary conditions have made the interconnections between national identity and democratic communication into an issue of growing salience. The defense of national identity—and the politics of collective identities more generally—are central to struggles in the political culture of all European states. Nor are such conflicts limited just to the *interiors* of existing states; rather they traverse political frontiers, and indeed are part and parcel of the present reconfiguration of the state system in Europe.

The present analysis offers a viewpoint on the current state of debate about media and collective identity in the European context, with sideward glances at related debates elsewhere. I shall suggest that it is increasingly evident that an analytical connection exists between how we approach questions of cultural identity and those of communicative democracy. Although the two distinct debates about these issues are not commonly theorized in relation to one another, their relationship merits further academic exploration.

THE QUESTION OF COLLECTIVE IDENTITY

The politics of collective identity has become a major issue in today's Europe, with nationhood as a key focus of collective loyalty. However, as nationhood and statehood in Europe do not invariably coincide, the growing salience of the national question offers an inherent challenge to the existing state system and to the stability of our geopolitical image of the continent. Culture and polity in Europe are not congruent with one another and, at a time of uncertainty, culture—in a broad sense—takes center stage as a battleground for the elaboration of identity politics. The case of Canada is similar, as illustrated in Stephen D. McDowell's chapter in this volume.

The upsurge of nationalist consciousness in Europe has been notable since the definitive collapse of the Soviet bloc in 1989–1990. Key benchmarks have been the reunification of Germany, the collapse of the Soviet Union and of Yugoslavia, and Czecho-Slovakia's separation into two states. There has been a notable upsurge in xenophobic and racist politics in Western Europe, generally focused on migrants and ethnic minorities. Neo-Nazi nationalism has reentered the political scene in several states—most notably, France, Germany, and Belgium—whereas in Italy neo-fascists have for the first time since World War II formed part of a Western government. Strongly decentralist—if not actually secessionist—tendencies are noticeable too, prominently in Belgium, Spain, Italy, and the United Kingdom. Unquestionably, the post–Cold War period has produced a general crisis of political identity in Europe, at the heart of which has been an accentuated concern with the nation as the locus and focus of collective sentiment and interest.

Collective identities are relatively fluid constructions rather than eternal essences. Their social making is an active, dialectical process that involves the continual construction and reconstruction of a sense of themselves by self-identifying communities using the signs provided by their cultures. The construction of a collective identity also generally involves active strategies of inclusion and exclusion whereby the boundaries of a given collectivity are policed. Hence, collective identities may be sustained not only by the auto-identification of a group but also by hetero-identification. Both how we define the Other, and how the Other simultaneously defines us, is part of the unavoidable game of identity politics. *We* are defined in part at least by being different from how *They* are. And *Their* difference from *Us* depends on our being what we think we are. Collectivities are therefore sustained and propelled by their reflexivity. The media are a prime site in which such reflexivity is elaborated (Morley and Robins 1995).

The process sketched out above extends through time, deploying both collective memory and collective amnesia. Thus the struggles over various versions of history at any given moment become crucial for the eventual self-understanding of a collectivity's formation. What is understood to be either typically "national" or "ethnic" about a given group is usually drawn from a highly selective account (see Fentress and Wickham 1992; Gellner 1983; Hall 1998; Hobsbawm and Ranger 1983; Namer 1987; Judt 1992). Analogously, the same process also extends through space. Since the nation-state became the "normal" political form in Europe some two centuries ago, this has been paradigmatically conceived in nationalist thought as a self-determining collectivity located in a specific national territory endowed with meanings (Kedourie 1985).

"EUROPEANIZATION"

National identity politics in today's Europe are unavoidably shaped by the region's encounter with the supranational level. Political, economic, and cultural change are in various ways affected by what may be termed "Europeanization," a process that includes institutional change at the macropolitical level, shifts in the sense of belonging and identity at the level of the group, and the reshaping of political understanding in the new, uncertain political geography (Pieterse 1999).

The European Union is at the center of current processes of Europeanization, being a contemporary attempt to move from an integrated market to a political formation, potentially a supranational form of state. Although this development process is uncertain and full of reversals, its ultimate logic (if successful) would be to create a new instance of political legitimacy. Given Europe's diversity, and its historical legacy of conflicting nationalisms, such an entity could not readily be built on the classic simplifying nationalist criteria of ethnicity, consanguinity, language, or religion. The uneven process toward ratification of the Maastricht agreement in 1992–1993 made it quite apparent that the road is not free of obstacles. Emergent Europeanness will probably have to be rooted in a gradualist saga of growing together through institutional sedimentation in the long term rather than the quickfire product of technocratic rationalism.

Plainly, "Europe" is not a single politico-cultural space; nor is "Europeanness" an unambiguous attribute (Schlesinger 1992, 1993, 1994a, 1994b). In thinking about whether and how—if at all—media might construct "Europeanness," it is important to note that Europe's geocultural scope is far from clear. Although there might be little dispute that the continent begins at the Atlantic coastlines, there is far less agreement about precisely where it ends. At the heart of the debate about "Europeanness" are questions about what kinds of political, economic, and cultural attributes both individuals and collectivities require in order to make a claim to "belong" to Europe. Who are and will be the "insiders" and who the "outsiders"? And what role may media play in the processes of definition both within given states and on the broader European level? Such considerations make the attempt—even the aspiration—to construct a European identity so vitally important. In this connection, it seems particularly appropriate to lay special emphasis on the expectations that have centered on the audiovisual media of television and the cinema. These are the principal contemporary diffusers of popular culture, and they are surrounded by assumptions about their implications for the exercise of political, economic, and cultural power. It is the audiovisual media and their ostensible role in European identity-construction that have been the focus of most policy and academic debate.

THE NATION-STATE AS IMPLICIT FOCUS

Research and debate about questions of political communication and democracy have generally (if rather implicitly) concerned themselves with the question of the nation (Dahl 1994: 552). That is because—as in other areas of social scientific research—the underlying framework until quite recently has been that of a national society institutionally delimited by a state. Histories of the press and of broadcasting, and of such communicative practices as advertising, are almost invariably national histories in which there is an overarching interest in how such institutions contribute to the shaping of the national culture, economy, and polity. Arguments about questions of ownership and control of the media or about "bias" in the news have also presupposed a relevance in virtue of a given country's political system for the functioning of which such matters are important. Does the concentration of ownership and control affect the possibility of pluralism within a given (national) polity? Does a systematic bias in news coverage toward the status quo adversely affect the public perception of reformist or revolutionary political forces within a given national political system? Even if we shift the ground somewhat and pose questions about the impact of foreign films or television programs on the public, such concern has been largely fuelled by worries about the preservation of the *national* culture, where "culture" has been held to be the embodiment of some distinctive collective configuration of values, beliefs, and practices. The combined anchorage points of nation-state and national society are very hard to escape, even in undertaking comparative research: In actual fact, these are normally the very terms of comparison.

INTERNATIONALIZING PRESSURES: THE 1980s TO DATE

Although it would be true to say that most academic research in the field of media studies is still conducted within a national-state framework, it also noticeable that some work is being increasingly driven beyond the state's confines by policy demands deriving directly from government, parastatal regulatory bodies, and cultural agencies, as well as by the market requirements of the big commercial media enterprises. There has been a growing recognition of the transnational, even global, framework as relevant for media analysis. States and media enterprises operate within both national and transnational frameworks, so the scope of their need to know about the media environment has become more extensive. Inasmuch as they are attempting to analyze the key players in the international media game, the explanatory and interpretative efforts of social scientists have also ramified in line with the broadening concerns and fields of action of their objects of study, as is illustrated throughout this book.

The tendency to escape from the national level as the governing framework has become particularly marked during the past decade during which time "Europeanization," most notably through the development of the European Community/Union (but also through the activities of the Council of Europe), has had an increasing impact on thinking and research. The emergence of a supranational legal framework, the transnationalization of media ownership and control in Europe, the differential impact of deregulatory policies, the breaking down of East-West divisions in the post–Cold War era—all of these have contributed to the momentum of redefinition.

However, considering mass communication by reference to a supranational context is by no means simply an artifact of the mid-1980s and after. Looking back to the 1970s, the first major stirrings of interest in questions of transnational media flow became evident, influenced by broader social science debates about center/periphery relations, economic and political dependency, and neo-imperialism. Much of this work crystallized around initiatives taken by UNESCO. Thus, for instance, in Latin America, the critique of U.S. cultural dominance via popular media and consumerism began to develop through the platform of UNESCO in the early 1970s (Marques de Melo 1988; Roncagliolo 1994). One outcome of this explicit engagement was the development of the idea of pursuing national communication policies via the state, one that still remains powerful in Latin America and elsewhere. It is certainly a central matter of debate in Europe today. It was in the early 1970s, too, that the first major study of international television flows was published and the academic debate began to gather some steam (Nordenstreng and Varis 1974; Tunstall 1977). By the later 1970s, it could reasonably be said that the question of media, state, and national identity was firmly on the academic agenda, but in a highly specific form, and debated in ways that differ significantly from today's discussion.

The arguments centered on the debate about the New World Information and Communication Order, initiated by the Movement of Non-Aligned Nations and again conducted through UNESCO. This framework of assumptions, which paralleled the desire to create a New World Economic Order deriving from the nonaligned countries, was primarily concerned with the unequal cultural trading relations between the core capitalist countries of the West (especially the United States, Britain, and France) and the Third World. It was anticolonial in spirit. There was a secondary (somewhat muted) concern, too, with the cultural role of the Soviet Union inside the Second World.

The arguments centered mainly on the impact of transnational flows of two cultural modes of expression: the fictional (whether films or television programs) and the factual (news, whether in image, sound, or print).

Above all, the concern at the heart of UNESCO's intervention was with the defense of national cultures in weak and dependent nations, and with the pursuit of greater equity and balance in the flow of facts and images in international journalism. The official position was summed up by the Mass Media Declaration made in Paris in November 1978. This essentially *normative* statement concerned itself with the "Fundamental Principles of the Mass Media to Strengthening Peace and International Understanding, to the Promotion of Human Rights and to Countering Racialism, Apartheid and Incitement to War." The Declaration stipulated the existence of a variety of rights to freedom of information and expression and was couched in antiracist and anti-imperialist language (Nordenstreng 1984; Gerbner, Mowlana, and Nordenstreng 1993; Vincent, Nordenstreng, and Traber 1999). The decisive step in further focusing the arguments was the publication in 1980 of the so-called MacBride Report, *Many Voices, One World* (International Commission for the Study of Communication Problems 1980).

Inevitably, the role of journalism (not least U.S.-, U.K.-, and French-owned international news agencies) was central to this debate. The news agencies were seen as exercising monopolistic control over news flow and as screening out "South-South dialogue." The question of domination over entertainment by U.S., U.K., French, and German television producers also entered the agenda as did the role of advertising in spreading consumerism.

Both the U.S. and U.K. governments (then under President Reagan and Prime Minister Thatcher) chose to interpret UNESCO's initiatives as an attack on freedom of information as interpreted by liberal doctrine and as sufficient grounds to withdraw from the organization in 1984 (Golding and Harris 1997; MacBride and Roach 1993). In many respects, therefore, this debate prefigured subsequent attempts to think about an international public sphere. The idea of an international order implied a transnational communicative space, regulated in the interests of more equal dialogue—a theme that in recodified terminology has become central to contemporary debate about public communication.

THE EUROPEAN CONTEXT

The UNESCO debates were essentially premised on a conception of the flow of media products from the First World to the Third. When we place a "European," First World frame on the question of cultural and national identity, the metropolitan center of cultural monopoly reconfigures before our eyes. The game becomes one played principally *between* Europe and the

United States. The First World becomes a complex of international relations rather than (as viewed from the outside) a hegemonic source of cultural power. This has major implications for thinking about the relations among national identities, states, and the media.

Surveying developments since the early 1980s, we see that these relations have become increasingly complex and ramified. There are a number of reasons for this. First, in Western European states, there had been considerable postwar experience in dealing with monopolistic (or, as in Britain, duopolistic) public service broadcasting systems, but no real experience of dealing with commercialism outside of a public service framework (other than, as in the case of radio piracy, to try and suppress it). The widespread reregulation of broadcasting has had to accommodate the emergence of commercial systems throughout the European continent. Second, although as noted above, there had been concern with the imbalances of global media flow, the 1980s saw the full-fledged emergence of the transnational multimedia enterprises and of the "media moguls" as new actors on the scene; these have produced novel problems of regulation and control for states and raised questions about how we should now think of communication sovereignty (Guillou and Padioleau 1988; Tunstall and Palmer 1991; Tomlinson 1997). Third, state media policies had tended to focus on broadcasting (from a broadly cultural perspective) and in some countries on the press (as part of the regulation of pluralism in print). The 1980s saw a concern with industrial policy become increasingly paramount in the field of broadcasting. The deregulation of telecommunications and the rise of satellite, cable, and video distribution further complicated the scene, as did growing cross-media ownership and control centered on the emergence of new media "baronies." By the end of the decade, these various tendencies had become pronounced in the West. A further key complication in the European media landscape was occasioned by the breakdown of the communist bloc in 1989–1990. This has meant that the European communicative space has extended, simply by virtue of the demise of the former Cold War divisions.

A EUROPEAN AUDIOVISUAL SPACE

European Union policymakers have turned their attention to how a common culture might be created among the member states. The role of media in the journalistic construction of public debates and also in the wider field of the production and distribution of fictional representations assumes major salience in this context, as do the ways in which the consumption of media products feeds into the construction of public opinion concerning national and cultural identities and their "proper" boundaries. It is precisely here that the analysis of the scope of cultural and media policy and its implementation becomes an issue. The rationalist approach of EU policymakers to cultural management highlights the sources of continuing cultural difference in Western Europe and the evident absence of any shortcut in surmounting these.

The European Commission's *Television without Frontiers*, published in 1984, set the context as follows:

> Information is a decisive, perhaps the only decisive factor in European unification. . . . European unification will only be achieved if Europeans want it. Europeans will only want it if there is such a thing as European identity. A European identity will only develop if Europeans are adequately informed. At present, information via the mass media is controlled at national level. (Commission of the European Communities 1984)

This perspective has had an enduring impact on subsequent thinking and debate. First of all, it assumes, simplistically, that there is a strong, unilinear, and homogenizing causal connection between media consumption and collective identity formation. Next, the national level of media production and distribution is seen as an obstacle to be transcended in the interests of forging "Europeanness." And finally, the desired shaping of a new cultural identity is linked to the transnational distribution of information, that is, to the formation of a European public sphere (Paterson 1993).

In the early and mid-1980s, before the deregulatory trend in broadcasting became predominant, it was still possible to think of radio and television as the cultural arms of nation-building and as providing a public forum for the elaboration of divergent, party-based projects within a political community composed of citizens. The project of building a European culture through television was simply extended from one political level to another, without any serious consideration of what might be involved in moving from a national community defined by the boundaries of a single state to an international community defined by integrationist political economics. However, increasingly since the late 1980s this public culturalist model has been widely supplanted by an individualizing economistic conception of audiences as consumers and of programming as, above all, a commodity.

The role of audiovisual media in constructing a European identity has been officially defined in opposition to a culturally invasive Other, namely the United States. French policymakers have been most eloquent in articulating this point of view. The then president of the European Commission, Jacques Delors, pointedly asked: "Doesn't the defense of freedom, elsewhere so loftily proclaimed, include the effort of each country, or each ensemble of countries, to use the audiovisual sphere to ensure the protection of their identity?" (cited in Burgelman and Pauwels 1993: 176).

By the end of the decade, the EU's television directive, *Television without Frontiers*, was enacted with the goal of ensuring that equality of access to the market applied to television broadcasting across national frontiers. It began to be implemented in October 1991. The cultural logic was complemented by an underlying industrial logic. The purpose of opening up the market was to create greater opportunities for European audiovisual production in a *global* market. Creating the internal market was coupled with an attempt to impose a quota on importation from the external market. The directive's Article 4 stipulates that "Member States shall ensure where practicable and by appropriate means, that broadcasters reserve for European works . . . a majority proportion of their transmission time" (European Union 1989). These words are echoed in the "cultural objectives" of the Council of Europe's subsequent *European Convention on Transfrontier Television*, published in January 1990. This document aimed to supersede state power and ensure that EU member states did not create restrictions aimed against the reception and retransmission of programs from other member states. The official conception of what constitutes "European" audiovisual production in Europe includes programs and films produced in EU member states, or by signatories to the Council of Europe Convention, or in countries belonging to European Free Trade Area.

Although the EU context in some measure has begun to affect the scope for autonomous media policymaking at the level of the nation-state, Western Europe is still far from having homogeneous media systems. Media institutions remain nationally specific, strongly influenced in their internal regulatory regimes by domestic political determinants (Blumler 1992; Østergaard 1997; Pohoryles, Schlesinger, and Wuggenig 1990). Moreover, states still remain the most significant spaces for political communication (Wolton 1993). In fact, the national political level is everywhere of crucial importance in shaping the economic rules of the media game.

But at another level it is important to analyze the impact of internationalizing tendencies in European media. For instance, the reconstruction of domestic audiovisual markets has been driven to a considerable extent by the rise first of advertising and then of subscription-financed private television during the past decade. The proliferation of distribution systems, including satellite and cable, has increased the total European demand for programs enormously. In the case of the press, there have been significant crossnational acquisitions and some evidence, as for instance, in the magazine market, of the internationalization of product. The South Korean market is undergoing a similar process, as is detailed in the chapter by Kim and Hong in this book.

However, there are problems in generalizing about the patterns of media consumption across the EU and the European continent more generally. For instance, there is low newspaper readership in some Latin countries compared with northern Europe. According to research conducted before Austria, Finland, and Sweden joined the EU in January 1995, media consumption was then clustered around nine language areas. Only in the smaller countries bordering larger neighbors with the same language has there been significant transborder media consumption (Commission of the European Communities 1992a). These variations are important features of persisting cultural difference. It is possible that the policy-driven concentration on the European dimension of audiovisual communication has overshadowed the crucial importance of national and regional print media in sustaining diverse patterns of communication.

Although both the EU and the much broader regional grouping, the Council of Europe, have seen the elaboration of a "European audiovisual space" as a matter of policy, cross-border media developments, whether in television, newspapers, or magazines, have actually often been the product of private corporate initiative rather than governmental action. The European mediascape is traversed by actors such as Murdoch's News International, the Luxembourg-based CLT, Germany's Bertelsmann, and Italy's Mediaset. The process of transnationalization and economic integration resulting from the private actions of enterprises must be weighed alongside that of national governments and Euro-bureaucracies (Silj 1992). This raises the question not only of how multimedia enterprises operate within the European space but also how their strategies toward Europe may also articulate with their wider global strategies (Hoskins, McFadyen, and Finn 1997). It also raises the question of how plausible it is to analyze the state as an instance of rational policymaking.

The development of European television programming has been encouraged via regional regulatory measures and conventions. The production and distribution of audiovisual products has been stimulated by means of a number of EU-funded ventures. Undoubtedly, the EU and Council of Europe's promotional efforts have had some impact in developing a European audiovisual market by stimulating new production and in enhancing cross-national collaboration (Beltrame 1998; European Communication Council 1997; Mele 1990). But such support for production is dwarfed by what is spent by European countries on imports of nondomestically produced programs from the United States. In 1992, the EU member states spent $3.7 billion on importing audiovisual products, which far outweighed the $288m spent on European productions in the United States (Gardner 1993; Godard 1993). In 1995, the United States had a surplus of $6.3 billion with the EU.

THE SPECTER OF "AMERICANIZATION"

The scale of U.S. imports of television programs and films has been a cause of official concern. The very popularity of the U.S. product (hardly something new, given the historic global dominance of Hollywood) has been represented as posing a danger of "Americanization." Ever since World War I,

American popular culture has been seen in official circles and by cultural elites as constituting a threat to the *national* culture (Dickinson and Street, 1985; Wagnleitner and Tyler May 2000). In recent years, this line of argument has been most clearly articulated in France, where the issue has been supercharged by its perception as part of the global clash between *la Francophonie* and the Anglo-Saxons (see Mattelart, Delcourt, and Mattelart 1984; Wolton 1990; Grantham 2000). Now, transposed to a supranational level, in official thinking "Americanization" is represented as a threat to *European* culture. This is a complicated topic and the views of governments and cultural elites have not coincided with the popular cultural consumption patterns in which "Americanness" has been syncretically transformed (Hebdige 1988).

It is not surprising, therefore, as so emphatically signaled by Jacques Delors, that the forging of a common European culture through television and cinematic production should be conceived of as a form of cultural defense, and it is not unusual to encounter military metaphors in this context—and not just in official circles. Speaking for the creative community, the celebrated German film director Wim Wenders has opined that "Europe will become a Third World continent because we will not have anything to say on the most important medium. . . . There is a war going on and the Americans have been planning it for a long time. The most powerful tools are images and sound" (Carvel 1993).

This rhetoric of cultural war connects to the other major logic of the European audiovisual space, namely its industrial and commercial goal of creating a European market capable of stimulating the production of hardware as well as of software, thereby also confronting the Japanese challenge in media technologies.

The integrationist model of audiovisual space, however, has had a notable defect. In the effort to rationalize the management of culture, its initiators have underestimated the refractoriness of national television audiences. Television programs (and films) produced in Europe tend to be so nationally specific as to offer limited scope for audience identification elsewhere on the continent. On the whole, with the exception of productions in the English language, they do not travel extensively outside their language area. There is no *European* market as such for the products of European producers, "merely a collection of distinct domestic markets" and major European producers' strategies are primarily concerned with strengthening their positions within their national markets (Silj 1992: 16, 37). Given that preferences both for national styles and contents in television programs are generally high (Dziadul 1993), and that these are coupled with a widespread lack of popular interest in the product of other European countries, we are faced with a somewhat paradoxical outcome. To the extent that it exists at all, the real common currency of the European audiovisual space is actually the output of the *American* television and film industries. The United States produces—and has long produced—the moving images that most easily traverse *any* European national barriers. Although American product does not dominate the prime-time television schedules, it does have an unrivalled ability to enter each and every national market, and Hollywood unquestionably dominates the European cinema box office.

It is this reality that gave such force to Europeans' dispute with the United States over the character of audiovisual goods during the GATT Uruguay Round negotiations concluded in December 1993. Indeed, such was the importance of the issue that it almost proved to be a stumbling block to the final agreement and had to be set aside for future resolution when neither side would give way. Underlying this trade dispute are deeply rooted differences of view about the role of culture in the constitution of the national polity and identity.

For the United States, moreover, films and television are, along with aircraft, the top dollar exports earners. It is hardly surprising that the U.S. lobby, led by the Motion Picture Association of America, fought to remove Europe's trade barriers on audiovisual services (Valenti 1993). The main argument used has been that movies and programs are commercial products just like any other, and thus that Article 4 of the EU's *Television without Frontiers* directive is "anti-competitive." Moreover, European countries have been accused of censorship by excluding U.S. media materials, and the sovereignty of the consumer has been invoked for good measure. This, it should be said, occurs in television markets in which U.S. films and television programs are ubiquitous—taking an average share of 80 percent in the European market (Buchan 1993)—and where the national film industries' outputs are consequently uniformly dwarfed, if not utterly marginalized, by American success at the box office (Hoskins, McFadyen, and Finn 1997: 62).

However, Article 4 is not in fact a juridically enforceable quota, rather it represents a political aspiration, to be attained "where practicable." The European position, in a nutshell, has been that films and television programs are cultural artifacts and are not thought to be the same as other traded commodities. Consequently, it has been argued that a principle of "cultural exclusion" should apply to the audiovisual sector, which is officially represented as at the center of European cultural and democratic life (European Broadcasting Union 1993; Ralite 1993). The Europeans argue their case against the background of a fall in some 25 percent of filmmaking activity since 1980, and with an increasing proportion of such output dependent on coproduction deals. Quite how to resolve this shortfall in production remains a point of some contention within the European Commission.

THE PERSISTENCE OF LANGUAGE

The European linguistic order persists because, characteristically, the development of official languages in Europe has been intimately connected not only with the educational system but also with the creation of state-supported mass media. Officially adopted languages are protected, and linguistic competence is largely coterminous with citizenship. It has been observed that the "robustness of European states and their languages makes it extremely unlikely that further political integration will be accompanied by language unification" (de Swaan 1991: 321). A relevant factor is language competition in the EU, with English and French the de facto Community languages, and with a long-standing background of rivalry between French and German from the earliest days of the Community. Undoubtedly, though, English is the "first second language," and the current state of foreign language competence among young Europeans shows that "English is paramount as the medium of wider communication" in the EU and looks set to serve the needs of international communication. That is not to exclude the likely regional importance of German and French (de Swaan 1993: 245, 250). Nor is it to ignore the continuing resilience of the other official national languages of state, alongside which are also the efforts to upgrade the linguistic status of nations without states (the Catalans in Spain being the most notable instance here) as well as attempts to foster "lesser used" languages by means of broadcasting (Gifreu 1992; Cormack 1993).

Linguistic and sociocultural differences substantially account for the failure to create a pan-European televisual market via direct broadcast satellite (Collins 1990). The initial pan-European aspirations of satellite operators have decanted into distributing television programming either by national markets or by homogeneous language areas, notably the English, German, French, and Scandinavian (Richeri 1992). As Joseph Straubhaar's discussion of cultural proximity in chapter 8 of this volume would predict, the vast bulk of the European audience prefers programs in its own language and looks for cultural-linguistic affinities, and similarity of outlook and lifestyle in television's offer. To consume in another language runs against the line of least resistance, and it is the case that even in the smaller European states national programming tends to be at a higher quality than overseas material. Moreover, although English is the most widely spoken second language, it is not a lingua franca (Richeri 1993: 79–80).

To date, much official thinking about the European audiovisual space, therefore, has been prone to what I have elsewhere labeled the "fallacy of distribution," according to which it is supposed that making available the same cultural product leads to an identity of interpretation on the part of those who consume it (Schlesinger 1993). But this is to ignore the context of reception of culture, and, not least, the syncretic capacities of any given collectivity. In the interpretation of audiovisual culture, nationality is of signal importance (Liebes and Katz 1990), not to speak of the differences within nations based on factors such as class, gender, and ethnicity (Schlesinger et al. 1992). The evidence suggests official national languages offer a key source of resistance to wider processes of sociocultural homogenization. Those cultural forms that are least nationally bound in their appeal—notably music and sport—are the ones most likely to succeed at the pan-European level. However, it is an open question whether, for example, music videos distributed across Europe will leave an enduring sense of "Europeanness" among those millions of young people who consume them once they leave the category of consumers of youth culture. Moreover, the discourses of national identity (and also passionate regionalism and localism) are still actively at play in the field of European sport (Blain, Boyle, and O'Donnell 1993).

EUROPEANIZATION AND THE CONSTRUCTION OF PUBLIC SPHERES

While there is now increasing recognition of the problems faced by constructing European identity through television, the rhetoric about creating an audiovisual space has been paralleled by arguments—albeit much less prominently aired—about the difficulties posed by the creation of a European "public sphere," a term much used in contemporary debates about communicative democracy.

A common starting point in discussion about democracy and the media has been Jürgen Habermas's (1989) classic account of the formation of the bourgeois public sphere. In a nutshell, the key idea is that from the late eighteenth century through to the mid-nineteenth century a space emerged in which private individuals could debate the regulation of civil society and the conduct of the state, underpinned by the rise of the political press and of new social milieux wherein discussion could occur. The commercialization of the press and the advent of organized corporate interests in the economy, Habermas contends, has led to the "refeudalization" of the public sphere and the loss of its critical function. It should be added that this conception has concerned itself above all else with the formation of *national* spaces for political debate and criticism.

Contemporary debate has been reconstructive, attempting to develop the analysis beyond Habermas's original formulation: It has sought to make the concept of the public sphere relevant to the profound reshaping of the media landscape that has occurred in the past two decades or so (Dahlgren 1991). The public sphere is used as a concept to be employed in *normative* criticism of the present organization of the media and its consequences for democracy. A major concern has been with the participation of citizens in political life in virtue of their access to adequate information for the conduct of rational public action.

Whereas the argument about a European audiovisual space has been mainly concerned with controlling the inflow of *entertainment*, those concerning the possibility of a European public sphere, above all, have focused on the role of *information*. Of course, to counterpose the two, entertainment and information, as if they could be conceived of as hermetically sealed from one another, is merely an analytical exercise.

Arguments about the public sphere tend to presuppose the political form of the sovereign state, assuming that the role of information is to assist the conduct of the citizen within the *national*, democratic polity. However, as EU policymakers began to think about regional media space, public sphere questions came onto the agenda in the shape of an evaluation of how pluralistic are the structures of mass communication in individual member states and what kinds of action the Union needed to take to ensure that a diversity of media would exist (Commission of the European Communities 1992b). In this connection, we are witnessing a renewed interest in questions of transnationalization originally signaled in the UNESCO debates but focused on Europe as opposed to the globe. When "Europe" becomes the arena, concentrations of power may be seen as tolerable *across* states that would simply be unacceptable on a nation-state basis.

In current EU policy debate, particular attention has been given to the role of public service broadcasting in providing a forum for a range of views and interests to be articulated, a diversity of cultural forms to be represented, and, thus, a framework for the national culture to be reproduced in ways accessible to the generality of citizens (Elliott 1982; Pauwels 1999; Scannell 1989).

The focus on broadcasting should not overshadow the variations in national press structures and different views of print journalism in different national political cultures. One line of argument has drawn attention to the internal differentiation in the national press according to which readers addressed by elite or quality newspapers receive a radically different account of the world from those who read the mass or popular newspapers. Indeed, by this account, it no longer makes sense to think of "the newspaper" as a useful term, given that it embraces everything from the establishment organ to the most sensationalist tabloid (Sparks 1988). However, such a perspective (much influenced by the British experience) ignores other press traditions, such as those in Norway and Sweden, where a policy of state subsidy is underpinned by explicit normative considerations: In effect, there is an ideology of public service allied to a recognition of the power of the market.

In both sets of arguments, whether concerned with the press or broadcasting, typically the present obstacles to full communicative openness are rehearsed. Such constraints are located within both the political economy and the sociology of the media. Well-substantiated developments such as the concentration of media ownership and control, restriction of new entries into the market by cost, the weight of advertising in the construction of public opinion, the attrition of public-sector broadcasting, the internationalizing and centralizing tendencies of media production and distribution, and the professionalization of relations between news sources and media are variously presented as evidence of the shortcomings of the present system (Golding and Murdock 1991; Garnham 2000; Goldsmiths Media Group 2000; Keane 1991; McQuail and Siune 1998). Such material considerations obviously play into normative arguments about the relationship between citizenship (conceived as rational, therefore informed action) and media performance (McQuail 1992).

To address the question of democracy, we clearly need to go beyond the rhetoric of national and cultural identity, which really has not considered the *internal* political character of the community it purports to defend. The simple establishment of an audiovisual space, a minimal common currency of the moving image produced by Europeans and addressed to European audiences, is only a highly one-dimensional vision of a putative European public sphere. Making commonly available a range of audiovisual products might begin to create some of the preconditions of a fully articulated public sphere. Crucially, however, this provision does not necessarily relate to the *critical* function whereby political conduct is appraised by the citizen, supported in his or her judgment by a flow of adequate information about the actions of government.

Interestingly, as in the case of cultural identity, arguments about a potential European public sphere do keep coming back to audiovisual media. And there is a good reason for this: Television has a communicative potential to cross frontiers (shared with radio) that is lacked by the press. Newspapers, with few exceptions, are tied to national markets and political systems. It is true that a new kind of "international press" has been developing in recent years, with papers such as *The European, The Financial Times, The International Herald Tribune* and *The Wall Street Journal* consciously addressing international political and economic elites in the nearest thing we have to a European lingua franca, namely English. In recent years, sections of the quality press in various countries have also begun to produce "European" supplements, compiled from reports and features selected from like-minded newspapers across the continent; this has been complemented by cross-national syndication on a rather modest scale.

The consolidation of this kind of press signifies the emergent presence of a transnational domain of elites and decision makers, which is becoming increasingly visible as processes of globalization shift certain powers away from the national level and create new ranks of professionals. To be sure, elite information-sharing formations can hardly be considered as constituting a

fully fledged public sphere as such, given that the costs of entry for participants are rather high in terms of the requisite cultural and economic capital
(Garnham 1986: 52–53). In this regard, arguments about the class-based
structure of press consumption are certainly relevant not only at the national
level but at the transnational too (Schlesinger 1999).

The complex of administrative, executive, and legislative arrangements
that constitutes the European Union could provide the kernel of a public
sphere. It could also be imagined that the "pilgrimage" of functionaries
through the organs of the nascent Eurostate may eventually confer loyalties
on an administrative group that might supersede those of their nation-state
of origin, and, moreover, that a sole Union language will eventually take
clear precedence. To think this, however, is to envisage a long drawn-out and
linear process. And in that process, there can be little doubt, media would
play a role, perhaps not least by representing the EU's political dimension.
Such a role, however, needs to be a popular one, serving the wider "European" public that lies beyond the transnationalizing elites that might eventually cohere into a "European" ruling class.

The launching of Euronews in January 1993 was an attempt to reach such
a broader public. This project, supported by a consortium of European public service broadcasters and the European Parliament, arose in the context of
global competition to dominate the international news agenda and reflected
the desire in some quarters to produce a "European" perspective on this.
The race became especially marked after the Gulf War in 1991, when CNN's
success marked out new territory subsequently also entered by the BBC's
World Television News. Although global in reach, both Anglo-American
companies are firmly rooted in their national bases, which obviously helps
give them their distinctive corporate journalistic identities. By comparison
with Euronews, which broadcasts in six languages (Arabic, English, French,
German, Italian, and Spanish), both are monolingual channels, broadcasting
solely in English. The development of this form of transnational news
broadcasting precisely embodies the contradictions of the European cultural
space. Transnationally broadcast television (with news and journalism at its
center) is part of a global struggle for commercial and political hegemony
that certainly needs to be watched, not least because of its perceived impact
on national sovereignty and political and cultural identities.

National broadcast news still tends to be the preferred form in Europe and
for the foreseeable future will compete for public attention with Euronews
or any successor effort to address a "European" public. National news still
generally speaks with an institutional, public service voice and has the signal
advantage of addressing a bounded community. The gradual and uneven
emergence of the "multichannel universe" in various parts of Europe is putting this privileged news broadcasting form under pressure to change. To the
extent that transnational news broadcasting becomes routinely more impor-

tant—whether via CNN, the BBC, or Sky News—national television journalism will have to change both its form and content. This will have consequences for the ways in which national political communities are addressed and defined.

EUROPE'S EXPANDED COMMUNICATIVE SPACE

Any discussion of "Europeanization" and the media would be incomplete if it did not consider some of the emergent implications of media developments in Central and Eastern Europe. These point to further practical and conceptual difficulties for the construction of a European public sphere and an overarching cultural identity.

In the postcommunist states of East-Central Europe the media have been profoundly affected by the wide-scale collapse of a system of communist party-state media control and its replacement by postcommunist regimes. This has evidently led both to change and continuity. The change is perhaps most evident in the case of print media, where the ending of party-state rule has ushered in the privatization of the press and its large-scale commercialization. Due to the chronic economic weakness of the former Soviet bloc's economies, a lack of domestic capital has led to an influx of foreign capital. Where it has been judged to be profitable, a rapid growth of transnational ownership and control by mainly Western European media corporations has occurred. However, the extent of foreign capital penetration has varied significantly, in part determined by the extent to which governments have seen foreign ownership as desirable or as a threat to the national culture (Sparks 1998; Splichal 1992, 1993; Jakubowicz 1994). A crucial point is that where the press has been marketized and commercialized there has been a consequent loss of direct political control (Høyer, Lauk, and Vihalemm 1993; Zernetskaya 1994).

Because of this, the role of the audiovisual media has become even more important to the political classes of the postcommunist regimes—and given the significant collapse of film production in East-Central Europe, television has assumed added prominence. Here, continuity with the past in modes of control is much more evident, even though there has been a formal shift from party-state–controlled broadcasting to a public service model inspired by Western European practice. Ironically, just as it is being adopted in the postcommunist states, the very survival of classical public service broadcasting is in some doubt in Western Europe (not least in the case of the once iconic BBC) in an audiovisual environment increasingly reshaped to favor the commercial imperative. Given the weak economic condition of East-Central Europe, we may reasonably wonder whether public service goals will survive the fiscal crisis of the state and global media competition.

In general, the new regulatory bodies for radio and television are directly dependent on political patronage, and the control of appointments extends to key managerial positions (a practice by no means unknown in several Western European countries). The kinds of struggle that may ensue over the political direction of broadcasting were most publicly exemplified in Hungary's media war, in which the presidents of Hungarian Radio and Television were unconstitutionally, and very controversially, ousted by the ruling party for taking public service autonomy too seriously (Hankiss 1994).

For the foreseeable future, however, even where privatization of the audiovisual sector is occurring, television, and to a lesser extent radio, are seen by East-Central European politicians as central to the building of the postcommunist state and the maintenance of the national culture. Once again, we see exemplified the profound belief in—especially—televisual power and its connection with *national* space.

CONCLUSION

The policy driven attempt to create some audiovisual framework for achieving a "European" mode of address seems destined to continue. Destined to continue, that is, if the European Union does indeed develop further as a form of state organization, whether federal or confederal. To the extent that the integration process is maintained (however contradictorily), there will still be a problem of collective representation to be solved at the European level. The changing institutional structure of the European Union has begun to provoke thinking about whether or not a European public sphere might be emerging, albeit one that because of its heterogeneity cannot model itself on the classical conception of the nation-state. It has been suggested that for this to be feasible, "participation in the life of public institutions takes precedence over nationality; that, whatever the citizen's cultural or national identity, his or her insertion in public political space is elective and not 'native.' " (Tassin 1992: 189). Whatever the eventual form of such a political community, there is a case for recognizing that the emergence of the supranational dimension poses a different kind of challenge to communicative practices from that of cultural defense alone.

Meanwhile, the examples of both Western and Eastern Europe indicate how communicative space may be used to reinforce the boundaries of national communities. They open up a more general question about how other spaces might in the future be reshaped by broader processes of change. The reconfiguration of communicative spaces in the post–Cold War period on the basis of the national principle is directly analogous to the conscious attempt to "Europeanize," but evidently much more easily effected. This again directs our attention to the role of the state in controlling its communicative environment. We must also consider the role of private enterprise in seeking attractive market opportunities within given cultural-linguistic spaces.

The continuing nationalization of media space remains in contradiction with the ongoing project of creating a continental communicative space. Whether this core tension can be overcome is an open question. It depends, among other things, on whether the process of European state creation will significantly diminish the importance of the nation-state as a locus of power and citizen loyalty. Related to this is whether or not a distinctive Europolitical culture can emerge that offers a potential focus for a new level of political identity. That, in turn, presupposes the calling-into-being of a transnational citizenry with equal and widespread communicative competences that is able to tame and democratize the Euro-elite. On all of these counts, the signs are decidedly ambiguous.

NOTE

This chapter is revised and updated from "Europeanization and the Media: National Identity and the Public Sphere," Working Paper no. 7/95. ARENA (Advanced Research on the Europeanisation of the Nation-State), The Research Council of Norway, University of Oslo, February 1995.

7

The Unsovereign Century: Canada's Media Industries and Cultural Policies

Stephen D. McDowell

Canadian communications and cultural policymakers have long struggled with a number of questions and problems similar to those being confronted in discussions of state sovereignty and the implications of globalization. The Canadian case contributes in several ways to a reconsideration of why the state matters in discussions about globalization and sovereignty. First, it contains elements relevant to both the internal and external components of sovereignty definitions and debates. Second, it demonstrates that the role of the state may be contested and contradictory, and that the state may serve simultaneously both as a forum for promoting sovereignty and as a conduit for expanding integration with continental and regional economies. Third, it illustrates that symbolic discourses about sovereignty can be accompanied by economic and political policies that may actually narrow the national public sphere, complicating the task of assessing globalization and sovereignty. Finally, the role that uncertainty has played in justifying a role for the Canadian state points to implications for state responses to globalization.

Canadian sovereignty has long been in question, whether in terms of creating solid federal governance or in the efforts to build and protect a Canadian sphere from outside influences. In Canada in the twentieth century, these questions were first associated with the goal of escaping a colonial relationship with the United Kingdom, and then with efforts to cope with highly asymmetric bilateral relations with the United States (as John Holmes called it, "Life with Uncle"). Due to the cultural, linguistic, and geographic proximity to the United States, the first part of this chapter argues, some of the dynamics associated with discussions of globalization in the late twentieth century were accelerated and concentrated in Canadian debates (Barnet and Cavanaugh 1994; Deibert 1997; Ferguson 1992, 1995; Galperin 1999).

Alongside an external focus in debates on sovereignty, Canadians have also continually struggled with internal questions such as the meaning and character of community, nationality, and federal governance. Questions about tenuous Canadian sovereignty—such as the integration of the national economy, external economic linkages, foreign-owned manufacturing, the role of Canadian elites in promoting either nationalism or continentalism, and the support of national media—have been the hardy perennials in Canadian policy research. Equally resilient streams of research address the nature of Canadian identity, bilingualism, multiculturalism, self-governance by First Nations' peoples, and the federal-provincial division of governing powers. The second part of the chapter, then, reviews the threads that have formed the backdrop of Canadian communications and cultural policies.

The third part of the chapter traces the explanation for the formation of Canada's cultural policies to historical conflicts and conditions, and notes how long-standing positions and problems were recast in a move to a neoliberal or neomercantilist trade and investment strategy in the 1980s and 1990s. It points to an activist state, in both national and international spheres associated with sovereignty. Rather than responding timidly to challenges to Canadian communications sovereignty, the Canadian state has engaged in restructuring domestic social bargains and has tried to create niches in which Canadian-based media firms can prosper nationally and internationally.

SOVEREIGNTY, POLITICAL ECONOMY, AND CULTURAL POLICY DEBATES

Sovereignty in Canada has never been fully assumed, whether sovereignty is seen as a legitimate internal governing authority or a Canadian political sphere that is secure from outside influences. Historically, this is not a new problem. Escaping the ambit of the United Kingdom with the granting of "dominion" status in 1867 still left the country within the British Commonwealth of nations. The Queen of England was and still remains the Queen of Canada, and it is her representative that is the Canadian head of state.

While moving away from one external colonial power over the 100 years after being granted dominion status in 1867, Canadians also tried to establish a sovereign nation-state in the context of a highly asymmetrical bilateral relationship with the United States. However, it should be noted that, as Glen Williams and Wallace Clement (1989) have argued, Canada occupied a privileged position in both of these empires: a high-income, resource-rich, white-settler colony in the British Empire, and a geographically and culturally close junior partner in the American Empire, with much elite intermingling.

Thus, it could be argued that some of the dynamics associated with globalization in the late twentieth century were more accelerated and concentrated in the Canadian debate. Globalization in media refers to many things, but four processes are often emphasized: transnational media flows, ownership and investment patterns across borders, media content that originates in other countries, and cultural patterns or media uses that evidence transnational preferences or tastes. Globalization in the twenty-first century is also associated with long-standing and structured relationships among states, whether interdependence, asymmetric interdependence, dependence, or imperialism and cultural imperialism.

While the policy discourses on the challenges to sovereignty and the rise of globalization grew in importance in the 1990s, several concurrent developments are instructive. First, while sovereignty has been called into question in the late twentieth century, more and more states have been created. Second, while multiethnic states often had tumultuous histories in the twentieth century, it is states that have defined nationality in nonethnic terms that are able to deal most adequately with migration and shifts in group identity. For these additional reasons, the examination of Canada's cultural policies provides a useful case to explore the relationships among globalization, nation-states, sovereignty, and media.

EXTERNAL FACTORS AFFECTING CANADIAN SOVEREIGNTY

A number of questions and debates have reflected the sense of a tenuous Canadian sovereignty. (See chapter 1 for a discussion of elements of sovereignty.) These themes have each been dealt with in extensive detail in policy research and public debate in Canada, and hence this discussion illustrates only some of the parameters of these issues.

The lack of integration of the national economy is a concern that has been addressed in numerous studies and policies, culminating in federal government action in the 1960s and 1970s. The dependent ties to the United States were noted, as was Canada's position as a branch plant economy and a resource economy. The sectors in which national ownership strongholds have been developed traditionally in the Canadian economy, either through private ownership by Canadian firms or by public ownership by Canadian public (or Crown) corporations, include resource extraction (agriculture, mining, petroleum, forestry), but with little additional processing in Canada associated with these activities. Telecommunications equipment, supported by a national monopoly service provider, was a notable exception (Amesse, Seguin-Dulude, and Stanley 1994). The most important crown corporation developed in the 1970s and 1980s was not a manufacturing firm, but a petroleum company, PetroCan. The major upshot of the National Energy Policy was to create this public-sector national firm to produce, distribute, and retail petroleum products. Private and public Canadian firms have also had strength in utilities, often due to state protection or Canadian ownership requirements. These include firms in electricity generation, insurance, securities, trust companies, banking, transportation, and communications. Ownership requirements ensured a Canadian private sector in telecommunications and broadcasting; this was supplemented by public agencies in telecommunications and broadcasting, as well as by agencies to support the arts and culture.

The Canadian economy's lack of domestic integration and vulnerabilities to external pressures were also demonstrated by a high level of exports as an overall portion of economic activity. The export dependence was also an export dependence on the United States, so that access to the U.S. market was seen as essential. Dependence on U.S. technology and investments were important factors in Canadian economic growth as well.

The role of the Canadian elite has also been questioned in debates about those economic strategies that were being pursued versus those that should be pursued: nationalist versus continentalist strategies. While the state and the private sector have made use of, and been the beneficiaries of, a nationalist mythology—such as with the granting of concessions to a private company to build the Canadian Pacific Railway across the country in the nineteenth century—a significant portion of the political and economic elite has retained a vision for integration into the North American economy. This perspective is referred to as continentalism. This vision saw Canada's best domestic options arising through running U.S. branch plants and providing tertiary services to U.S. companies. If Canadian capital were to retain a Canadian economic sphere, it would be through seeking monopolies, concentration, high profitability, and local distributorships.

Given the unique conditions of economic dependence, the appropriate types and level of support for the national media has also been an important theme in a number of Canadian policy debates. The nature of the problem of sovereignty and the autonomy of states, as well as the role of media and communication policies in supporting the growth and development of the nation-state, have been debated in periodic cycles. What goals were appropriate? How important were Canadian ownership and/or Canadian content to the maintenance of a distinctive Canadian culture? What means would be the most useful? What means are allowable now given bilateral relationships and commitments to international trade agreements?

The strongest support for national media has come in direct government programs for broadcasting. The Canadian Broadcasting Corporation was the public-sector organization, apart from the post office, with a direct and daily role in Canadians' lives and identity formation. It was founded in the context of a struggle over the nature of broadcasting in Canada and a debate over whether there would in fact be a meaningful Canadian broadcasting sector, as opposed to a broadcasting industry that was an appendage of commercial broadcasting in the United States (Collins 1995; McChesney 1999; Raboy 1990).

Alongside direct state and public-sector involvement in media, private media industries have also been supported as part of a public policy to support a Canadian space. The newspaper industry has had, because of legislative restrictions on ownership, a continuing pattern of Canadian ownership. Successive Canadian proprietors—Lord Beaverbrook, Lord Thompson, Conrad Black—have used the Canadian base as a springboard to becoming press barons in the United Kingdom. Book publishing, on the other hand, has been dominated by foreign titles, and Canadian publishing houses and publications have required consistent support through tax incentives and publication grants. Canadian publishing houses gradually have become more concentrated, but have maintained a portion of readership by supporting Canadian authors. Magazine publication has been supported by postal subsidies for distribution, by limitations on split runs of foreign magazines (with foreign editorial content and Canadian advertisements), and by tax laws limiting advertising expense deductions to advertisements placed in Canadian magazines (Acheson and Maule 1999). The Canadian magazine industry has been increasingly concentrated in two large firms, which also have cross-ownership interests in other media activities. The support programs used by the Canadian state to ensure the viability of the magazine sector have been portrayed as protectionist and successfully challenged by trading partners in the 1990s, calling into question the role of the state in supporting a Canadian-based private media sector.

These policy issues have contributed to a series of ongoing debates about sovereignty in Canada. In these debates, sovereignty is primarily represented as a preexisting and natural national sphere, which will flourish if only left to its own dynamics and devices away from outside influences. Retaining a Canadian economic, political, and cultural space against outside influences has always been a central part of political economy analysis. The focus has not been solely on culture, but rather on basic efforts to control the economy as well as media in such a way as to provide the basis for any meaningful political choices. These debates had certain periods in which they were most intense: the post-1945 period, the 1970s nationalist initiatives, the MacDonald Commission report in the 1980s, and the Canada-U.S. Free Trade debate in the mid- to late 1980s.

THE INTERNAL DEBATE ON SOVEREIGNTY AND THE LEGITIMACY OF GOVERNANCE

However, just as there have been debates about the nature of external influences on Canadian sovereignty, the internal elements of a sovereign community, or nation-state—the elements contributing to the acceptance of membership, citizenship, and a legitimate governing authority—have not been assumed in Canada. Like the externally oriented debates on how to protect a Canadian sphere, there has also been an internally oriented debate about what constitutes and how to create an appropriate identity and community, and the role of the state in relation to the nationalities and social groups that make up Canada. Five of the most important parts of this debate on the internal characteristics of sovereignty include the nature of Canadian identity, the policy of official bilingualism, the policy of multiculturalism, self-governance by First Nations' peoples, and the federal-provincial division of governing powers.

Conscious and expressed doubts over the nature of Canadian identity have almost themselves become one of the defining characteristics of Canadian identity. That is, national identity is in part constituted by the continuing struggles to define and assert identity, and by the struggles over the inability to arrive at a crystallized and uncontested shared definition. While these struggles continue, there has grown up a common body of symbols and experience, including hockey, snow, the north, and vastness. Canadian identity includes positive images, associated with geography, climate, and efforts to overcome the geography and the climate and to build a community of survival and prosperity. The positive elements of identity also include tolerance for diversity, and a support for multilateralism in international organizations and a middle power role in international affairs. Another dimension of Canadian identity comprises a comparison with the United States: Canadians are said to be less nationalistic, less assertive, less jingoistic than Americans.

The question remains whether settling the ongoing identity problematic is more important to the state or to social groups in Canadian civil society. Some market-oriented critics of cultural policies and programs have argued that the cultural producers who are supported by these programs have a vested interest in settling the identity question, or possibly in keeping it alive. The private media sector is also a direct beneficiary of policies and programs aimed to build and support identity, through the foreign ownership restrictions for non-Canadians in communications and cultural industries.

Official bilingualism was introduced by the government of Prime Minister Pierre Elliot Trudeau in the 1970s, and it recognizes English and French as official languages in Canada. This meant that federal government services would be provided in both official languages, as would publications and internal departmentwide memos in federal government departments. Civil servants would have to learn both official languages at a specified level of proficiency to obtain certain positions. Federal offices, including post offices, would provide services in English and French in all parts of the country, even where there were few speakers of one of the languages. Labels on products sold in Canada would include both official languages. Publicly supported language training and language immersion programs became summer options for all Canadians, especially students (Canada 1967).

The policy was designed to deal with, in part, one of the ongoing struggles in Canada: one state with two founding nations (France and England). Although Francophones have always been well represented in the federal governments, the English minority in Quebec had been dominant in the economic life of that province, until the awakening in the 1950s and 1960s began an assertion of French political and economic power. The struggle over the appropriate role for Quebec within Canada, and the challenge of promoting a sovereign Quebec, has been one of the most difficult and defining questions in Canadian political economy. Rather than managing this conflict, official bilingualism has often been seen as a problem by various parties in Canada.

Accompanying official bilingualism, multiculturalism was also a policy that arose in the 1970s. The oft-quoted phrase of former Prime Minister Trudeau was that Canada sought to be a cultural "mosaic," rather than a cultural "melting pot" (like its neighbor to the south). Canadian levels of immigration have been high throughout the nineteenth and twentieth centuries, with the initial European migrants—French, British—joined by southern Europeans in the post-1945 period, and by Asians and South Asians and many others from the 1970s onward. Efforts were made in cultural policy to recognize and support the diversity of cultural identities and forms of expression in Canada. The Canadian census included a number of check-off boxes to allow citizens to indicate their ethnic identity (leading to the complaint by some that "Canadian" was not included as an ethnic identity). This information was also used as a basis for support for cultural organizations associated with different ethnic communities. Although multicultural programs did not initially have the same level of support as the mainstream support for high culture or mainstream cultural programs, over the past two decades as the composition of the Canadian population has changed, the multicultural agenda has become a mainstay of all cultural debates and policies. The net result of this effort according to the mainstream account—although there are many dissenters to the view put forward here—has not been to diminish or dilute Canadian identity, but to attempt to define multiculturalism as part of Canadian identity. While it may mean that Canadian debates and popular sensibilities have a more nuanced and complex appreciation of identity, community, and sovereignty, this adds a further qualification to a simple or unitary notion of Canadian identity.

The negotiations over First Nations' or aboriginal peoples' self-governance are a fourth important debate affecting the internal constitution of sovereignty in Canada. After pursuing a long-standing policy of assimilation until the late 1960s, in the early 1970s the Canadian government shifted direction. The state recognized First Nations as having distinct and collective rights within Canada, and began to negotiate more seriously to settle long-standing land claims or treaty obligations. Greater funding, self-governance, and management and control over land were promised.

With the recognition of First Nations' identity and right to self-governance, Canadian identity is once again placed in question. Canadian identity with a recognition of First Nations includes subsets or parcels for which the rights of citizenship mean something different. A simple notion of Canadian identity is thwarted by the official acknowledgment of those who lived in this land prior to the formation of Canada as a colony and then as a state, and the stipulation that the government and other Canadians must recognize their special role.

A final defining element, which, depending on one's perspective, makes Canada possible or makes it horribly complicated, is the federal-provincial division of governance (Atkinson 1993; Blair and McLeod 1993). Federalism was in vogue when Canada was given dominion status in the nineteenth century. In the British North America Act (BNA), the powers of revenue collection and taxation were reserved primarily for the central—or federal—government. Many of the responsibilities for service provision were assigned to the provincial governments, such as education, and later health care. The residual power—those issues not specifically identified—lies with the federal government rather than with the provincial governments. There was no formal constitution in Canada until 1982. There have been a constant stream of federal-provincial struggles and conferences, some related to Canada and Quebec, some related to revenue transfers, and some related to resource management.

Federal-provincial issues also had an effect on communications regulation and policy. The Canadian Radio-Television Telecommunications Commission (CRTC) regulated companies that operated in more than one province, and after 1989 it regulated even provincially based telephone companies as they became privatized. There is little formal role for provinces in communications policy and regulation (Babe 1990). Even though provincial government education departments had educational television channels, and even though the rights of ways of cities and towns are used in cable television distribution, licensing and regulation is controlled entirely at the federal level. Provinces do have culture ministries or departments, and in Ontario this was joined with issues of citizenship in the Ministry of Citizenship and Culture.

The internal elements of sovereignty usually include formal legal control over a territory and the monopoly on the use of force. Legitimate governing authority is constituted by more than that, and it is the nature of legitimate governing arrangements and authority that have been ongoing struggles in Canada. What constitutes Canada in whole or in its parts? The state has tried to maintain legitimacy in the cultural sphere by engaging in active "nation-building" efforts; this was the mission statement of the federal Department of Communication in the late 1980s. The state has also tried to deepen legitimacy by building up and supporting civil society groups of various sorts. These measures recognized and officially gave some kind of group identity and subnational construction of legitimacy, while at the same time trying to include these groups in the national project. Sovereignty is not abstract in Canadian cultural debates. Legitimate governing authority has been parceled together as a set of theoretically untidy but justifiable historical bargains— from the recognition of two nations in the BNA and the special role of the French language, to multiculturalism, First Nations' self-governance, and federal-provincial struggles. The reciprocal relationship between citizenship and sovereignty has led to a well-developed recognition of diversity in public discourse on cultural policies. Canada, then, while designed as a white settler colony in the British Empire, has in some senses emerged as unreflective of the modern nation-state.

EXPLANATIONS OF THE FORMATION OF A CULTURAL POLICY STRATEGY

What does this background mean for the development of a cultural policy? Prior to liberalization in the 1980s, the strategy for cultural policies included support for the public broadcaster, protection for nationally based private broadcasters in exchange for their production of Canadian voices and themes relevant to Canadians, and a number of grant and tax subsidy programs to support a space for cultural production in Canada. At no time was the cultural sphere significantly closed off from outside content or influences; the attempt was merely to maintain access to "Canadian voices" for audiences in Canada (Communications Canada 1992).

This public funding was seen as an easy target when programs to cut were considered in the 1980s. As well, some ideological critics of public cultural institutions argued that these agencies had been colonized by the special but shared interests of cultural bureaucrats and cultural producers; institution building and protection of agencies and specialized constituencies had taken the place of effective policymaking. Similarly, bilingualism and multiculturalism were portrayed as misguided and ineffective, typified by pandering to special interests. A low point in the 1980s came with the prime minister's appointment of an advocate of abolishing the Canadian Broadcasting Corporation (CBC) to the CBC board of directors.

Long-standing positions and policy problems were recast in the move to a neoliberal or neomercantilist trade and investment strategy in the mid-1980s and 1990s. The rhetoric of cultural policies was retained, although actual support for programs and agencies was cut. Attempts were made to advance the interests of the extraction and industrial sectors by participating actively in the formation of liberal trade and investment agreements in North America and international organizations. While seeking openings in other sectors, Canada sought an exemption for cultural activities. Firms like Northern Telecom needed open access to the United States to remain a viable world companies (Amesse, Seguin-Dulude, and Stanley 1994). The increasing size of telecommunications and technology firms was seen also to require a national strategy that would provide both a national base and allow and encourage strategies to encourage alliances with leading companies in other countries (such as the purchase of 20 percent of Bell Canada by Ameritech in 1999).

As many critics had predicted, the effort to advance the cultural exemption principle has proven to be less than effective in trade disputes with the United States, whether in motion pictures or magazines. As Vincent Mosco has argued (1997), the move to markets nationally has actually resulted in greater concentration and national monopolies (cable television, newspaper publishing, magazine publishing), while at the same time the state seeks to treat culture as a unique and nontrading sphere in international organizations.

Canadian communications and cultural policy strategy in the 1990s could be defined as a neomercantilist approach. While adhering to regional and multilateral agreements on free trade, the power of the state is used to advance the prospects of Canadian-based multinational firms. The state has been activist in promoting this neoliberal agenda and is not merely rolling back commitments to support national culture. In telecommunications, it is trying to engage in the development of international trade agreements to create a rule-based trading regime. This is seen as the best way to gain access to the U.S. market and other national markets for Northern Telecom (Amesse et al. 1994) and Teleglobe (Bradford 1999). Access provides the possibility of Canadian firms gaining the size they need to remain global players in telecom from a small national market base.

But in broadcasting, sound recording, motion pictures, and publishing, the effort is to try to retain a Canadian space (Canada, Information Highway Advisory Council 1995; Canadian Heritage, 1999, 1998, 1997; Direct-to-Home 1995; Ellis 1992). For instance, although Seagram's was nominally a Canadian company involved in media, its headquarters and primary activities were outside the country. The definition of Canadian cultural firm is not the same as with a telecommunications firm. Cultural policy objectives are framed as building a Canadian industrial space for the production, distribution, and consumption of Canadian content: expressions, images, and sounds. Also, through support for the enhancement of cultural exports and coproductions, there are efforts to build cultural markets in other countries to enlarge the relevant market size for Canadian cultural products (Attallah 1996; Dorland 1996).

This strategy sought market access for some communications sectors in other countries while trying to hold onto protection for the national communications and cultural space in others. It also treated cultural and communications activities as an industrial sector for the purposes of national policy research and national debates over the importance of cultural production, while treating cultural activities and expression as noneconomic and unique to Canadian identity and Canadian character in other respects. The policy approach also supported cultural production more and more through private sector and market mechanisms, reducing the role of state agencies and the public sector, while at the same time claiming that these activities constitute a Canadian public and political space that is essential to the maintenance of Canadian sovereignty.

The risks of this kind of approach are already evident in magazine publishing. Trading partners may not respect cultural exemptions in trade agreements (Mosco 1990). Trading partners may use the World Trade Organization (WTO) rather than the NAFTA, choosing a forum that is more advantageous to a broad liberalization agenda, or they may continue to press for more liberalization. This is not unusual in that "progressive liberalization" is a stated process of international trade agreements, with each round only a step in that direction.

The shift to the market may in fact undermine the uniquely Canadian elements of programming and cultural expression that arise from publicly funded programs and public institutions to which experience and identity are attached. Public television programming and public television as an institution are significantly and qualitatively different than private, commercially oriented television. It may be that the content derived through the mandates and decision making of the public institution gave rise to the unique forms of expression related to the development and support of Canadian identity. That is, as stated by the Parliamentary Committee report, "Canadian content" may not be precise enough a term to get at the core of this question. Canadian content actually has some significant differences depending on why and how that content is designed, whether as a public service or as an attempt to aggregate audiences to sell their attentions to advertisers. These are not equivalent for the purposes of supporting Canadian culture and identity. The upshot of all of this is that the move to the market may undermine the sense of legitimacy of the governing authority that was an offshoot of the nation-building and other aspects that cultural programs and public institutions were designed to create.

RECASTING CULTURAL POLICY

Two policy reviews and the government response completed in 1999 provide comprehensive consideration, assessment, and recommendations for recrafting cultural policies. The first review is situated in the context of international developments, while the second focuses on the internal aspects of the cultural policy debate.

The first review, completed in February 1999, is the report of the Cultural Industries Sectoral Advisory Group on International Trade (SAGIT) to the Canadian Department of Foreign Affairs and International Trade (Cultural Industries SAGIT 1999). The report initially reviews the reasons for Canadian cultural objectives, stating that globalization makes these objectives even more important.

Culture is "the heart of a nation," and "globalization is manifesting itself in the reaffirmation of local cultures." The report claims:

> Canadian books, magazines, songs, films, new media, radio and television programs reflect who we are as a people. Cultural industries shape our society, develop our understanding or one another and give us a sense of pride in who we are as a nation. Canada's cultural industries fulfil an essential and vital role in Canadian society. (Cultural Industries SAGIT 1999: i)

The report is also premised on an assessment of the technical and economic developments at the international level that "are creating both opportunities and challenges for our cultural industries." These include, according to the report's authors, digitalization and convergence, which allow new technologies to "compete with existing distribution systems," but also provide for opportunities "to distribute Canadian content both at home and abroad." While national policies have tried to address "the growth of multinational corporations and the vertical integration of entertainment, distribution and delivery systems and products," an increasingly important need when negotiating open trade agreements is to "recognize cultural diversity and the unique nature of cultural products" (Cultural Industries SAGIT 1999: ii).

The SAGIT report proposes that rather than pursuing the "cultural exemption strategy used in the past, which takes culture 'off the table' in international trade negotiations," a strategy should be initiated that would try to negotiate "a new international instrument that would specifically address cultural diversity, and acknowledge the legitimate role of domestic cultural policies in ensuring cultural diversity." The report argues that a strategy to promote "cultural and linguistic diversity" is appropriate at this point in time, and that this would reflect a more assertive strategy than efforts in the past to seek cultural exemptions, and would allow Canada to collaborate with other nations (Cultural Industries SAGIT 1999: iii).

The report provides an overview of different cultural activities and the policies of the Canadian government that have been and are being used to support Canadian culture. It also examines similar types of policies elsewhere, in building the case that efforts to protect cultural diversity are already evident in other countries. After reviewing a number of approaches, it argues in favor of pursuing the cultural diversity instrument in international trade negotiations:

> A new cultural instrument would seek to develop an international consensus on the responsibility to encourage indigenous cultural expression and on the need for regulatory and other measures to promote cultural and linguistic diversity. The instrument would not compel any country to take measures to promote culture, but it would give countries the right to determine the measures they will use (within the limits of the agreement) to safeguard their cultural diversity. (Cultural Industries SAGIT 1999: 31)

The second report, *A Sense of Place—A Sense of Being,* was completed in June (Canada, Standing Committee on Canadian Heritage 1999). It was from the Parliamentary Standing Committee on Canadian Heritage and reflected two years of hearings and consultations that the Committee had undertaken at the request of the Minister of Canadian Heritage to review "the evolving role of the federal government in support of culture in Canada."

Rather than presenting a sector-by-sector review of cultural policies, the report was organized around the themes of cultural production and distribution. Chapters covered issues associated with cultural creators, training, production and distribution, preservation, and consumers and citizens, especially in the context of new technologies, globalization, and changing demographics. The report also reflected on the model for cultural support that had been used in the past and the ways in which this model may need to be changed to respond to contemporary challenges. The "Canadian model of cultural affirmation . . . focuses on the development of a healthy cultural marketplace, freedom of choice for consumers and the principle of access to Canadian cultural materials. It emphasizes partnerships with other governments, organizations, and the private sector." As well, the report argued, the Canadian model was flexible in responding to changing circumstances and conditions. In its discussion of "the shifting balance between domestic and foreign influences," the emphasis of the report on an internal policy could also be seen as trying to minimize the transaction costs for cultural production, distribution and consumption, in order to try to complete a market link between Canadian cultural producers and consumers (Canada, Standing Committee on Canadian Heritage 1999).

Connecting to the Canadian Experience: Diversity, Creativity and Choice, the November 1999 government response to the report of the Parliamentary Standing Committee, also made reference to the SAGIT report and noted that the recommendations regarding a cultural diversity initiative had been accepted by the government.

A new international instrument on cultural diversity would lay out the ground rules for cultural policies and trade, and allow Canada and other countries to maintain policies that promote their cultural industries. The objective continues to be to preserve and promote domestic cultural policies within our international obligations. (Canadian Heritage 1999)

It is notable that this policy approach tries to address the contradictory aspects of past approaches. It remains to be seen whether the new approach can resolve the contradictions and risks of the previous approach. The "cultural diversity" agenda connects well with themes in Canada's domestic cultural policy, serving to tie together bilingualism, multiculturalism, and First Nations' self-governance. At the same time, Canadian national identity can be defended as one element of a culturally diverse world. As a political initiative, it puts forward a positive agenda and could serve as a basis for debate and discussion at a number of levels in Canada and internationally, rather than the indistinct and defensive "cultural exemptions" approach (presuming the general acceptability of trade but seeking exceptions) or the tactical approach of not including cultural sectors in a schedule of offers in a multilateral trade negotiation.

Given that this approach will be advanced in international trade organizations, it also needs to be seen at this level as a set of ideas and questions around which bargaining and coalition building can take place. The focus on cultural diversity may connect well with progressive forces in countries like the United States, where there are some—most often quietly murmured— concerns about mergers, acquisitions, and cross-ownership in media activities. It has the strength of possibly being used as an attempt to mobilize domestic civil society forces in a number of countries. The concept of cultural diversity fits well in a liberal pluralist political culture; how it will translate in other national environments or be used by other states remains to be seen. Finally, the civil society forces that this agenda must connect with in other countries if it is to be efficacious are not likely to be represented in the delegations that the U.S. administration sends to trade negotiations.

There will no doubt be efforts to portray cultural diversity as the 1990s equivalent of "free and balanced flow" of news and information, harking back to the alarmist opposition raised by media firms and some northern states in UNESCO debates over the New World Information and Communication Order. The cultural diversity approach may also draw support from numerous other administrations that are concerned about the predominance of transnational media firms. This is, as Canadian negotiators are no doubt aware, in no way assured. Each of these countries that are potential supporters or members of a possible coalition, like Canada, may also have a national champion firm in the cultural sector that has extensive international operations. As Philip Schlesinger discusses in chapter 6, the European Union participates as one entity, despite differing perspectives its members may have on questions of cultural policy. As well, countries may have subsidiaries of transnational media firms that are able to work to shape the agenda of trade negotiators.

Nevertheless, the domestic consumption of this policy initiative, and the fact that it presents a positive agenda for coalition-building action in multilateral organizations (consistent with Canadian efforts in past negotiations), will make this a potentially important initiative to track and evaluate on the next round of international trade negotiations in the WTO and in considering the emerging role of states with regard to media.

CONCLUSION

This discussion of Canada's cultural policy development leads to four claims about ways in which the framing of debates on sovereignty and globalization should be reconsidered.

First, both the internal and external aspects of sovereignty need to be considered in conceptualizations of sovereignty. The discussion above has pointed to the importance of cultural policy in attempting to build and maintain the legitimate governing authority for the Canadian state within Canada. This has resulted in a number of state-civil society arrangements that are best understood historically rather than through any syllogistic approach to sovereignty. These efforts also are supported by measures to protect a Canadian economic space.

Second, the role of the state may be contested and contradictory. The state may serve simultaneously as a forum for promoting sovereignty and as a conduit for expanding integration within continental and global economic ties. The shift toward a neoliberal trading and economic strategy in the 1980s did not mean that the rhetoric of cultural support was ended. The rhetoric of support for Canadian culture continued while actual public expenditures on cultural programs were frozen or reduced. At the international level, the match between policy statements and the direction of resources must also be examined. It will remain to be seen to what extent the shift to cultural diversity in international trade and investment negotiations is actually matched by difficult choices if this strategy is opposed by large trading partners.

Third, symbolic discourses about sovereignty that are accompanied by economic and political policies that may narrow the scope of the public sphere complicate the task of relating globalization and communications sovereignty. The public sphere and participation in decision making in Canada have been supported by cultural institutions promoting Canadian identity in a variety of forms. In recent decades, cultural policies shifted toward more use of the private sector as the vehicle to promote Canadian communications and culture. While this has provided an opportunity for Canadian-owned companies and private-sector producers, the actual content of the messages has become less relevant to Canadian themes, but especially less relevant to the maintenance of a public life (versus a private life defined by consumer choice and consumption).

Fourth, the role that uncertainty has played in justifying a role for the Canadian state points to several implications for state responses to globalization. The state can structure policies to support certain services that markets will not deliver, such as communications services to rural or sparsely populated areas. Robert Horwitz discusses such a policy in South Africa in chapter 3. Similarly, the state can serve to encourage certain forms of private action through the use of granting programs or tax incentives for certain expenditures or investments. During the 1980s, the Canadian state went some way to reduce the role of the public sector in culture through partnerships with and support for private firms. These policies can contribute to structuring internal markets to try to close the creativity, production, distribution, and consumption loop, and to create an organic market for cultural products and services in Canada. However, the market economy is dynamic, and this dynamism is accentuated by the rapid introduction of new technologies in a number of sectors and by the continuing concentration of ownership. Whether the strategy of cultural diversity will acknowledge that the uncertainties posed by global communications markets are such that state and public agencies are an essential part of a strategy supporting cultural diversity remains to be seen.

8

Brazil: The Role of the State in World Television

Joseph Straubhaar

The electronic media are an increasingly complex system with global, regional, national, provincial, and local players and flows. There are global channels like CNN that reach a few people in almost every country and there are media empires or global operations, like those of Rupert Murdoch, that reach a number of people in many countries. Further, there is a globalization of models, genres, and systems, such as advertising and soap operas, which have spread to most of the world's television systems. However, there is also an even more rapid growth of channels, operations, genres, and models at the level of "regions" defined by culture, language, and geography. Within a cultural-linguistic region like Latin America, the evening soap operas or *telenovelas* have a much broader impact than CNN, MTV, or even the regional satellite channels of Murdoch or Hughes.

Clearly things are changing so that more parts of the world interact more frequently and more intensely. More people travel, more migrate looking for work. More companies operate transnationally. Cultures around the world also interact more, especially via media like television, radio, and film. There is a world system of television, just as there is a world economic system. However, world system and global are not the same. Several scholars argue that the world includes regional, national, and local phenomena; it is not just a globalized system in which everything is homogenized and blended (Ianni 1992; Ortiz 1994). There is an important difference between globalization and world perspectives. The world capitalist economy described by Immanuel Wallerstein (1979) includes subnational, national, supranational or regional, and global economies, which all interact. Wallerstein sees national and local actors as unequal; core countries dominate the periphery, such as Africa, or the more developed semiperiphery, such as Brazil. This chapter takes a "world" perspective, arguing that national and regional television systems are just as important, if not more important, than global systems, and that the state matters because it plays a significant role in shaping national television systems.

Concern with both globalization and cultural-linguistic regionalization should not obscure the fact that, as this chapter demonstrates, television remains primarily a national phenomenon. Most television is watched via national systems. Further, unlike the situation observed in the early 1970s by Nordenstreng and Varis (1974), much, if not most, of that television, particularly in the prime-time hours when most people watch, is produced at the national level (see table 8.1 on page 146). To take the examples of TV Globo and Televisa, both are far more powerful and important in their home markets, Brazil and Mexico, than they are as partners in Sky Latin America, their regional broadcast joint venture with Rupert Murdoch (Sinclair 1999). However, much of this national programming is produced using regionalized or globalized genres or formats, such as the telenovela variation of the increasingly global commercial television reliance on soap opera. This contradiction echoes Robert Robertson's (1995) idea that we are increasingly using globalized forms to produce the local. More recently, a number of places are beginning to produce local or subnational television. This can be at the level of a large province (such as Quebec); a city, like most local television in the United States; or even a neighborhood, as frequently happens with alternative video productions like TV Maxambomba in Rio de Janeiro.

Culture is clearly not just a force acted on by technologies like television, institutions like the nation-state, and economic patterns like advertising. This chapter explores this cultural process as hybridization, the synthesis of local cultures with the imported elements of culture brought in by globalization. This happens through specific processes like electronic media flows, migration, inflow of cultural genres and models, and entrepreneurial actions of global or national corporations, within the structural context set by economics, technology, and national institutional acts.

THE NATIONAL STRIKES BACK

We focus here on the national as a layer of structure, cultural/informational production, and identity that endures strongly, even when various technologies, such as satellite TV, video, and the Internet, enable new layers such as the global, the cultural-linguistic regional, and the local to potentially strengthen as well. Almost all television broadcast days reflect productions from global, cultural-linguistic regional, and national/local levels. Most people now have some awareness of the global, with levels of identity that correspond to global, regional, national, and local. For example, a Brazilian peasant interviewed by the author several times between 1995 and 1998 in a remote land-reform settlement near Ilheus, Bahia, reflects a small level of global awareness. Mostly, he is aware of the World Wildlife Fund, which funds a community agent who talks to him about ecological farming and provides a truck his community can use sometimes. He also knows a little about the Latin American cultural-linguistic region, because his wife likes Mexican soap operas, which they can sometimes see on the community TV set. He has lived in several parts of Brazil, knows quite a bit about Brazil, and primarily thinks of himself as Brazilian. He also knows about local issues, personalities, and conditions, and thinks of himself as being from the state of Bahia.

Much of most people's identity is national or local and that very nationalism or localism provides a strong source of resistance to globalization. Even though technology now allows the global and regional broadcast of satellite television, other factors such as national economics, policy controls, and audience preferences continue to make national television broadcasts more important. While people have multilayered identities and interests, there is still a tendency toward preferring cultural proximity, that is, preferring cultural products from a culture similar to one's own (Straubhaar 1991a). However, as we see below, that similar culture is also the evolving hybrid of local, national, regional, and global forces.

People are increasingly acquiring multilayered identities that correspond in many ways to the multiple layers of world media: global, cultural-linguistic regional, national, provincial, and local. These layers of identity, framed by language, cultural history, and personal cultural experience, define markets for culture in ways that even global firms must respond to. The state and national culture are still powerful in this process, because through schooling, national media, language policy, and national organization of institutions like militaries, education, and commercial associations, the state in many countries continues to reinforce and define these nationally based conceptual frames.

THE INTERACTION OF GLOBAL AND NATIONAL TELEVISION

All of these levels of electronic media—global, cultural-linguistic regional, national, and provincial or local—are important and they interact with each other in complex ways. There is a tendency recently to stress globalization, but we should not overestimate the importance of global levels and elements compared to regional, national, provincial, and local ones. There is in fact powerful globalization based on technology, capitalist markets, investments, media flows, travel, migration, employment, advertising, and language/ culture diffusion. However, almost all of those factors also work to reinforce regionalism, nationalism, and localism, especially in media production and identity. When technology and economics do sometimes seem to favor globalization over other possibilities, they are often opposed by other forces. For example, Castells sees the forces of globalization, based essentially in technology and economics, challenged and ultimately transformed by identity, based in "a multiplicity of sources, according to different cultures, histories and geographies" (1997: 3).

Globalization is different in different regions. For example, while most European and African countries continue to import most television programs from the United States and relatively little from each other, that is less true in Latin America and the Middle East, where cultural trade within cultural-linguistic regions is large and growing. Latin American markets are more likely to import U.S. production ideas and genres than U.S. programs. So they are still engaged in globalization, but in a different way.

One of the main current limits on globalization in media and culture is that very few people have a primarily global identity. Identity tends to be based in language, religion, geography, history, ethnicity, collective memory, and political power apparatuses (Castells 1997). Those elements of identity tend to be local, or, especially when the state has been capable of mobilizing and reinforcing them, national. In many cases, national governments have intervened fairly effectively to support or reinforce these cultural boundaries to define national media markets. The combination of strong states and effective national broadcast entities has helped reinforce a strong sense of national identity in countries like Brazil and Mexico. However, when governments have tried to delineate national media markets without the existence of historical cultural boundaries defined by language, it has proven far more difficult. Robertson (1995) has aptly noted that we now tend to see the global replication of ideas and models for how to express nationality and national identity. This produces contradictions such as the expression of local identity through imported genres. A good example is the way the global genre of soap opera has been transformed into the Latin American telenovela. Although the telenovela has a recognizable regional form as a genre, most of the major national producers—Mexico, Argentina, Brazil, Colombia, Peru, and Venezuela—have created national forms of the genre that are characteristically different (Hernández 1999). This has been encouraged by national states in Brazil, Mexico, and elsewhere.

WORLD MEDIA SYSTEMS, STRUCTURE, AND CULTURE

This chapter proposes an analytical structure for understanding global, regional, national, and provincial systems, in this case, those of television and the Internet. This builds on the idea of Appadurai and others that there are various levels or forms of international interaction. Appadurai (1996) calls these levels "scapes": technoscapes (technology), ethnoscapes (migration, etc.), mediascapes, financescapes, and ideoscapes (government and other ideological institutions). This chapter argues that different forms of interaction or "scapes" are unevenly globalized or nationalized. Whereas technology, financial capital, and economic models tend to be increasingly globalized, media policy, cultural policy, market definition, and cultural identity are often still very nationally focused.

To help understand these distinctions, it is useful to distinguish the structural from the cultural. Television has both structural and cultural components. Its main structural elements are economic frameworks, technological bases, and institutions. A majority of the relevant institutions are most completely developed at the national level. At the macro level, the main cultural issue is modes of interaction between cultures, such as homogenization versus hybridization. Here the state often acts as a gatekeeper, acting to bar certain kinds of programs or program formats, or to provide incentives for local production. At the micro level, the main cultural components are program and program model importation, producer creativity, content genres and themes, and audience reception. Again, many of these processes are structured by the actions of national state institutions.

THE EXAMPLE OF TELEVISION IN BRAZIL

Television in Brazil is a complex blend of the national, the global, and the local. Television has contributed to the unification of a national culture and national marketplace. This signifies a great deal of success for a nationalization project begun in the 1950s, accelerated under the military regimes that ruled Brazil after 1964, and continued by subsequent civilian governments.

Before television, Brazilian cultural, political, and even economic life was far more localized and regionalized. Even by the 1950s, ethnographies such as Conrad Phillip Kottak's in Arembepe showed that villagers and rural people were little aware of national holidays, national cultural figures, national foods, and even national sports (1990, 1994). In the first years of television, until roughly 1968, television was also localized. The memorable drama experiments of the 1950s, the early development of Brazilian popular music programming, and early telenovelas were primarily developed on stations limited to the major cities of Rio de Janeiro and São Paulo, such as TV Rio, TV Record, and TV Excelsior. However, after the 1964 military coup, television, particularly TV Globo, was successfully used by the military to reach across the country and create a broader sense of national identity throughout the diverse regions of Brazil.

Other military development projects, such as a highly developed state sector in the economy, were substantially changed by post-1985 civilian governments. However, the consolidation and national extension of the television system has persisted. By 1984, the military intervention had set the essential boundary conditions for the present system: an almost complete national penetration of television broadcasts; predominance of private commercial nationally owned networks and dominance of audiences and advertising revenues by TV Globo; relatively strong minor network challengers in SBT, TV Bandeirantes, and, more recently TV Record; development of popular program genres that reflect a nationalism favorable to the regimes; and development of a news style also essentially favorable to the regimes.

In Brazil as elsewhere, television has been seen has having a "nationalizing vocation." Brazilian television is in many ways one of the world's most prominent national television system success stories. A number of comparative studies have noted the relative success of Brazilian television in producing most of its own programming. Others challenge whether Brazil has innovated or copied foreign models in its programming (Oliveira 1993; Schiller 1991). Even more have criticized the political uses of Brazilian television in mobilizing support for both military and civilian regimes (Lima 1993). Others have criticized the creation of a consumer culture via television, even though that was precisely what military and civilian development planners in the 1960s and 1970s had in mind, engaging increasing numbers of the Brazilian population in the market economy (Salles 1975).

STRUCTURAL FACTORS

Technology tends to enable new developments. It can also present constraints, but the result over time tends to be a layering, additive effect of new possibilities. New technologies, such as broadcast or satellite television, don't necessarily eliminate other options based on earlier technologies. For example, although VCRs and satellite/cable television bring in the possibility of many new U.S. movies and programs for Latin Americans, only relatively small proportions have access to these technologies and many of them don't necessarily use them to watch the "new" U.S. content. In almost all Latin American countries, other than perhaps Argentina, a clear majority of the population still primarily watches broadcast television (Straubhaar forthcoming), which is still very responsive to state rules and incentives, particularly in news, but also in entertainment (Sinclair 1999). In Brazil, for example, only 5–6 percent of television households have cable or satellite TV, a proportion that has been fairly stable for several years, even though a substantially larger number could afford those services (Pay TV 1999).

Economic factors both enable and limit cultural developments, as well as the use of new technological developments. Economic relations with other countries and economic growth can enable new possibilities, such as bringing television broadcasting into a country, or expanding the funds available for local production. By the mid-1960s in Brazil, the economy had been growing rapidly as the government invested in infrastructure and basic industries, such as steel, and as multinational and local manufacturing firms had been investing and growing in capacity. This led to an acceleration of the growth of a consumer economy within Brazil. With this, the television audience grew to embrace the middle class and lower middle class in an increasing number of cities. The number of television sets in Brazil went from 760,000 in 1960; 6,746,000 in 1970; 19,602,000 in 1977; to 33,000,000 in 1990 (Getino 1990: 56). This growth of a mass audience for marketing mass consumption products began to attract more advertising revenues. As in other countries, the new multinational and domestic advertisers favored television over other media as a means to reach the mass of consumers (Tunstall 1977: 56). This led to an expansion of network coverage, and national program production (table 8.1 on page 146).

However, economic patterns can also limit possibilities. For example, advertising as an economic system for financing television broadcasts both enables and limits the possibilities of the medium. Advertising tends to enable by increasing the money available for production. It also tends to limit broadcast program genres to certain types, predominantly entertainment, which often puts other kinds of programming, like development education, high culture, and extensive information programming, out of bounds. In Brazil, only a very small set of state government and national channels developed educational programming, while the commercial networks developed soap operas, variety shows, musical variety, comedy, talk shows, and sports, all classic commercial genres (Straubhaar, LaPastina, and Rego 2000).

Advertising, the dominant means of financing television in most countries, typically represents a complex interaction of forces between the state, multinational advertisers, national advertisers, and national broadcasters. In most countries outside North America, the state acts both as an advertiser (for state-owned companies) and as a regulator of advertising rules. In Brazil, for example, the effective control of much of the economy by state companies for most of the 1960s-1980s made the bestowal or withholding of state company advertising an extremely effective lever of power over national broadcasters (Mattos 1982). That enabled the state to favor national production over imported programs, favor certain genres over others, reinforce favored and cooperative TV networks (especially TV Globo), and influence news content (Straubhaar 1988). The state could also set the macroeconomic rules within which other advertisers operated, as well as regulate certain forms of advertising (Mattos 1982).

One of the main economic constraints on technology and its uses is the limit placed on access to new media by the inequitable distribution of income. This is the case in the United States as well as most Latin American countries. In Latin America, access to newspapers, magazines, books, satellite/cable television, and the Internet is limited in many countries to the upper middle class or even the elite. In Mexico, 1.5 million out of 90 million have access to the Internet and 18–20 percent have satellite or cable TV. In Brazil, the Internet has grown faster, to 8 million out of 170 million, but cable/satellite TV access has grown more slowly, remaining fairly static at 5–6 percent. In both cases, there seems to be a global elite who can afford access to the Internet and to satellite and cable TV.

At the political or institutional level, the dominant structure is still the state, although globalization analysts like to point out its decline relative to other more global actors, like multinational corporations. States still structure most ground rules of media, such as national market structures, ownership rules, production incentives and subsidies, financial rules, frequency assignments, technical standards, and content rules. In Brazil, for example, the military governments initially tolerated a joint venture between TV Globo and Time-Life that violated foreign ownership restrictions in the constitution. The delay in enforcement for four crucial years (1964–1968) in TV Globo's early establishment and consolidation of its basic network was seen as a military government financial favor to TV Globo. Government loans were then used to repay Time-Life (Straubhaar 1981). Recently, some regional groups are beginning to exercise power, and in certain policy arenas, like economic restructuring, international organizations like the World Bank, International Monetary Fund (IMF), and World Trade Organization can exercise considerable power as well. (Daeho Kim and Seok-Kyeong Hong's chapter in this volume considers the influence of the IMF in South Korea.)

The Brazilian military governments were far more active and interventionist in media, including the financial aspects. They financed microwave, satellite, and other aspects of television network infrastructure. The government favored certain networks, particularly TV Globo, with government advertising, which was considerable, because government or state corporations, banks, trading companies, mines, steel mills, and the like constituted nearly half the GNP for a couple of decades. As Mattos (1984) noted, the state had become the main advertiser.

At the cultural level, this chapter focuses on the formation of language and cultural communities and the creation and flow of media, particularly television, within and across those communities. The key elements in the formation of communities are their own historical dynamics, particularly the development of language and cultural themes, the creation and maintenance of group cultural identities as a locus of meaning, and cross-cultural interpersonal interactions such as travel and migration between communities. The nation-state has to build on these historical dynamics. It is easier for the state to reinforce a historical sense of national identity than to create a state that attempts to bridge differences between stronger primary loyalties. This has been a problem for composite states as diverse as India, Nigeria, and the former Yugoslavia, and a challenge for the emerging supra-state entity of the European Union, as Philip Schlesinger discusses in chapter 6.

In the early and mid-1960s, while television was still turning from an elite urban medium into a truly mass medium in Brazil, several stations and networks began to turn toward a mass audience with programming that was linked to national popular culture. National music began to be more prominent on variety shows. National character types and images began to be more prevalent on the telenovelas, such as *Beto Rockefeller*, which featured a typical Rio type, the good-lifer ("boa vida") in 1968. These developments made sense within the dynamics of the commercial media system within Brazil, building on its own popular culture and history. But they were elements that the government could also use and reinforce for its own modernization and national identity projects.

The military governments encouraged this trend toward national television program production. In the early 1970s, several government ministers pushed the commercial networks hard to develop more Brazilian programming and reduce their reliance on imported programs, particularly those that contained violence (Straubhaar 1981). TV Globo, in particular, increased national production considerably, because it had discovered that audiences, and consequently advertisers as well, preferred nationally produced musicals, comedies, and telenovelas over all but a few imported programs. Government also intervened to close programs that it considered immoral or in bad taste. In some cases, it would censor a theme from a telenovela but not cancel the entire program (Straubhaar 1984, 1989).

The media build on, reinforce, and, by dint of the agency of both media producers and consumers, sometimes contradict both this cultural context and the larger structural context of economics, technology, and institutions. For example, several television stations, particularly TV Rio, TV Excelsior, and TV Globo, responded to the commercial opportunity of the 1960s economic growth by changing their programming to appeal to a broader mass audience. They began to create or import programs that would sell products like soap, tobacco items, textiles, food stuffs, and fairly simple appliances (Sodré 1978). In doing this, they were also responding to the economic policy guidance of the military government, which itself built on the growth policies of the preceding governments. But more than anything, they were taking initiative to exploit a commercial opportunity and, for the creative producers, to produce new national programming that employed their talents and gave them an opportunity to create.

NATIONAL TELEVISION PRODUCTION FORCES

Most television is watched on national systems. States as diverse as China and Brazil work to protect the national market for national broadcast television. Many states in Asia (Chan 1994) and the Mid-East (Boyd 1993) specifically restrict international Direct Broadcast Satellite (DBS). Others, like Brazil, focus on providing incentives to national broadcasters to ensure their competitiveness (Straubhaar 1991a).

There are a number of crucial structural conditions that greatly facilitate national media production. These structural conditions enable national cultural producers to resist the contrasting advantages of global and regional producers. Some of these are inherent to the size and type of economy in question, which are structural conditions that limit or enable the state itself to act in regulating or structuring media industries.

Market size is a crucial limit to whether national industry grows. Very few small countries produce a great deal of television, even in Europe. Conversely, most large developing countries eventually become significant producers of television because the size of the market supports greater production. Brazil is a prime example of this. As the largest country in Latin America and the eighth largest economy in the world, it had the population base and economic wealth to create national programming.

Wealth of a market is also a crucial condition. It can compensate for market size, per se, if the market, like Japan, Taiwan, or Hong Kong, is wealthy enough. Aside from East Asia, however, wealth is still unequally distributed in countries like Brazil, so most major developing nation producers are large countries like Brazil, Egypt, India, and Mexico.

Some structural conditions are the result of interaction between global economic forces and national governments. While the global market pushes for certain kinds of commercial or financial structures (Herman and McChesney 1997), the state can still make certain decisions about how media institutions or industries are to be structured. As noted above, the Brazilian government, like that of Mexico, decided to structure national media as private commercial networks, but used both rules and incentives make them responsive to government programs and goals (Sinclair 1999).

National commercial structure limits what kind of media products will be produced. If commercial success in a market is imperative, the most commercially successful program models will be adopted, local or foreign. Depending on the strength of the national state, it can shape national commercial structures by defining rules for ownership structure, foreign ownership limits, advertising, subsidies for production, and import quotas.

In Brazil, the television networks formed since 1964 tended to have a fairly close working relationship with government officials, communicating government messages in frequently informal and sometimes subtle ways. Brazilian scholars such as Tarso de Castro (1984: 9–10) or Cohn (1977) have singled out TV Globo as being particularly responsive to the government. For example, in the early 1980s, TV Globo broadcast a Sunday evening prime-time program that featured speeches and answers to questions by the president, and TV Globo's news coverage was widely assumed by these scholars to reflect, or at least not contradict government viewpoints. That function of TV Globo has clearly continued into the post-1985 civilian regimes, in the view of most scholars and press critics. TV Globo was very supportive of the first two postmilitary civilian governments, Sarney and Collor. In fact, some scholars attribute Collor's election victory in 1989 to TV Globo's support (Lima 1993), although others felt that TV Globo's support was only one factor among several (Lins da Silva 1990; Marques de Melo 1992; Straubhaar 1996).

The national financial base likewise places boundaries around what kind of programming will be produced. Reliance on advertising tends to constrain programming options to those genres that are commercially successful—for instance, those that draw the largest or most economically attractive audiences. This has been the case in Brazil: The program genres that proliferated were indeed those that were most commercially successful (soap operas, variety shows, comedies, music, reality shows, and sports).

Competition among media in a national, regional, or global markets may spark creativity but it also tends to disperse resources among a number of competitors. Growth in infant national or regional television industries may sometimes be enhanced by limiting the number of competing stations or networks. This is often defined by the state. In Brazil, the military governments after 1964 clearly favored TV Globo as a preferred partner, killing one rival, TV Excelsior, which favored other political forces. The government supported TV Globo as a quasi-monopoly until the late 1970s, when it began to fear that Globo had become too powerful. So in 1981, the government issued two license packages to create competitors SBT and TV Manchete.

Government policies are crucial for shaping industries and enabling them to act independently of foreign pressure, but the style of government involvement may limit industry growth. The state can be a media actor on its own. It can be a facilitating or obstructive regulator and can create favorable conditions, such as subsidies for construction, R&D or other needs.

After the 1964 Brazilian revolution, the government initiated a low interest loan program for the purchase of television sets, built a microwave network that enabled television networks to reach the more remote parts of the country, and contributed a good deal of revenue through advertising by government-owned corporations and banks. The development of the telecommunications system, radio, and television was a high priority directly related to the military regime's perception of national security needs. The military governments saw telecommunications as vital economic infrastructure. They perceived broadcasting, in particular, as a means of reinforcing a sense of national identity (particularly in the more remote regions of the country), communicating government development plans and messages to the people and assuring a supportive political climate (Mattos 1982, 1984).

Other cultural industries can also support or limit television industries. Television draws heavily on the strength of related local cultural industries (film, music, theater, press/news, written fiction, and recordings). If those are underdeveloped too, that places another boundary on television production. In Brazil, much of the talent that helped national television production flourish came from other national cultural industries, particularly film and theater, but also music, publishing, and even the circus (Sodré 1977).

Within the boundaries placed by these political economy structures, developments tend to be nonlinear and hard to predict, but we do see patterns among the groups of actors involved. The key groups of people include those involved in the management and direction of television, the entrepreneurs; those involved in the actual program planning and production, the producers; and the audiences.

Producer behavior follows commercial imperatives but tends to follow the demands of the domestic market or audience when resources allow. Entrepreneurial behavior likewise tailors operations to the programming interests of domestic (or regional or global) audiences and to domestic and foreign business needs and markets, with considerable differentiation among larger markets/systems. Two key developments in the Brazilian industry came in with TV Globo in the late 1960s. It adapted most economic elements of the U.S. network television model, especially in finance and network operations, to the extent of convincing a contracted Time-Life financial advisor, Joe Wallach, to naturalize as a Brazilian citizen so he could work directly for TV Globo instead. However, within this economic framework, TV Globo ignored Time-Life's programming advice and brought in program managers from Brazilian advertising agencies and other television networks. They sifted through emerging Brazilian genres, such as telenovelas, variety shows, comedy and music to find the national genres that worked best with the audience within a frankly commercial framework (Straubhaar 1981).

National audiences tend to prefer national production, due to cultural proximity. National cultures vary in their appeal to domestic audiences, although this tends to be a crucial local advantage. National media's ability to compete with foreign imports varies depending on homogeneity and acceptance of local culture.

Over time, the patterns of action and behavior by these kinds of actors tend to stabilize and form culturally defined boundaries. Among industry professionals, those tend to take the form of "the way we do things here," and among audiences, they tend to take the form of preferences for certain kinds of programming. Theoretically, these are both forms of reflexive cultural structuring (Giddens 1984) and hybridization (García Canclini 1995). Giddens argues that social actors, both institutions and individuals, participate reflexively at various levels of awareness in the structuring of their own action. While states may be constrained by global actors as various as the U.S. government, the World Bank, Hollywood producers, and multinational advertising agencies, states still create rules, license and regulate national broadcasters, place their own advertising, and negotiate with whatever force they command. Together with global and regional actors, states effectively costructure the environment within which national media operate. That sort of structure sets the stage for cultural production that is almost necessarily hybrid. As television networks produce programming, they respond to global advertising trends and demands, to economic conditions both global and national, and to state interests in fostering national identity. This production targets a culture that, at least in the case of Brazil, is already a hybrid of over 500 years of interaction among European, African, and indigenous cultures. Both producers and consumers in Brazil focus on genres, like the telenovela and the variety show, that are also the result of a synthesis of influences. These come from European genre heritages, U.S. commercial formats, and the content specifics of a culture that Martín-Barbero (1993) calls *mestizo* and García Canclini (1995) calls hybrid.

NATIONAL TELEVISION PRODUCTION

Television genres have developed remarkably over the last twenty to thirty years. For example, a number of people have remarked on the changes the soap opera/serial/telenovela has experienced over time and the variety of forms it has taken in various settings (Allen 1995). More important, in some ways, is that a number of very low cost genres have evolved that can be produced almost anywhere with the simplest and cheapest of equipment: news, talk, variety, live music, and games. More and more countries are producing an increasing proportion of their own programming using such genres. Table 8.1 shows that a significant number of countries are doing over half of their own programming, both in the total broadcast day and during prime time, where audience viewing is concentrated and the most popular programs are usually placed.

In Brazil, like most countries, programming had to be live in the 1950s and consequently had to be local. Telenovelas were introduced in Brazil in 1952 and were popular throughout the decade, along with live drama, variety, and news. Imported television programs (feature films, adventure series, and cartoons/children's programs) flooded Brazil in the 1960s. They were cheap, slickly produced, and popular. In the 1960s, the most popular shows

Table 8.1 Percentage of Nationally Produced Programming in Prime Time and Total Broadcast Day

	1962		1972		1982		1991–1992	
	Prime	Total	Prime	Total	Prime	Total	Prime	Total
Asia								
Japan	81%	92%	95%	90%	96%	95%	92%	94%
South Korea	73	76	80	79	89	87	89	86
Hong Kong	23	26	64	62	92	79	95	83
Taiwan	74	64	98	79	89	88	97	78
India	—	—	98	80	89	88	97	78
Europe								
France	100	100	87	88	83	82	60	66
Spain	80	74	60	72	73	73	44	50
Sweden	75	81	68	79	74	86	50	52
Mid-East								
Israel	—	—	63	82	64	55	64	56
Lebanon	66	60	46	38	37	34	34	24
Latin America								
Dominican Republic	38	45	33	55	21	32	—	—
Colombia	65	77	81	75	83	66		
Chile	63	65	54	52	58	48	58	44
Brazil	70	69	86	55	64	63	72	64
NAFTA								
Hispanic U.S.	—	—	3	66	14	43	0	43
Puerto Rico	—	—	27	35	48	37	29	43
Mexico	63	59	68	62	58	57	46	67
Ang. Canada	22	47	31	45	39	45	46	45
Fr. Canada	26	32	33	33	29	32	30	27
Caribbean								
Trinidad	26	24	46	42	31	18	30	19
Jamaica	17	30	30	29	37	20	29	25
Barbados	16	16	13	51	10	16	—	—

Note: In this study, we look empirically at television programs broadcast on major VHF television stations (with at least 5 percent of the viewing audience) during sample weeks from 1962, 1972, 1982, and 1991–1992 for twenty-two countries and cultural regions. Television program listings for those weeks were analyzed in a simple content analysis.

In Canada, Anglophone (Ang.) Canadian channels are distinguished from Francophone (Fr.) Canadian channels.

The coding for data in tables 8.1 and 8.2 was done by experts familiar with program content for the market and the year in question, so that programs could accurately be assigned into origin categories. Thanks to the people who coded schedule information: Claudio Avendaño, Kristina Cahoon, Consuelo Campbell, Lucia Castellon, Karen Champagnie, Min-Chuan Chen, Scott Clarke, Luiz Guilherme Duarte, Michael Elasmar, Veronica Gonzalez, Patricia McCormick, Ritin Singh, Joseph Straubhaar, Makiko Takahashi, Sug-Min Youn.

were imported series, imported feature films, telenovelas, live variety shows, musical variety, and comedy programs (table 8.2).

In the 1960s, the average length of telenovelas story lines was increased to about nine months, the shows were placed daily in prime viewing time, the plots were increasingly nationalized, and sophistication was added by bringing in writers, actors, and directors from theater and cinema. Telenovelas developed during this period into a considerably more sophisticated genre at TV Excelsior in São Paulo and TV Globo in Rio. By the 1970s, telenovelas were the most popular programs and dominated prime time on the major networks, TV Globo and TV Tupi. TV Globo, in particular, began to attract major writers and actors from both film and theater to also work in telenovelas.

Telenovelas increasingly drew on popular novels, such as those by Jorge Amado. The dominant themes were upward mobility, consumption goals, and urban lifestyles. These messages appealed broadly to the mass audience in a growing consumer society. At TV Globo at least, the production values in telenovelas became high enough to rival programs imported from the United States or Europe. The Brazilian telenovelas are good enough, as commercial television entertainment, to be exported throughout Latin America and even recently into Europe and Africa (Antola and Rogers 1984).

In the 1980s, three other Brazilian television networks attempted to break into telenovela production to compete with Globo for a broader general audience. Neither SBT nor Bandeirantes had commercial success producing telenovelas, but TV Manchete achieved fairly high ratings for an ecology-oriented serial, "Pantanal," set in Brazil's western subtropical region. SBT resorted to importing telenovelas from Mexico, instead of producing them. TV Globo had also begun coproduction of telenovelas with international partners to lower costs and reach other markets. TV Globo has produced twelve to fourteen hours of programming a day since the late 1970s.

Imports were gradually replaced in prime time and many other time slots by domestic production, however. The audience definitely seemed to prefer the Brazilian production to the available alternatives. In 1982, only 22 percent of Brazilian audience time was spent watching imported programs, down from about 48 percent in 1965 (Straubhaar 1984). The major surviving demand in the 1980s was for an occasional imported action adventure series or feature film once or twice a week in prime time on TV Globo. Imported programs had been pushed onto the smaller independent stations, and, on TV Globo, into the morning and late evening hours—filler material, in essence, for those hours in which local production is not profitable. That changed slightly in the late 1980s, when TV Globo began to use more feature films in late prime time (9 or 10 p.m.) to counter increased competition from other channels that were showing feature films. In the 1990s, patterns shifted again as Brazilian stations began to import formats, such as reality and game

Straubhaar

Table 8.2   Percentage of U.S.-Produced Programming in Prime Time and Total Broadcast Day

	1962		1972		1982		1991–1992	
	Prime	Total	Prime	Total	Prime	Total	Prime	Total
Asia								
Japan	19%	7%	5%	9%	3%	4%	6%	5%
South Korea	27	24	20	19	7	10	5	9
Hong Kong	72	69	30	28	2	9	0	2
Taiwan	26	36	2	21	6	9	3	20
India	—	—	0	3	0	0	0	0
Europe								
France	0	0	8	3	7	6	33	22
Spain	21	13	35	24	17	11	37	31
Sweden	12	8	3	2	8	4	36	34
Mid-East								
Israel	—	—	13	13	19	15	21	15
Lebanon	23	24	40	41	22	34	29	29
Latin America								
Dominican Republic	9	14	35	22	31	36	—	—
Colombia	31	18	11	10	14	23	—	—
Chile	0	4	22	38	16	28	18	22
Brazil	30	31	14	44	36	37	9	20
NAFTA								
Hispanic U.S.	—	—	3	66	14	43	0	43
Puerto Rico	—	—	55	28	37	24	27	22
Mexico	31	38	26	26	37	35	42	24
Ang. Canada	71	49	56	50	56	53	52	51
Fr. Canada	35	35	42	38	37	38	41	39
Caribbean								
Trinidad	26	29	50	50	57	59	58	69
Jamaica	42	30	54	46	40	55	63	65
Barbados	53	31	39	31	52	52	—	—

Note: In Mexico, the study distinguishes national (Mexican), U.S. (including U.S. Hispanic), regional/Latin American cultural-linguistic (including Puerto Rico), and other international levels. On Hispanic U.S. stations, we separated national/U.S. (including U.S. Hispanic), regional/Latin American cultural-linguistic (including Mexican), and other internationallevels. We treat Puerto Rico as a cultural region separate from U.S. Hispanic. In Canada, Anglophone (Ang.) Canadian channels are distinguished from Francophone (Fr.) Canadian channels.

shows, which provided new, local ways for other networks to compete with the continuing life of telenovela production on TV Globo.

CULTURAL CAPITAL AND CULTURAL PROXIMITY

Cultural proximity is a disposition toward the use of cultural capital in a certain way. Forms of cultural capital, in terms of what one knows about other countries and cultures, can lead people toward or away from cultural proximity, the tendency to prefer media products from one's own culture or a similar culture. Cultural capital focuses on the sources of knowledge that permit people to make choices among media and other sources of information and culture.

Individuals and groups build on their own personal experience and their mediated experiences to build a sense of cultural capital. The concept of cultural capital can be used to sum up a series of identifiable sets of knowledge and dispositions that people tend to use when deciding what they want to watch on television. While a number of studies have focused on the role of language in defining television markets (Wildman and Siwek 1988), a number of cultural factors also define television markets, by defining what audiences' cultural identities and cultural capital lead them to prefer. Those are specific things like humor, gender images, dress, style, lifestyle, knowledge about other lifestyles, ethnic types, religion, and values. Cultural groups defined by their differences on these kinds of factors often overlap greatly with language groups. The aspects of cultural capital that are most relevant to audience choices about global, cultural-linguistic regional, and national television, form a historical framework within which states must act if they wish to preserve or strengthen national television production. Nationally focused cultural capital is also something that states can contribute to building, through national educational programs, museums, censuses, cultural programs, book publishing, film subsidies, theatrical financing, and support for broadcast and print media.

Cultural capital, identity, and language tend to favor an audience's desire for cultural proximity. However, cultural proximity is itself limited by social class stratification. Groups united by language and/or culture seem to be increasingly fragmented by both economic and cultural capital in the senses defined by Bourdieu (1984). Economic capital gives some people in the economic elite of many countries access to television channels, particularly those delivered by satellite or cable, that the vast majority or the population cannot afford (Porto 1997). Even more subtly, in most countries, only the elite or upper middle classes have the education, employment experiences, travel opportunities, and family backgrounds that give them the cultural capital (Bourdieu 1984) required to understand and enjoy television programs or Internet content in other languages. This also extends beyond language to culture: The cultural capital required for wanting to watch many kinds of imported programs tends to be concentrated in middle and upper classes. That is due in large part to the fact that their wealth provides opportunities for education, travel, and personal contact with outsiders. Thus, while cultural capital is separable from economic capital, the former is bounded and constrained by the latter, the economic aspects of social class.

While cultural factors tend to be associated with language, they frequently span similar cultures with differing languages. That often has to do with shared histories and geographic proximities, like those of Iberia, which unite Spanish and Portuguese cultures in many ways. While Brazilians speak Portuguese, they have a great deal in common with Spanish-speaking Latin Americans in terms of underlying culture inherited from Iberia and further developed and hybridized with other cultures in Latin America. So even though a Brazilian television program might have to be dubbed from Portuguese into Spanish, it will otherwise tend to look far more familiar to a Venezuelan than will one from New York. Likewise, even though Brazil mostly imports cheap American feature films and series to use as filler in off-hours, it also imports a certain amount of programming, particularly telenovelas, from elsewhere in Latin America, particularly Mexico and Argentina.

Education is a principal source of cultural capital (Bourdieu 1984). In the case of Brazil, basic education is often very nationally focused, reflecting national languages, nationally authorized and focused textbooks, and teacher training. States like Brazil (and the United States, for that matter) have used primary and secondary education as a deliberate means for building nationally focused cultural capital. Interviews reflect that such schooling has helped install nationally focused cultural capital across social classes in almost all people. However, postsecondary education, as the interviews conducted in Brazil also reflect, tends to increase exposure to a more globally focused set of knowledge. Basic education might then accentuate an audience focus on cultural proximity, while higher education might open interests to a more global set of media choices and a larger global level of identity.

These are the major channels of cultural capital: schooling, family practices, family networks, personal networks, travel, religion, groups, or associations. These help determine or mediate mass media choices (Martín-Barbero 1993). However, the media themselves are also a source of cultural capital. The relationship is not a simple one of effects, either of media affecting values and ideas, or even of values and ideas from other sources cleanly determining media choices and likewise determining interpretations of media contents. Mass media like television are a source of cultural capital. However, other sources of cultural capital also mediate choices for mass media, like television. The interaction is complex.

Together with education, family, networks, travel, and religion, media help form specific types of cultural capital. In particular, these channels of communication all help construct meanings for three other principal bases of cultural capital: ethnicity, age, and gender. While ethnicity, age, and gender consist in some part of physical characteristics, the meanings assigned those characteristics is socially constructed (Maccoby and Jacklin 1966). The meanings constructed for these characteristics becomes part of the cultural capital used by people in making media choices.

Ethnicity is important in the construction of national or "regional" cultural-linguistic markets. In fact, ethnic identity can be seen as constituting a type of cultural capital. The ethnic makeup of a television program cast affects its visual appeal to audiences. If people can recognize themselves or a familiar or desired ethnic type on screen, that adds to the cultural proximity of a program. Ethnic appeal can come from actual ethnicity or ethnic ideals. Within Brazil, for example, there is divergence among broadcasters over whether to broadcast an ethnic ideal that appeals to the more affluent consumer classes, largely European in ethnicity, or whether to appeal to the larger television audience, which is around half Afro-Brazilian. The main network, TV Globo, has often been accused of under-representing Afro-Brazilians in both programming and commercials (Leslie 1991). In an effort to segment the national audience and compete with the dominant national network, two other networks, SBT and Record, are creating interview, "reality," game, and variety show programming. These genres address working and lower classes' sense of identity or cultural capital by using participants who are ethnically more representative of the diversity of the Brazilian audience.

Cultural affinities create forms of cultural capital that inform cultural proximity. Such affinities could be seen in very specific factors such as linguistic commonalties, shared religious histories, gender roles, moral values, common aspirations, common histories with colonialism, shared art forms, shared music forms, similar forms of dress, character types and stereotypes, and ideas about genre, storytelling, and pacing. Perceived cultural similarities also might include ethnic types, gender types, dress, style, gestures, body language, and lifestyle. Perceived cultural relevance seems to include news and discussion topics, definitions of humor, familiar stars and actors, and audience knowledge about other lifestyles. Images and values include perceptions of other countries and peoples, opinions or evaluations of them, and values about marriage, family relationships, importance of material goods, work, where and how to live. These specific kinds or forms of cultural capital add up.

CONCLUSION

Globalization is a powerful force, driven by economic and technological developments. Those structural developments set a powerful context for changes in culture and media. Structural factors like economics and technology can expand or shrink the boundaries of cultural development, presenting both opportunities and challenges to nation-states and national broadcasters. Making advertising the main financial base for media, for example, places some forms of cultural expression, like formal education or development education, almost out of bounds for commercial television. However, the advertising income may also enable a number of new types of commercial programming to be created. Those commercial forms will likely follow commercially successful global patterns, but be adapted or hybridized with local culture. Both national entrepreneurs and national artists, working within boundaries also set by the state, can work to express nationally relevant themes and ideas within those hybrid forms.

The notion of the narrow determination of culture by economics and technology that both Marxists and McLuhanites have often observed is an incomplete explanation of the complex employment of television by national actors in the world system. Two possible theoretical correctives have been analyzed here. One is the idea of cultural proximity (that people tend to prefer media and cultural products similar to their own familiar culture, even when new technologies make imported cultural products available). The other is the theory of cultural hybridization (that imported cultural elements tend to be synthesized with local ones, with the latter tending to determine the mix). These latter patterns of culture show that culture itself also bounds, enables, and patterns what technologies and economic forces can do within a certain culture. A new technological force, like television, or a new economic force, like advertising, introduces changes, but the outcomes will be hybrids, synthesized and blended with national and local cultures.

The action of the state can also place powerful boundaries on the forces and forms of globalization, if that state has certain conditions to work with. The Brazilian case examined here highlights some of the structural and cultural conditions that can enable the state to take action. Both formal structures, such as economic conditions, and less formal structures, such as culture, can provide rules, patterns and resources that the state can utilize, as well as constraints that it must live with (Giddens 1984). These include the size of the audience/market and its wealth. It also can include the commercial structures and entrepreneurial abilities of television broadcasters as well as the strength and breadth of historically developed cultural traditions, human resources, and cultural industries. In particular, one specific resource for national broadcasting is nationally focused cultural capital within the members of the audience. That seems to build the base for a sense of cultural proximity, of preferring to see one's own culture on the small screen, rather than U.S. imports, whether broadcast locally by a national network or via satellite by something like Murdoch's Sky Latin America. Through processes like education, the state can do a great deal to construct and shape the cultural capital that is the base for this sense of cultural proximity and identity, rather like Anderson's (1983) imagined community.

The nature of the state also matters. The national state of Brazil is quite large, well-organized, and powerful by the standards of the developing world. However, many states have some of these same resources to work with, to shape conditions to assist national broadcasters. Governments must recognize that their actions are both constrained and enabled by structural and cultural conditions, and work intelligently within those conditions.

The world is not being culturally homogenized in depth, but as Robertson (1995) observes, we are increasingly producing the national or local in forms or patterns adapted and hybridized from the global. That means the state, and national broadcasters, must work within global forms. The Brazilian state and TV Globo used the globally diffused, commercialized soap opera as the genre vehicle to construct a form of television fiction that could help articulate and develop a stronger sense of national identity. But as critics like Oliveira (1993), and Herman and McChesney (1997) note, this happens within a frame set and is limited by the demands of commercial advertisers, both foreign and domestic. The national broadcasters and state must also work within the boundaries and resources of national culture. Brazilian tele-novelas used resources from national fiction (especially the novels of Jorge Amado, many of which were adapted into telenovelas and mini-series), film (most actors work in both feature films and telenovelas), theater (likewise), and the broader themes of Brazilian history. These provide both audience and television producers a common pool of reference, imagery, and themes that both bounds and fuels the genres of Brazilian television.

Epilogue

Kaarle Nordenstreng

The contributions to this volume convincingly demonstrate that the conventional wisdom of globalization as a process toward a stateless world is quite misleading; that nation-states continue to matter both in global reality and in studies about it, while at the same time the state as a concept remains shamefully underanalyzed; and, hence, that there is a burning need for rethinking in the field. So this book sends a needed warning to the scholarly community not to be carried by conventional wisdom—in the same vein as was recently done in another landmark volume whose editors paraphrase Mark Twain by noting that the rumors of the nation's death are greatly exaggerated (Curran and Park 2000: 16). And I wish to add that this warning sign is particularly welcome in the community of media scholars who too often rush after fashionable mantras such as globalization.

One might find it ironic that such emphatic support for caution concerning a fashionable mantra comes from somebody who is known as a proponent of the conventional wisdom of the 1970s: media imperialism. I admit that it was another mantra in its time, but I refuse to deny all of its validity. The idea of media imperialism, with the notion of information sovereignty as an integral part of it, was a paradigm that was badly needed at that stage of understanding the world of communications. Seen from the angle of the history of ideas one may even say that it was a necessary step in the continuous intellectual project of understanding the world. Like all paradigms that convert sensitive social realities into scientific and/or political narratives, media imperialism and its cousin, the New World Information and Communication Order (NWICO), were turned into mantras serving political agitation rather than scientific analysis (see Nordenstreng 1993). But this does not undo its vital contribution to the big project, and it should not be used as a weapon to accuse and condemn its early proponents, who typically were less one-sided in their claims than was perceived by later critics.

Hence new and even fashionable paradigms do have a useful function to

155

play in the historical project of constructing an ever more appropriate under-standing of the world (let us leave the functionalist and objectivist aspects of this sentence for another debate). Therefore I am not ashamed but rather proud of having been an early proponent of the information imperialism framework—in the way articulated by my coeditor of the two "Sovereignty" volumes, the late Herbert Schiller (2000). Our pushing for that particular paradigm was instrumental in a gradual growth of collective wisdom, while it was vital that it was met by critical arguments and alternative paradigms such as those generated by cultural studies, which hit media imperialism with findings of the active audience, and so on. In the same way we can see that globalization as a contemporary paradigm has been instrumental in pro-viding the intellectual arena new perspectives—but only to the extent that it does not turn into a mantra.

That is where this book enters the arena of the history of ideas. The edi-tors see it as a follow-up to the "Sovereignty" volumes that I edited with Schiller, but one should look further and specify the paradigmatic context into which each enters.

HISTORICAL CONTEXTS

Our first edited volume, *National Sovereignty and International Communi-cation: A Reader* (1979), was a package of articles inspired by an anti-imperi-alist approach, highlighting broad themes of national development and inter-national law as well as specific issues of direct satellite communication and foreign news, with a subtext of supporting ordinary people and their demo-cratic rights against commercial pressures coming increasingly from "the business system, operating globally" (quoted in the introduction to this vol-ume). This was indeed a subtext, because we did remarkably little to elabo-rate the concepts of people, citizens, democracy, nation-state—and even sov-ereignty. In fact, our volume would have deserved harsh criticism for neglecting to define its conceptual foundations, and in hindsight we may say that it traveled too easily on the waves of then-conventional wisdom. A nota-ble exception was a devastating critique from Daniel Lerner himself (Lerner 1980), but that was not based on the intellectual weaknesses of our work but on our political line, spelling out a veteran's disgust with a whole generation of "the New Left" in communication studies that we came to represent for him.

Our second volume, entitled *Beyond National Sovereignty: International Communication in the 1990s* (1993), was put together in the early 1990s, when it had become clear that the collapse of Soviet-style socialism had not only brought welcome new political space for Eastern Europe but had also diminished the moral and material support that the Third World received from the international community. Accordingly, not only was the idea of a New International Order dropped by the United Nations and its specialized agencies such as UNESCO (across the board from economy to communication) but also an opposite New World Order was advocated by the U.S. regime that led the Gulf War. This meant the demise of an international system based on sovereign nation-states—the foundational philosophy of the UN as well as of the anti-imperialist paradigm of the 1970s. In this context it was logical that the volume had a new subtext: support for civil society, including a global civil society (for the latter, see my postscript "Sovereignty and Beyond"). But again we failed to provide theoretical elaboration for our central concepts, and civil society remained as hazy as the concepts of sovereignty and state had been in the earlier volume. As pointed out in the preface, our original ambition had been to put together an update of international communication theory, but the rapidly moving landscape did not facilitate that and thus we had to settle for an eclectic reader.

The present book is situated in a context where globalization sets the parameters for TINA ("There Is No Alternative," a slogan promoted by Margaret Thatcher)—aptly used by Robert Horwitz in chapter 3. Ideologically, this represents a further swing of the pendulum to the Right from where we were in the early 1990s, but on the other hand there are countertrends particularly from two directions. First, environmental problems have been recognized as truly global problems by intergovernmental forums in Rio 1992 and Kyoto 1997 (notwithstanding the setback at The Hague follow-up conference in 2000). Second, civil society made a breakthrough at the World Trade Organization meeting in Seattle in 2000 as nongovernmental movements stopped the proceedings of one of the most influential organizations in the contemporary world—demonstrating that even TINA is questionable. Clearly, globalization is far from a simple concept, inviting contradictory reflections. The contemporary forces of global capitalism are paralleled by those of peace and development movements that only recently justified anti-imperialist politics precisely as "global problems" (and with emphatic support of the Soviet-led socialist countries of the time!).

Today—the shift of the millennium—is the time when globalization is coming under critical scrutiny, in all fields. Therefore this book is not only timely but also vital for anyone who wants to understand the state of affairs in international communications studies. Yet, while praising its topic I have to note that—like collections such as the two "Sovereignty" volumes typically do—this book provides stimulation for further study rather than a comprehensive analysis of the globalization/state problem. In this respect I may wryly note that it is indeed a follow-up to the two "Sovereignty" volumes.

THE NATURE OF THE STATE

The focus on the state invites me to make a fundamental point: The state is always a composite of social, political, and economic interests rather than an isolated entity. A Marxist way of making this point is to speak about "the class nature of the state." Western scholarship has a tendency to go along with a libertarian view whereby the state is typically seen as an inherently repressive bureaucracy based on military and police force, buttressed by secret service agencies, and dominated by a law and order culture. Such a demonization of the state effectively eliminates the democratic aspirations of ordinary people, which, after all, constitute the leitmotif for a state in original theories of democracy (Held 1996).

In the democratic view, the state is truly meant to be a mechanism to facilitate governance in accordance with the people's will. Its basic nature is democratic and popular instead of repressive and elitist—in theory. In practice, however, most states have limited at least part of the mandate of the people and turned themselves into less democratic bureaucracies. The Soviet and other former East European states are textbook examples of how theoretical "people's democracies" in practice may end up with undemocratic state structures. The current power struggles between politicians and "oligarchs" in these countries—with accompanying media wars mostly concerning the control of television—furnish us with evidence of how important the state continues to be even in the neoliberal conditions of postsocialism, and also how contradictory its political line may be (for the Russian case, see Nordenstreng et al. 2001).

The chapters of this book provide illuminating examples of the nature of the state, helping us to deconstruct the original concept of the state as a mechanism of democracy. Take South Africa (see chapter 3): A state "owned" by a narrow apartheid regime moved almost overnight into the hands of a broadly based democratic government. In both cases the state does matter, but the color of the state changes—not only in racial terms but also in almost all respects. Or take India (see chapter 4): a state operating as a platform to balance conflicting socioeconomic forces from both within and outside of the country. These are persuasive cases in point for today's Marxists: The state indeed has a class nature.

Another example comes to mind. At the height of the NWICO battles in the 1980s, the coalition dominated by U.S. press proprietors and led by the World Press Freedom Committee (WPFC) engineered "The Declaration of Talloires," which advocated the U.S. First Amendment notion of media freedom and attacked the NWICO for ostensibly advocating state control of the media. This call by the self-proclaimed voice of the "independent news media" was endorsed by a letter from President Ronald Reagan, the highest representative of the U.S. state (Nordenstreng 1999: 257). The Talloires group went around proudly quoting the letter, without seeing the paradox: the state actively advocating a denial of state involvement in the media.

The ideological struggle around NWICO exposed the central role that the concept of the state occupies in media policies, both national and international. Given the libertarian bias held even by many leftist media intellectuals, it was relatively easy to construct the big lie that NWICO promoted state control (such as licensing of journalists). A demonized notion of the state traveled so well that many professional and academic experts failed to see that while opposing state control and supporting media freedom they were in fact subscribing to a corporate initiative, conspicuously directed against democratic interests.

True, the situation was quite complicated in the international arena, with the Soviet-led socialist countries as well as several less democratic Third World countries supporting the NWICO. Later, when Eastern European countries became fellow travelers of Western powers, the balance also shifted at UNESCO, which switched from advocating to opposing NWICO. This reversal reveals another paradox: The United States had left UNESCO, citing among other reasons its displeasure with NWICO as an instrument of state control of the media, while in the post-NWICO period the United States, formally a nonmember, gained significant influence over UNESCO's liberal media policies, mainly through the surrogate body of WPFC.

Yet the bottom line is clear: First, states and intergovernmental organizations are not sociopolitically neutral or inherently biased in one or another direction, but always represent the forces that happen to be in power (leaving aside here the many questions about types of power). This is evident throughout this book, notably in the chapters on Canada, India, Australia, Korea, and the EU. Second, there is a lot of ideological baggage in the media field, capitalizing on the notion of a solid and suspicious state, which is seen as fundamentally opposed to the ideals of freedom and democracy. Contributions like this book are vital steps toward getting rid of that ideological baggage.

A FINAL NOTE

My focus above—like in most of the chapters in this book—has been on the state as a political-administrative entity surrounded by the forces of globalization. But a nation-state contains much more than formal structures of governance: It leads us to consider the social welfare state, cultural identities, and collective psychologies. In other words, it invites us to focus on the life world of ordinary people—on real civil society and not just those nongovernmental organizations that are vocal in its name (and often elitist even though they are fighting for democracy).

Such a focus on people is part and parcel of the new and genuine importance placed on human rights in international law and politics. But we should not place human rights in opposition to the nation state. Rather we should see that the state is a guarantor of human rights, democracy, and rule of law.

Moreover, the state remains crucial for development in the Third World. The welfare state may have nearly completed its task in industrialized countries, and thus may have exhausted much of its progressive role. Indeed, in the view of some interest groups, it has overreached itself and should be rolled back, with civil society and the so-called third sector assuming a greater role in the management of society. But the developing countries are far from ready for this. In these countries it is mainly the state that can ensure that poverty and inequality can be seriously tackled; relying on civil society or NGOs would be largely wishful thinking. In this respect globalization does stand against development.

Historically, a strong state is a legacy of the colonial powers. While the state was to a large degree democratized in the industrialized West, it remained largely undemocratic in the developing South. What developing countries need is not to replace an undemocratic state with an undemocratic global market but to democratize their states and to retain national development as top priority.

It is with this spirit—focusing on both people and development—that we should continue to examine the concept of the state.

Bibliography

AAP Newsfeed. 1999 May 26. "Australian government gets Internet bill and good-will of Brian." <http://www.lexis.com> (accessed June 6, 2000).

Acheson, Keith, and Christopher Maule. 1999. "Canadian Magazine Policy: International Conflict and Domestic Stagnation." Paper prepared for the World Services Congress, November 1–3, Atlanta, Georgia.

Adler, Glenn, and Eddie Webster. 1995. "Challenging Transition Theory: The Labor Movement, Radical Reform, and Transition to Democracy in South Africa." *Politics & Society* 23: 75–106.

———, eds. 2000. *Trade Unions and Democratization in South Africa, 1985–1997.* New York: St. Martin's Press.

African National Congress. 1992. *ANC Policy Guidelines for a Democratic South Africa.* Adopted at National Conference, Johannesburg, May 28–31.

African National Congress. 1994. *The Reconstruction and Development Programme: A Policy Framework.* Johannesburg: Umanyano Publications.

Allen, Robert C. 1995. *To Be Continued: Soap Operas Around the World.* London: Routledge.

Alleyne, Mark D. 1995. *International Power and International Communication.* New York: St. Martin's.

Almond, Gabriel. 1988. "The Return to the State." *American Political Science Review* 82: 853–874.

Amesse, F., L. Seguin-Dulude, and G. Stanley. 1994. "Northern Telecom: A Case Study in the Management of Technology." In *Canadian-Based Multinationals*, ed. S. Globerman. Calgary: University of Calgary Press.

Anderson, Benedict. 1983. *Imagined Communities: Reflections on the Origin and Spread of Nationalism.* London: Verso.

Antola, Livia, and Everett M. Rogers. 1984. "Television Flows in Latin America." *Communication Research* 11 (2): 183–202.

Appadurai, Arjun. 1996. *Modernity at Large: Cultural Dimensions of Globalization.* Minneapolis: University of Minnesota Press.

Archibugi, Daniele, David Held, and Martin Köhler. 1998. *Re-imagining Political Community: Studies in Cosmopolitan Democracy.* Stanford: Stanford University Press.

Armes, Roy. 1987. *Third World Film Making and the West*. Berkeley: University of California Press.

Atkinson, M. M. Ed. 1993. *Governing Canada: Institutions and Public Policy*, 2d ed. Toronto: Harcourt Brace.

Attallah, Paul. 1996. "Canadian Television Exports: Into the Mainstream." In *New Patterns in Global Television: Peripheral Vision*, ed. J. Sinclair, E. Jacka, and S. Cunningham, 161–191. New York: Oxford University Press.

Audley, Paul. 1994. "Cultural Industries Policy: Objectives, Formulation, and Evaluation." *Canadian Journal of Communication* 19 (3/4): 317–352.

Australian Broadcasting Authority. 2000 April 19. "Internet complaints scheme—the first three months." <http://www.aba.gov.au/about/publicrelations/newrel2000/27nr2000.htm> (accessed June 5, 2000).

————. n.d. "Online services content regulation: Background/history of regulatory scheme." <http://www.aba.gov.au/what/online/background.htm> (accessed June 26, 2000).

Babe, R. E. 1990. *Telecommunications in Canada: Technology, Industry and Government*. Toronto: University of Toronto Press.

Bangemann, Martin. 1994. Europe and the Global Information Society: Recommendations to the European Council, 26 May.

Bardhan, P. 1984. *The Political Economy of Development in India*. Oxford: Basil Blackwell.

Barnet, Richard J., and J. Cavanagh. 1994. *Global Dreams: Imperial Corporations and the New World Order*. New York: Simon & Schuster.

Baskin, Jeremy. 1991. *Striking Back: A History of Cosatu*. Johannesburg: Ravan Press.

————, ed. 1994. *Unions in Transition: COSATU at the Dawn of Democracy*. Johannesburg: National Labour & Economic Development Institute.

Bauman, Zygmunt. 1998. *Globalization: The Human Consequences*. New York: Columbia University Press.

Beltrame, Francisca. 1998. "Creating a Directive on Pluralism and the Media Concentration: A Case Study of the European Union Legislative Process." In *Lawmaking in the European Union*, ed. Paul Craig and Carol Harlow. London: Kluwer Law International.

Beltran, Luis Ramiro, and Elizabeth Fox de Cardona. 1979. "Latin America and the United States: Flaws in the Free Flow of Information." In *National Sovereignty and International Communication*, ed. Kaarle Nordenstreng and Herbert I. Schiller, 33–64. Norwood, N.J.: Ablex.

Benkler, Yochai. 2000. "Internet Regulation: A Case Study in the Problem of Unilateralism." *European Journal of International Law* 11: 171–185.

Benzie, R. 1997. " 'Zundelsite' Attacked; Tribunal Ponders Website Hate," *Toronto Sun*, October 15: 32.

Bertelsmann Foundation. 1999. "Risk Assessment and Opinions concerning the Control of Misuse on the Internet." <http://www.stiftung.bertelsmann.de/internetcontent/english/framesethome.htm> (accessed June 24, 2000).

Bird, Roger, ed. 1988. *Documents of Canadian Broadcasting*. Ottawa: Carleton University Press.

Blain, Neil, Raymond Boyle, and Hugh O'Donnell. 1993. *Sport and National Identity in the European Media*. Leicester: Leicester University Press.

Blainey, Geoffrey. 1982. *The Tyranny of Distance: How Distance Shaped Australia's History*, 2d ed. Melbourne: Macmillan.

Blair, R. S., and J. T. McLeod, eds. 1993. *The Canadian Political Tradition: Basic Readings*, 2d ed. Scarborough: Nelson.

Blasi, Vincent. 1977. "The Checking Value in First Amendment Theory." *American Bar Foundation Research Journal* 1977: 521–650.

Blaustein, Albert P., and Gisbert H. Flanz, eds. 1999. *Constitutions of the Countries of the World*. Dobbs Ferry, N.Y.: Oceana Publications.

Block, F. 1977. "The Ruling Class Does Not Rule." *Socialist Review*, 33.

Blumler, Jay G., ed. 1992. *Television and the Public Interest: Vulnerable Values in West European Broadcasting*. London: Sage.

Bollinger, Lee. 1986. *The Tolerant Society. Freedom of Speech and Extremist Speech in America*. New York: Oxford University Press.

Bosniak, Linda. 1999. "Citizenship denationalized." School of Law, Rutgers University, Camden, seminar paper. Mimeo.

Bourdieu, Pierre. 1984. Trans. Richard Nice. *Distinction: A Social Critique of the Judgement of Taste*. Cambridge, Mass.: Harvard University Press.

Bousquet, N. 1980. "From Hegemony to Competition: Cycles of the Core." In *Processes of the World System, Political Economy of the World System Annuals*, ed. Terence Hopkins and Immanuel Wallerstein, 43–83. Beverly Hills, Calif.: Sage.

Boyd, Douglas. 1983. *Broadcasting in the Arab World: A Survey of the Electronic Media in the Middle East*, 2d ed. Ames: Iowa State University Press.

Boyd-Barrett, Oliver. 1997. "International Communication and Globalization: Contradictions and Directions." In *International Communication and Globalization*, ed. Ali Mohammadi, 11–26. London: Sage.

Boyne, R. 1990. "Culture and the World System." *Theory, Culture and Society* 7, 57–62.

Bradford, Meriel V. M. 1999. "From Monopoly to Global Telecommunications Enterprise: The Teleglobe Case." Paper prepared for the World Services Congress, November 1–3, Atlanta, Georgia.

Briggs, J., and D. Peat. 1989. *Turbulent Mirror: An Illustrated Guide to Chaos Theory and the Science of Wholeness*. New York: Harper and Row.

Buchan, David. 1993. "Lights, Camera, Reaction!" *Financial Times*, 18/19 September.

Burgelman, Jean-Claude, and Caroline Pauwels. 1993. "Audiovisual Policy and Cultural Identity in Small European States: The Challenge of a Unified Market." *Media, Culture and Society* 14 (2): 176.

Busfiled, Steve, and Dan Glaister. 1998. "They Know What's Good for You." *Guardian*, March 27: 19.

Bustamante, Enrique. 2000. "Spain's Interventionist and Authoritarian Communication Policy: Telefónica as Political Battering Ram of the Spanish Right." *Media, Culture & Society* 22 (4): 433–445.

Cafruny, A. 1995. "Class, State, and World Systems: The Transformation of International Maritime Relations." *Review of International Political Economy* 2 (2).

Cameron, Bruce. 1995. "Cabinet Guide to Privatisation Held Back." *Cape Times*, June 29.

Canada, Information Highway Advisory Council. 1995 September. *Connection Community Content: The Challenge of the Information Highway.* Final Report of the Information Highway Advisory Council. Ottawa: Supply and Services.

Canada, Royal Commission on Bilingualism and Biculturalism. 1967. Report, Book I: *The Official Languages.* Ottawa: The Queen's Printer.

Canada, Standing Committee on Canadian Heritage, Parliament of Canada. 1999 June. *A Sense of Place—A Sense of Being: The Evolving Role of the Federal Government in Support of the Culture of Canada.* Ottawa: Parliament of Canada. <http://www.parl.gc.ca/InfoComDOC/36/1/CHER/Studies/Reports/cherrp09-e.html> (accessed July 15, 2000).

Canadian Heritage. 1997. *Canadian Television in the Digital Era*, January. Ottawa: Canadian Heritage.

———. 1998. *A Review of Canadian Feature Film Policy*, February. Ottawa: Canadian Heritage.

———. 1999. *A Report of the Feature Film Advisory Committee.* Ottawa: Canadian Heritage.

Cardoso, Fernando Henrique. 1973. "Associated Dependent-Development: Theoretical and Practical Implications." In *Authoritarian Brazil*, ed. Alfred Stepan, 142–176. New Haven: Yale University Press.

Carvel, John. 1993. "Plea for Europe Film Industry." *The Guardian*, 14 October.

Castells, Manuel. 1997. *The Power of Identity.* Malden, Mass.: Blackwell Publishers.

Chalmers, Damian. 2000. "Post-nationalism and the Quest for Constitutional Substitutes." *Journal of Law and Society* 27: 178–217.

Chan, Joseph M. 1994. "National Responses and Accessibility to Star TV in Asia." *Journal of Communication* 44 (3): 70–88.

Chase-Dunn, C. 1989. *Global Formation: Structures of the World Economy.* Oxford: Basil Blackwell.

Cho, Pack-Je. 1992. "New Media Policy in Korea: Issues and Policy Suggestions." In *Changing International Order in North-East Asia and Communications Policies*, ed. Kang Hyeon-Dew, 283–305. Seoul: Nanam.

Choi, Yung Joo. 1995. *Interpenetration von Politik und Massenmedien: Eine theoretische Arbeit zur politischen Kommunikation.* Munster: Lit. (in Korean)

Chossudovsky, Michael. 1997. "The IMF Korea Bailout." <http://kimsoft.com/1997/ sk-imfe.htm> (accessed July 1998).

Cohn, Gabriel. 1977. Comunicação e Industria Cultural. São Paulo: Companhia Editora Nacional.

Collins, Richard. 1990. *Television: Policy and Culture.* London: Unwin Hyman.

———. 1995. "Reflections across the Atlantic: Contrasts and Complementaries in Broadcasting Policy in Canada and the European Community in the 1990s." *Canadian Journal of Communication* 20 (4): 483–504.

Collins, Richard, and Cristina Murroni. 1996. *New Media, New Policies.* Cambridge: Polity.

Colson, Ilsa. 1999 23 August. "Australia a global village idiot, US lawyer agrees." AAP Newsfeed.<http://www.lexis.com> (accessed June 6, 2000).

Commission of the European Communities. 1984. *Television without Frontiers: Green Paper on the Establishment of the Common Market for Broadcasting, Especially by Satellite and Cable* (COM, 84, 300 Final). Brussels: CEC.

———. 1992a. Study on Pluralism and Concentration in Media: Economic Evaluation. Brussels: Booz-Allen & Hamilton, 6 February.

———. 1992b. Pluralism and Media Concentration in the Internal Market: An Assessment of the Need for Community Action, Commission Green Paper (COM [92] 480 final). Brussels, 23 December, European Commission.

Communications Canada. 1992. *The Information Society: New Media, New Choices.* Ottawa: Supply and Services.

Communications Decency Act. 1996. Title V of the Telecommunications Act of 1996, Pub. L. No. 104–104, 110 Stat. 56.

Cormack, Mike. 1993. "Problems of Minority Language Broadcasting: Gaelic in Scotland." *European Journal of Communication* 8: 101–117.

Cox, R. W. 1986. "Social Forces, States and World Orders: Beyond International Relations Theory." In *Neorealism and Its Critics*, ed. Robert Keohane, 204–254. New York: Columbia University Press.

Creed, Adam. 1999 27 April. "Campaign against Australian Censorship Gains Steam." Newsbytes. <http://www.lexis.com> (accessed June 6, 2000).

———. 2000a 3 February. "Porn Site Evades Australian Censorship Laws." Newsbytes. <http://www.lexis.com> (accessed June 6, 2000).

———. 2000b 29 March. "Australian Net Freedoms Group Blocked In Censorship Inquiry." Newsbytes. <http://www.lexis.com> (accessed June 6, 2000).

Cultural Industries Sectoral Advisory Group on International Trade (SAGIT). 1999. *New Strategies for Culture and Trade: Canadian Culture in a Global World.* Ottawa: Department of Foreign Affairs and International Trade.

Cunningham, Stuart. 1992. *Framing Culture: Criticism and Policy in Australia.* Sydney: Allen and Unwin.

———. 1996. *Australian Television and International Mediascapes.* Cambridge: Cambridge University Press.

Cunningham, Stuart, and Elizabeth Jacka. 1996. "The Role of Television in Australia's Paradigm Shift to Asia." *Media, Culture & Society* 18 (4): 619–637.

Curran, James. 1991. "Mass Media and Democracy: A Reappraisal." In *Mass Media and Society*, ed. James Curran and Michael Gurevitch, 82–117. London: Edward Arnold.

Curran, James, and Michael Gurevitch. 1977. "The Audience." In *Mass Communications and Society*. Milton Keynes, U.K.: Open University Press.

Curran, James, and Myung-Jin Park. 2000. "Beyond Globalization Theory." In *De-Westernizing Media Studies*, ed. James Curran and Myung-Jin Park, 3–18. London: Routledge.

Dahl, Hans Fredrik. 1994. "The Pursuit of Media History." *Media, Culture and Society* 16 (4): 551–563.

Dahlgren, Peter. 1991. "Introduction." In *Communication and Citizenship: Journalism and the Public Sphere in the New Media Age*, ed. Peter Dahlgren and Colin Sparks, 1–24. London: Routledge.

Davies, Lars, and Chris Reed. 1996. "The Trouble with Bits—First Steps in Internet Law." *Journal of Business Law* 1996: 416–430.

de Castro, Tarso. 1984. "Padrão Global de Deformação de Verdade." *Boletim Intercom* 46: 9–10.

De Santis, Heather. 1998. *Measures Affecting Trade in the Cultural Sector: Focus on Cultural Policy in Latin America.* Hull: Department of Canadian Heritage.

de Swaan, Abram. 1991. "Notes on the Emerging Global Language System: Regional, National and Supernational." *Media, Culture and Society* 13 (3): 309–323.

de Swaan, Abram. 1993. "The Evolving European Language System: A Theory of Communication." *International Political Science Review* 14 (3): 241–255.

Deibert, Ronald J. 1997. *Parchment, Printing, and Hypermedia: Communication in World Order Transformation.* New York: Columbia University Press.

Delacourt, John T. 1997. "The International Impact of Internet Regulation." *Harvard International Law Journal,* 207–235.

Deutsch, Karl W. 1966. *Nationalism and Social Communication: An Inquiry into the Foundations of Nationality,* 2d ed. Cambridge: MIT Press.

Dickinson, Margaret, and Sarah Street. 1985. *Cinema and State: The Film Industry and the British Government 1927–84.* London: BFI Publishing.

Direct-to-Home Satellite Policy Review Panel. 1995. *Direct-to-Home Satellite Broadcasting: Report of the Policy Review Panel.* Ottawa: Heritage Canada and Industry Canada.

Dorfman, Ariel, and Armand Mattelart. 1972. *Para Leer el Pato Donald: Comunicación de Masa y Colonialismo.* Mexico: Siglo Veintiuno.

Dorland, Michael. 1996. *The Cultural Industries in Canada: Problems, Policies, and Prospects.* Toronto: James Lorimer.

Downing, John. 1996. *Internationalizing Media Theory.* London: Sage.

Duarte, Luis. 1997. "Social Class as a Mediator for Patterns of Viewership of International Programs." Unpublished paper. Michigan State University, East Lansing.

Durham, W. Cole Jr. 1993. "Rhetorical Resonance and Constitutional Vision." *Cardozo Law Review* 14: 893–906.

Dyson, Kenneth, and Peter Humphreys, eds. 1990. *The Political Economy of Communications: International and European Dimensions.* London: Routledge.

Dziadul, Chris. 1993. "Ready for Primetime." *Television Business International,* May: 52–61.

Economic Survey of India 1993–1994. Publications Division, Government of India, New Delhi.

Edelman, Murray. 1964. *The Symbolic Uses of Politics.* Chicago: University of Illinois Press.

Electronic Frontiers Australia. 2000 February. "FOI request on ABA." <http://www.efa.org.au/FOI/foiaba2000.htm> (accessed July 3, 2000).

Elliott, Philip. 1982. "Intellectuals, the 'Information Society' and the Disappearance of the Public Sphere." *Media, Culture and Society* 4 (3): 243–253.

Ellis, David. 1992. *Split Screen: Home Entertainment and the New Technologies.* Toronto: Friends of Canadian Broadcasting.

Emerson, Thomas I. 1970. *The System of Freedom of Expression.* New York: Random House.

European Broadcasting Union. 1993. "Statement on GATT Negotiations on Audiovisual Services." Geneva, 5 October.

European Commission. 1989. Council Directive 89/552 of 3 October 1989 on Television without Frontiers, 1989 O.J. (L298) 23.

———. 1994. Strategy Options to Strengthen the European Programme Industry in the Context of the Audiovisual Policy of the European Union, April.

European Communication Council. 1997. *Exploring the Limits: Europe's Changing Communication Environment.* Berlin and New York: Springer.

European Union. 1989. "Council Directive of 3 October 1989." Official Journal of the European Communities, No. L 298/23, 17 October.

European Union Council of Ministers. 1997. "Resolution of the Council and of the Representatives of the Governments of the Member States, meeting within the Council of 17 February 1997 on illegal and harmful content on the Internet." Official Journal C 070 (March 6), 1–2.

Evans, Peter. 1979. *Dependent Development: The Alliance of Multinational, State and Local Capital in Brazil.* Princeton: Princeton University Press.

———. 1997a. "The Eclipse of the State? Reflections on Stateness in an Era of Globalization," *World Politics* 50 (October): 62–87.

———, ed. 1997b. *State-Society Synergy: Government and Social Capital in Development.* Research Series/No. 94. Berkeley: International and Area Studies.

Evans, Peter, D. Rueschmayer, and Theda Skocpol, eds. 1985. *Bringing the State Back In.* Cambridge: Cambridge University Press.

FCC. 1999. Home page. <http://www.fcc.gov.> (accessed June 7, 2000).

Featherstone, Mike, ed. 1990. *Global Culture: Nationalism, Globalization and Modernity.* London: Sage.

Featherstone, Mike, Scott Lash, and Roland Robertson. 1995. *Global Modernities.* London: Sage.

Fejes, Fred. 1981. "Media Imperialism: An Assessment." *Media, Culture and Society,* 3 (3): 281–289.

Feldman, Saul D. 1979. "Nested Identities," *Studies in Symbolic Interaction,* 2: 399–418.

Fentress, James, and Chris Wickham. 1992. *Social Memory: New Perspectives on the Past.* Oxford: Blackwell.

Fenwick, Helen. 1998. *Civil Liberties,* 2d ed. London: Cavendish.

Ferguson, Marjorie. 1992. "The Mythology about Globalization." *European Journal of Communication* 7: 69–93.

———. 1995. "Media, Markets, and Identities: Reflections on the Global-Local Dialectic." *Canadian Journal of Communication* 20 (4): 439–459.

Finn, Adam, Colin Hoskins, and Stuart McFadyen. 1994. "The Environment in which Cultural Industries Operate and Some Implications." *Canadian Journal of Communication* 19 (3): 353–376.

Fletcher, Frederick J. 1998. "Media and Political Identity: Canada and Quebec in an Era of Globalization." *Canadian Journal of Communication* 23 (3): 359–380.

Florida Star v. B.J.F. 1989. 491 U.S. 524.

Fox, Elizabeth. 1975. "Multinational Television." *Journal of Communication* 25 (2): 122–127.

———. 1992. "Cultural Dependency Thrice Revisited." Paper presented at the International Association for Mass Communication Research, Guaruja, Brazil.

———, ed. 1988. *Media and Politics in Latin America: The Struggle for Democracy.* Beverly Hills: Sage.

Fox, Elizabeth, and Silivio Waisbord. 2001. *Global Media, Local Politics: Broadcasting Policies in Latin America.* Austin: University of Texas.

Frank, A. G. 1994. "Soviet and East European Socialism: A Review of the International Political Economy on What Went Wrong." *Review of International Political Economy* 1 (2).

Frederick, Howard. 1993. *Global Communication and International Relations.* Belmont, Calif.: Wadsworth.

Fried, Charles. 1992. "The New First Amendment Jurisprudence: A Threat to Liberty." *University of Chicago Law Review* 59: 225–253.

Friedman, Steven. 1987. *Building Tomorrow Today: African Workers in Trade Unions, 1970–1984.* Johannesburg: Ravan Press.

Galperin, Hernan. 1999. "Cultural Industries in the Age of Free-Trade Agreements." *Canadian Journal of Communication* 24 (1): 49–78.

Galtung, Johan. 1971. "A Structural Theory of Imperialism." *Journal of Peace Research* (2): 81–117.

García Canclini, Néstor. 1995. *Consumidores y Ciudadanos: Conflictos Multiculturales de la Globalización.* Mexico: Grijalbo.

Gardner, David. 1993. "EC Agreement on Formula to Protect European Culture under Uruguay Round." *Financial Times,* November 6/7.

Garnham, Nicholas. 1986. "The Media and the Public Sphere." In *Communicating Politics: Mass Communications and the Political Process,* ed. Peter Golding, Graham Murdock, and Philip Schlesinger, 37–54. Leicester: Leicester University Press.

———. 2000. *Emancipation, the Media, and Modernity: Arguments about the Media and Social Theory.* Oxford: Oxford University Press.

Gasher, Mike. 1995. "The Audiovisual Locations Industry in Canada: Considering British Columbia as Hollywood North," *Canadian Journal of Communication* 20 (2): 231–254.

Gellner, Ernest. 1983. *Nations and Nationalism.* Oxford: Blackwell.

General Agreement on Tariffs and Trade. 1994. *Final Act Embodying the Results of the Uruguay Round of Multilateral Trade Negotiations,* May 3. Geneva: GATT.

Gerbner, George, Hamid Mowlana, and Kaarle Nordenstreng, eds. 1993. *The Global Media Debate: Its Rise, Fall, and Renewal.* Norwood, N.J.: Ablex.

Getino, Octavio. 1990. *Impacto del video en el espacio audiovisual latinoamericano.* Lima, Peru: Instituto para América Latina.

Giddens, Anthony. 1984. *The Constitution of Society: Outline of a Theory of Structuration.* Berkeley: University of California Press.

———. 1985. *The Nation-State and Violence.* Cambridge: Polity.

Gifreu, Josep. 1992. "Estructura y política de la comunicación en Cataluña," *Telos: Cuadernos de Comunicación, Cultura y Sociedad* 30: 54–61.

Gigante, Alexander. 1996. "Ice Patch on the Information Superhighway: Foreign Liability for Domestically Created Content," *Cardozo Arts & Entertainment Law Journal* 14: 523–552.

Gilpin, R. 1981. *War and Change in World Politics.* New York: Cambridge University Press.

———. 1987. *The Political Economy of International Relations.* Princeton: Princeton University Press.

Giordano, Philip. 1998. "Invoking Law as a Basis for Identity in Cyberspace." Stanford Technology Law Review. <http://stlr.stanford.edu/STLR/Articles/98STLR1/index.htm> (accessed July 6, 2000).

Gittings, John. 1998. "Murdoch's Beijing Love Fest." *Guardian*, December 12: 14.

Gleick, J. 1988. *Chaos: The Making of a New Science*. New York: Penguin Books.

Godard, François. 1993. "Gatt Real." *Television Business International*. November/December: 14, Table 1.

Golding, Peter, and Graham Murdock. 1991. "Culture, Communications, and Political Economy." In *Mass Media and Society*, ed. James Curran and Michael Gurevitch, 15–32. London: Edward Arnold.

Golding, Peter, and Phil Harris. 1997. *Beyond Cultural Imperialism: Globalization, Communication and the New International Order*. London: Sage.

Goldsmiths Media Group. 2000. "Media Organisations in Society: Central Issues." In *Media Organisations in Society*, ed. James Curran. London: Arnold.

Goldsmith, Jack. 2000. "Unilateral Regulation of the Internet: A Modest Defence." *European Journal of International Law* 11: 135–148.

Gourevitch, Peter. 1986. *Politics in Hard Times*. Ithaca, N.Y.: Cornell University Press.

Gramsci, Antonio. 1971. *Selections from the Prison Notebooks*. Ed. and trans. Quintin Hoare and Geoffrey Nowell Smith. London: Lawrence and Wishart.

Grantham, Bill. 2000. *"Some Big Bourgeois Brothel": Contexts for France's Culture Wars with Hollywood*. Luton: Luton University Press.

Greenawalt, Kent. 1989. "Free Speech Justifications." *Columbia Law Review* 89: 119–155.

———. 1990. *Speech, Crime, and the Uses of Language*. Oxford: Oxford University Press.

Grieco, J. 1988 "Anarchy and the Limits of Cooperation: A Realist Critique of the Newest Liberal Institutionalism." *International Organization*, 42.

Gringras, Clive. 1997. *Laws of the Internet*. London: Butterworths.

Grinspun, Ricardo, and Maxwell A. Cameron, eds. 1993. *The Political Economy of North American Free Trade*. Montreal-Kingston: McGill-Queen's University.

Grossberg, Lawrence. 1998. "Globalization, Media and Agency." Paper prepared for Seoul and Tokyo Seminar 1997. *Media and Society*, N. 18, Seoul: Nanam.

Grubel, James. 1999. "Harradine cannot be ignored in Senate dramas." AAP Newsfeed, May 14. <http://www.lexis.com> (accessed June 6, 2000).

Guback, Thomas H. 1969. *The International Film Industry*. Bloomington: Indiana University Press.

Guback, Thomas, and Tapio Varis. 1986. "Transnational Communication and Cultural Industries." (Reports and Papers on Mass Communication No. 92). Paris: UNESCO.

Guillou, Bernard, and Jean-Gustave Padioleau. 1988. *La Regulation de la Télévision*. Paris: La Documentation Française.

Habermas, Jürgen. 1989. *The Structural Transformation of the Public Sphere*. Cambridge: Polity Press.

Habermas, Jurgen. 1998. *The Inclusion of the Other: Studies in Political Theory*. Cambridge: MIT Press.

Haggard, S., and B. Simmons. 1987. "Theories of International Regimes." *International Organization*, 41.

Haggard, Stephan, and Robert R. Kaufman. 1995. *The Political Economy of Democratic Transitions*. Princeton: Princeton University Press.

Hall, Allan. 1998. "Canada Unveils Plan to Limit US cultural Imperialism." *Scotsman* (Sept. 25): 13.

Hall, Eammon G. 1993. *The Electronic Age: Telecommunication in Ireland*. Dublin: Oak Tree Press.

Hall, John A. 1998. *The State of the Nation: Ernest Gellner and the Theory of Nationalism*. Cambridge: Cambridge University Press.

Hall, Stuart. 1991. "The Local and the Global: Globalization and Ethnicity." In *Culture, Globalization and the World-System: Contemporary Conditions for the Representation of Identity*, ed. Anthony O. King, 19–29. London: Macmillan.

Hamelink, Cees. 1988. *Cultural Autonomy in Global Communications: Planning National Information Policy*. London: Centre for the Study of Communication and Culture.

Hamilton, Sebastian. 1998. "Smith Vows to Defend Film Industry against EU Tax Break Cuts." *Scotland on Sunday* (Dec. 20): 8.

Han, Sang-Jin. 1991. *Research in Korean Middle Class Theory*. Seoul: Literature and Society. (in Korean)

Hankiss, Elemér. 1994. "The Hungarian Media's War of Independence: A Stevenson Lecture, 1992." *Media, Culture and Society* 16 (2): 293–312.

Harvard Law Review. 1999. "Cyberspace Regulation and the Discourse of Sovereignty." *Harvard Law Review* 112: 1680–1704.

Hayles, K. 1990. *Chaos Bound*. Ithaca, N.Y.: Cornell University Press.

Hebdige, Dick. 1988. "Towards a Cartography of Taste, 1935–1962." In *Hiding in the Light: On Images and Things*, ed. Dick Hebdige. London: Routledge.

Held, David. 1989. *Political Theory and the Modern State: Essays on State, Power, and Democracy*. Stanford: Stanford University Press.

———. 1995. *Democracy and Global Order*. Cambridge: Polity.

———.1996. *Theories of Democracy*, 2d ed. Stanford: Stanford University Press.

Hemming, R., and A. Mansoor. 1988. *Privatization and Public Enterprises*. Washington, D.C.: International Monetary Fund, Occasional Paper No. 56.

Henkin, Louis. 1996. *Foreign Affairs and the Constitution*, 2d ed. Oxford: Clarendon Press.

Heritage Canada. 1999. *Connecting to the Canadian Experience: Diversity, Creativity and Choice*. Ottawa: Heritage Canada.

Herman, Edward S., and Robert W. McChesney. 1997. *The Global Media: The New Missionaries of Corporate Capitalism*. London: Cassell.

Hernández, Omar. 1999. "Genre Differences in Mexican and Brazilian Telenovelas." Unpublished paper at University of Texas, Austin.

Heuval, Jon Vanden, and Dennis Everette. 1994. "Trends and Developments in the Media of South Korea." In *Elite Media amidst Mass Culture*, ed. Chie-Woon Kim, 1–26. Seoul: Nanam.

Hinsley, Francis Harry. 1966. *Sovereignty*. London: Watts.

Hirsch, Mario, and Vibeke G. Petersen. 1992. "Regulation of Media at the European

Level." In *Dynamics of Media Politics: Broadcast and Electronic Media in Western Europe*, ed. Karen Siune and Wolfgang Truetzschler, 42–56. London: Sage.

Hirst, Paul, and Grahame Thompson. 1995. "Globalization and the Future of the Nation State." *Economy and Society* 24 (3): 408–442.

———. 1996. *Globalization in Question*. Cambridge, England: Polity.

Hobsbawm, Eric, and Terence Ranger, eds. 1983. *The Invention of Tradition*. Cambridge: Cambridge University Press.

Holton, Robert J. 1998. *Globalization and the Nation-State*. New York: St. Martin's Press.

Hong, Seok Kyeong. 1999. "Bataille de l'image en Corée: la 'culture' contre le 'marché.' " Paper presented at the conference "Medias et Diversité: vive la différence," Paris, June 18–19.

Horwitz, Robert B. 1997. "Telecommunications Policy in the New South Africa: Participatory Politics and Sectoral Reform." *Media, Culture and Society* 19: 503–533.

———. 2001. *Communication and Democratic Reform in South Africa*. New York: Cambridge University Press.

Hoskins, Colin, Stuart McFadyen, and Adam Finn. 1997. *Global Television and Film: An Introduction to the Economics of the Business*. Oxford: Oxford University Press.

Høst, Sigurd. 1991. "The Norwegian Newspaper System: Structure and Development." In *Media and Communication: Readings in Methodology, History and Culture*, ed. Helge Rønning and Knut Lundby, 281–301. Oslo: Norwegian University Press.

Høyer, Svennik, Epp Lauk, and Peeter Vihalemm, eds. 1993. *Towards a Civic Society: The Baltic Media's Long Road to Freedom*. Tartu, Estonia: Nota Baltica Ltd.

Huntington, Samuel. 1996. "The West Unique: Not Universal." *Foreign Affairs* 75 (6): 28–46.

Hutchings, Kimberly, and Roland Dannreuther, eds. 1999. *Cosmopolitan Citizenship*. New York: St. Martin's Press.

Ianni, Otavio. 1992. *A Sociedade Global (The Global Society)*. Rio de Janeiro: Editora Civilização Brasileira.

Information Highway Advisory Council, Canadian Content and Culture Working Group. 1995a. *Ensuring a Strong Canadian Presence in the Information Highway*. Ottawa: Industry Canada.

Information Highway Advisory Council. 1995b. *Connection Community Content: The Challenge of the Information Highway Final Report of the Information Highway Advisory Council*. Ottawa: Supply and Services.

Innis, Harold A. 1951. *The Bias of Communication*. Toronto: University of Toronto Press.

———. 1952. *Empire and Communications*. Toronto: University of Toronto Press, reprinted 1972.

International Commission for the Study of Communication Problems. 1980. *Many Voices, One World*. Paris: UNESCO.

Internet Industry Association. 1999a. "IIA guide for ISPs: Internet content regulation checklist." <http://www.iia.net.au/guide.html> (accessed June 24).

———. 1999b. "Internet Industry Code of Practice: Codes for industry self regulation in areas of Internet content pursuant to the requirements of the Broadcasting Services Act 1992 as amended" <http://www.iia.net.au/code6.html> (accessed June 24).

———. 2000. "Guide for Internet Users: Information about online content." <http://www.iia.net.au/guideuser.html> (accessed June 24).

Internet Software Consortium. 2000. "Distribution by Top-Level Domain Name by Host Count (January 2000)." Available at <http://www.isc.org/ds/WWW-200001/dist-bynum.html> (accessed June 30).

iPrimus. 2000. "Filtering policy." <http://bess02.iprimus.net.au/s295/policy.html> (accessed July 14).

Iwabuchi, K. 1997. The Sweet Scent of Asian Modernity: The Japanese Presence in the Asian Audiovisual Market. Paper presented at Fifth International Symposium on Film, Television and Video—Media Globalization the Asia-Pacific Region, FuJen University. Taipei.

Izod, John. 1988. *Hollywood and the Box Office 1895–1986*. Basingstoke, England: Macmillan.

Jakubowicz, Karol. 1994. "Equality for the Downtrodden, Freedom for the Free: Changing Perspectives on Social Communication in Central and Eastern Europe." *Media, Culture and Society* 16 (2): 271–292.

Janus, Noreene. 1981. "Advertising and the Mass Media in the Era of the Global Corporations." In *Communication and Social Structure: Critical Studies in Mass Media Research,* ed. Emile McAnany and J. Schnitman, 287–316. New York: Praeger.

Jessop, Bob. 1985. *Nicos Poulantzas: Marxist Theory and Political Strategy*. London: Macmillan.

———. 1989. "Capitalism, Nation-States and Surveillance." In *Social Theory of Modern Societies: Anthony Giddens and his Critics*, ed. David Held and John Thompson, 103–128. Cambridge: Cambridge University Press.

Johnson, David R., and David G. Post. 1996. "Law and Borders—The Rise of Law in Cyberspace." *Stanford Law Review* 48: 1367–1402.

Judt, Tony. 1992. "The Past Is Another Country: Myth and Memory in Postwar Europe." *Daedalus* 121 (4): 83–118.

Kahn, Joseph, Cathy Chen, and Marcus W. Brauchli. 1996. "Beijing Seeks To Build Version of the Internet That Can Be Censored." *Wall Street Journal*, Jan 31: A1, A4.

Kakabadsiie, M. A. 1995. "The World Trade Organization and the Commodification of Cultural Products." *Media Asia* 22: 71–77.

Katz, Elihu, and George Wedell. 1976. *Broadcasting in the Third World*. Cambridge: Harvard University Press.

Katzenstein, Peter. 1985. *Small States in World Markets*. Ithaca, N.Y.: Cornell University Press.

———. 1996. "Regionalisation in Comparative Perspective." Working Paper 95/1. Oslo, Norway: ARENA.

———, ed. 1978. *Between Power and Plenty: Foreign Economic Policies of Advanced Industrialized Countries*. Madison: University of Wisconsin Press.

Keane, John. 1991. *The Media and Democracy*. Cambridge: Polity Press.

Kedourie, Elie. 1985. *Nationalism*. London: Hutchinson.

Keohane, Robert O. 1980. "The Theory of Hegemonic Stability and Changes in International Economic Regimes, 1967–77." In *Change in the International System*, ed. Ole Holsti et al., 131–162. Boulder, Colo.: Westview Press.

———. 1989. *International Institutions and State Power*. Boulder, Colo.: Westview Press.

Kim, Minnam, ed. 1993. *Rewriting History of the Korean Mass Media*. Seoul: Aachim. (in Korean)

Kindleberger, Charles Poor. 1973. *International Economics*. Homewood, Ill.: R. D. Irwin.

Kizza, Josep Migga. 1998. *Civilizing the Internet: Global Concerns and Efforts toward Regulation*. Jefferson, N.C.: McFarland.

Kohli, A. 1989. "Politics of Economic Liberalization in India." *World Development* 7 (3): 305.

Kolko, Gabriel. 1998. "Mais exportez donc! dit le FMI." *Le Monde Diplomatique*, May 1998.

Korea Information Society Development Institute. 1997. *Comprehensive Plan for the Information and Communication Industry*. Seoul: KISDI. (in Korean)

Korea Press Institute. 1997, 1998. *The Korean Press*. Seoul: KPI. (in Korean)

Korean Broadcasting Commission. 1998. *Report on the 3rd Regulatory Roundtable for Asia & the Pacific 1998*, Korean Broadcasting Commission, November.

Korean Society for Journalism and Communication Studies. 1993. *Research in Korean Communication Models II-Koreans and Communication*, Korean Society for Journalism and Communication Studies, May. (in Korean)

Kottak, Conrad Philip. 1990. *Prime-Time Society: An Anthropological Analysis of Television and Culture*. Belmont, Calif.: Wadsworth.

———. 1994. *Assault on Paradise*. Belmont, Calif.: Wadsworth.

Krasner, Stephen. 1976. "State Power and the Structure of International Trade." *World Politics* 28 (3): 317–347.

———. 1978. *Defending the National Interest: Raw Materials Investments and U.S. Foreign Policy*. Princeton: Princeton University Press.

———. 1991. "Global Communications and National Power: Life on the Pareto Frontier." *World Politics* 43 (3): 336–366.

Lapid, S. 1989. "The Third Debate: On Prospects of International Theory in the Post-Positivist Era." *International Studies Quarterly* 33 (3): 235–254.

Lee, Chin-Chuan. 1980. *Media Imperialism Reconsidered*. Beverly Hills, Calif.: Sage.

Leiner, Barry M. et al. 2000. "A Brief History of the Internet." Available at <http://www.isoc.org/internet-history/brief.html> (accessed June 30, 2000).

Lerner, Daniel. 1980. Book review of *National Sovereignty and International Community: A Reader*. *The Public Opinion Quarterly* 44 (1): 137–138.

Leslie, Michael. 1991. "Illusion and Reality on Commercial Television: A Comparison of Brazil and the U.S." Paper presented at the International Communication Association, Chicago, May.

Lessig, Lawrence. 1996. "The Zones of Cyberspace." *Stanford Law Review* 48: 1403–1411.

Liebes, Tamar, and Elihu Katz. 1990. *The Export of Meaning: Cross-Cultural Readings of Dallas*. New York: Oxford University Press.

Lima, Venicia A. de. 1993. "Brazilian Television in the 1989 Presidential Elections." In *Television, Politics, and the Transition to Democracy in Latin America*, ed. Thomas Skidmore, 97–117. Washington, D.C.: Woodrow Wilson Center.

Lins da Silva, Carlos E. 1990. "Indústria da Comunicação: Personagem Principal das Eleicoes Presidencias Brasileiras de 1989." *INTERCOM – Revista Brasileira de Comunicação* 18: 121–128.

Lloyd, Ian J. 2000. *Electronic Commerce and the Law*. Edinburgh: Edinburgh University Press (Hume Papers on Public Policy, vol. 7, no. 4).

Louw, P. Eric, ed. 1993. *South African Media Policy: Debates of the 1990s*. Bellville, South Africa: Anthropos.

MacBride, Sean, and Colleen Roach. 1993. "The New International Information Order." In *The Global Media Debate: Its Rise, Fall, and Renewal*, ed. Gerbner George, Hamid Mowlana, and Kaarle Nordenstreng, 168–174. Norwood, N.J.: Ablex.

Maccoby, Eleanor Emmons, and Carol Nagy Jacklin. 1966. *The Pyschology of Sex Differences*. Stanford: Stanford University Press.

Manger, Jason J. 1995. *The Essential Internet Information Guide*. London: McGraw-Hill.

Mann, M. 1983. "The Autonomous Power of the State." *Archives européenes de sociologie*, XXV.

Marais, Hein. 1998. *South Africa, Limits to Change: The Political Economy of Transition*. London: Zed Books.

Marques de Melo, José. 1988. "Communication Theory and Research in Latin America: A Preliminary Balance of the Past Twenty-five Years." *Media, Culture and Society* 10 (4): 405–418.

———. 1992. "Brazil's Role as a Television Exporter within the Latin American Regional Market." Paper presented at the International Communication Association. Miami, Florida, May.

Marshall, William P. 1995. "In Defense of the Search for Truth as a First Amendment Justification." *Georgia Law Review* 30: 1–39.

Martín-Barbero, Jesús. 1993. *Communication, Culture and Hegemony: From the Media to Mediations*. Trans. Elizabeth Fox and Robert A. White. London: Sage.

Mathieson, Rosalind and Fiona Hamilton. 1998. "Harradine calls for Internet crackdown." AAP Newsfeed, September 6, <http://www.lexis.com> (accessed June 6, 2000).

Mattelart, Armand. 1996. *La mondialisation de la communication*. Paris: Presse Universitaire de France.

Mattelart, Armand, Xavier Delcourt, and Michèle Mattelart. 1984. *International Image Markets: In Search of an Alternative Perspective*. London: Comedia.

Mattos, Sergio. 1982. "Domestic and Foreign Advertising in Television and Mass Media Growth: A Case Study of Brazil." Ph.D. diss., University of Texas at Austin.

———. 1984. "Advertising and Government Influences on Brazilian Television." *Communication Research* 11 (2): 203–220.

Maule, Christopher J., and Keith Acheson. 1994. "International Regimes for Trade, Investment, and Labour Mobility in the Cultural Industries." *Canadian Journal of Communication* 19 (3): 401–422.

Mayer, Franz C. 2000. "Europe and the Internet: The Old World and the New Medium." *European Journal of International Law* 11: 149–169.

McAnany, Emile, and K. T. Wilkinson, eds. 1996. *Mass Media and Free Trade: NAFTA and the Cultural Industries.* Austin: University of Texas Press.

McChesney, Robert W. 1994. *Telecommunications, Mass Media, and Democracy.* New York: Oxford University Press.

———. 1999. "Graham Spry and the Future of Public Broadcasting." *Canadian Journal of Communication* 24 (1): 25–48.

McChesney, Robert, and Edward Herman. 1997. *The Global Media: The New Missionaries of Corporate Capitalism.* London: Cassell.

McQuail, Denis. 1992. *Media Performance: Mass Communication and the Public Interest.* London: Sage.

———. 2000. *Mass Communication Theory,* 4th ed. London: Sage.

McQuail, Denis, and Karen Siune, eds. 1998. *Media Policy: Convergence, Concentration, and Commerce.* London: Sage.

Meiklejohn, Alexander. 1948. *Free Speech and Its Relation to Self-Government.* New York: Harper.

Mele, Marco. 1990. "Il mercato europeo dei programmi audiovisivi." In *Le Televisioni in Europa,* ed. Claus-Dieter Rath, Howard H. Davis, Francois Garçon, Gianfranco Bettetini, and Aldo Grasso, 331–361.Turin, Italy: Edizioni della Fondazione Giovanni Agnelli.

Miliband, Ralph. 1968. *The State in Capitalist Society.* London: Weidenfield & Nicholson.

Miller v. California (1973) 413 U.S. 15.

Mitchell, T. 1991. "The Limits of the State: Beyond Statist Approaches and their Critics." *American Political Science Review* 85 (1).

Mohammadi, Ali, ed. 1997a. *International Communication and Globalization.* London: Sage.

———. 1997b. "Communication and the Globalization Process in the Developing World." In *International Communication and Globalization,* ed. Ali Mohammadi, 67–89. London: Sage.

Morgenthau, H. 1956. *Politics Among Nations: The Struggle for Power and Peace.* New York: Alfred A. Knopf.

Morley, David, and Kevin Robins. 1995. *Spaces of Identity: Global Media, Electronic Landscapes and Cultural Boundaries.* London: Routledge.

Mosco, Vincent. 1990. "Toward a Transnational World Information Order: The Canada-U.S. Free Trade Agreement." *Canadian Journal of Communication* 15 (2): 46–65.

———. 1996. *The Political Economy of Communication: Rethinking and Renewal.* Thousand Oaks, Calif.: Sage Publications.

———. 1997. "Marketable Commodity or Public Good: The Conflict between Canadian Domestic and Foreign Communication Policy." In *How Ottawa Spends,* ed. Gene Swimmer et al. Ottawa: Carleton University Press.

Mowlana, Hamid. 1997. *Global Information and World Communication: New Frontiers in International Relations.* London: Sage.

Murdock, Graham, and Peter Golding. 1989. "Information Poverty and Political Inequality: Citizenship in the Age of Privatized Communications." *Journal of Communication* 39 (3): 180–195.

Murray, Andrew D. 1998. "Internet Domain Names: The Trade Mark Challenge." *International Journal of Law and Information Technology* 6: 285–312.

N2H2. n.d. "Solutions overview." <http://www.N2H2.com/solutions> (accessed July 1, 2000).

Namer, Gerard. 1987. *Mémoire et Société*. Paris: Méridiens Klincksieck.

Nandy, Ashis. 1989. "The Political Culture of the Indian State." *Daedalus* 118 (4): 1–26.

National Socialist Party v. Village of Skokie (1977) 432 U.S. 43.

National Telecommunications Policy 1994. Ministry of Communications, Government of India, New Delhi.

Nebraska Press Ass'n v. Stuart (1976) 427 U.S. 539.

New York Times v. United States (1971) 403 U.S. 713.

Niosi, Jorge, ed. 1991. *Technology and National Competitiveness: Oligopoly, Technological Innovation, and International Competition*. Montreal: McGill-Queen's University Press.

Noam, Eli. 1993. "Media Americanization, National Culture, and Forces of Integration." In *The International Market in Films and Television Programs*, ed. Eli Noam and Joel Millonzi, 41–58. Norwood, N.J.: Ablex.

Nordenstreng, Kaarle. 1984. *The Mass Media Declaration of UNESCO*. Norwood, N.J.: Ablex.

———. 1993. "New Information Order and Communication Scholarship: Reflections on a Delicate Relationship." In *Illuminating the Blindspots: Essays Honoring Dallas W. Smythe*, ed. Janet Wasko, Vincent Mosco, and Manjunath Pendakur, 251–273. Norwood, N.J.: Ablex Publishing Corporation.

———. 1999. "The Context: Great Media Debate." In *Towards Equity in Global Communication: MacBride Update*, ed. Richard Vincent, Kaarle Nordenstreng, and Michael Traber, 235–267. Cresskill, N.J.: Hampton Press.

Nordenstreng, Kaarle, and Herbert Schiller, eds. 1979. *National Sovereignty and International Communication: A Reader*. Norwood, N.J.: Ablex.

———, eds. 1993. *Beyond National Sovereignty: International Communication in the 1990s*. Norwood, N.J.: Ablex.

Nordenstreng, Kaarle, and Tapio Varis. 1974. *Television Traffic: A One-Way Street? A Survey and Analysis of the International Flow of Television Programme Material*. Reports and Papers on Mass Communication, No. 70. Paris: UNESCO.

Nordenstreng, Kaarle, Elena Vartanova, and Yassen Zassoursky, eds. 2001. *Russian Media Challenge*. Helsinki, Finland: Aleksanteri Institute.

Nordlinger, E. 1981. *On the Autonomy of the Democratic State*. New Haven, Conn.: Yale University Press.

Nussbaum, Martha Craven. 1996. "Patriotism and Cosmopolitanism." In *For Love of Country: Debating the Limits of Patriotism*, ed. Martha Nussbaum and Joshua Cohen, 2–20. Boston: Beacon Press.

O'Donnell, Guillermo, and Philippe C. Schmitter. 1986. *Transitions From Authoritarian Rule: Tentative Conclusions About Uncertain Democracies*. Baltimore: Johns Hopkins University Press.

Ohmae, Kenichi. 1995. *The End of the Nation-State: The Rise of Regional Economies*. London: Harper Collins.

Oliveira, Omar. 1993. "Brazilian Soaps Outshine Hollywood: Is Cultural Imperialism Fading Out?" In *Beyond National Sovereignty: International Communication in the 1990s*, ed. Kaarle Nordenstreng and Herbert I. Schiller, 116–131. Norwood, N.J.: Ablex.

Olssen, Tom. 1990. "Sweden's Via Media." In *Media Structures in a Changing Europe*, ed. Ronald Pohoryles, Philip Schlesinger, and Ulf Wuggenig, 269–286. Vienna: ICCR.

Ortiz, Renato. 1994. *Mundialização e Cultura*. São Paulo: Editora Brasiliense.

Østergaard, Bernt Stubbe, ed. 1997. *The Media in Western Europe: The Euromedia Handbook*. London: Sage.

Ostiguy, Elizabeth M. 1995. "The Benefits of More Choice in Distribution Channels for Cultural Programming." *Canadian Journal of Communication* 20: 329–334.

Palan, Ronen. 1992. "The Second Structuralist Theories of International Relations: A Research Note." *International Studies Notes* 17 (3).

Paterson, Richard. 1993. "Introduction: Collective Identity, Television and Europe." In *National Identity and Europe: The Television Revolution*, ed. Phillip Drummond, Richard Paterson, and Janet Willis, 1–8. London: BFI Publishing.

Pauwels, Caroline. 1999. "From Citizenship to Consumer Sovereignty: The Paradigm Shift in European Audiovisual Policy." In *Communication, Citizenship, and Social Policy: Rethinking the Limits of the Welfare State*, ed. Andrew Calabrese and Jean-Claude Burgelman, 65–76. Lanham, Md.: Rowman & Littlefield.

Pay TV. 1999. "Audiencias para Pay-TV." September. (São Paulo, Brazil).

Perrin, N. 1979. *Giving Up the Gun: Japan's Reversion to the Sword, 1543–1879*. Boston: D. R. Godine.

Petrazzini, Ben. 1996. "Telecommunications Policy in India: The Political Underpinnings of Reform." *Telecommunications Policy* 20 (1): 39–51.

Pieterse, Jan Nederveen. 1999. "Europe, Traveling Light: Europeanization and Globalization." *The European Legacy* 4 (3): 3–17.

Pohoryles, Ronald, Philip Schlesinger, and Ulf Wuggenig, eds. 1990. *Media Structures in a Changing Europe*. Vienna: ICCR.

Pool, Ithiel de Sola. 1983. *Technologies of Freedom*. Cambridge: Belknap Press.

Porto, Mauro Pereira. 1997. "New Political Strategies in Brazilian Television? Globo's 'Journal Nacional' in a Comparative Perspective." Latin American Studies Association, Guadalajara, Mexico.

Postman, Neil. 1986. *Amusing Ourselves to Death: Public Discourse in the Age of Show Business*. New York: Penguin.

Poulantzas, Nicos. 1969. "The Problem of the Capitalist State." *New Left Review*, 58: 67–78.

———. 1973. *Political Power and Social Classes*. London: New Left Books.

———. 1978. *State, Power, Socialism*. London: New Left Books.

Price, Monroe E. 1994. "The Market for Loyalties: Electronic Media and the Global Competition for Allegiances." *Yale Law Journal* 104: 667–705.

Price, Monroe. 1995. *Television, the Public Sphere, and National Identity*. Oxford: Clarendon Press.

Prigogine, I., and Stengers, I. 1984. *Order out of Chaos: Man's New Dialogue with Nature*. New York: Bantam.

Przeworski, Adam. 1991. *Democracy and the Market: Political and Economic Reforms in Eastern Europe and Latin America.* Cambridge: Cambridge University Press.

Przeworski, Adam et al. 1995. *Sustainable Democracy.* Cambridge: Cambridge University Press.

R. v. Fellows (1997) 2 All E.R. 548.

R.A.V. v. City of St. Paul (1992) 505 U.S. 377.

Raboy, Marc. 1990. *Missed Opportunities: The Story of Canada's Broadcasting Policy.* Montreal: McGill-Queen's.

Ralite, Jack. 1993. "Le GATT contre la culture: Danger pour la civilization." *Le Monde Diplomatique.* November: 32.

Red Lion Broadcasting Co. v. FCC (1969) 395 U.S. 367.

Reno v. American Civil Liberties Union (1997) 521 U.S. 844.

Republic of South Africa. 1989. *Summarized Report on the Study by Dr. W. J. de Villiers Concerning the Strategy, Policy, Control Structure and Organisation of Posts and Telecommunications.* Pretoria: Government Printer.

———. 1991a. *Post Office Amendment Act* (Act No. 85 of 1991). Pretoria: Government Printer.

———. 1991b. Task Group on Broadcasting in South and Southern Africa. *Report of the Task Group on Broadcasting in South and Southern Africa* (Viljoen Commission Report). Pretoria: Government Printer.

———. 1993a. *Constitution of the Republic of South Africa* (Act No. 200 of 1993). Cape Town: Government Printer.

———. 1993b. *Independent Broadcasting Authority Act* (Act No. 153 of 1993). Cape Town: Government Printer.

———. 1995a. *Independent Broadcasting Authority. Report on the Protection and Viability of Public Broadcasting Services; Cross Media Control of Broadcasting Services; Local Television Content and South African Music* (Triple Inquiry Report). Johannesburg: IBA.

———. 1995b. Ministry of Public Enterprises. "Discussion Document by the Government of National Unity on the Consultative and Implementation Framework for the Restructuring of the State Assets." Pretoria: Ministry, July 25.

———. 1996a. *Growth, Employment and Redistribution: A Macroeconomic Strategy.* Pretoria: Government Printer.

———. 1996b. Ministry of Posts, Telecommunications and Broadcasting. *The White Paper on Telecommunications Policy.* Pretoria: Government Printer, March 13.

Restatement (Third) of Foreign Relations Law. 1987. Philadelphia: American Law Institute.

Richeri, Giuseppe. 1992. "TV and New Technology—Satellite and Cable in Europe." In *The New Television in Europe*, ed. Alessandro Silj, 71–104. London: John Libbey.

———. 1993. *La tv che conta: Televisione come Impresa.* Bologna: Baskerville.

Rival, Laura. 1997. "Modernity and the Politics of Identity in Amazonian Society." *Bulletin of Latin American Research* 16 (2): 137–151.

Robertson, Robert. 1995. "Glocalization: Time-Space and Homogeneity-Heterogeneity." In *Global Modernities*, ed. M. Featherstone, S. Lash, and R. Robertson, 25–44. Thousand Oaks, Calif.: Sage.

Robinson, D. C., E. R. Buck, and M. Cuthbert, eds. 1991. *Music at the Margins— Popular Music and Global Cultural Diversity.* Newbury Park, Calif.: Sage.

Rogers, Everett. 1983. *Diffusion of Innovations,* 3d ed. New York: The Free Press.

Rogers, Everett, and Jorge Schement. 1984. "Media Flows in Latin America." *Communication Research* 11 (2): 305–319.

Roncagliolo, Rafael. 1994. "Communication and Development: The Latin American Challenge." In *Mass Communication Research: On Problems and Policies,* ed. Cees J. Hamelink and Olga Linné, 267–275. Norwood, N.J.: Ablex.

Rowe, W., and V. Schelling. 1991. *Memory and Modernity: Popular Culture in Latin America.* London: Verso.

Rudolph, L., and S. Rudolph. 1987. *In Pursuit of Lakshmi: The Political Economy of the Indian State.* Chicago: Chicago University Press.

Ruggie, John G. 1989. "International Structure and International Transformation: Space, Time, and Method." In *Global Changes and Theoretical Challenges: Approaches to World Politics in the 1990s,* ed. O. Czempiel and J. Rosenau, 21–35. New York: Lexington Books.

Salinas, R., and Paldan, L. 1979. "Culture in the Process of Dependent Development: Theoretical Perspectives." In *National Sovereignty and International Communications,* ed. Kaarle Nordenstreng and Herbert. I. Schiller. Norwood, N.J.: Ablex.

Salles, M. 1975. "Opinião Publica, Marketing e Publicidade no Processo Brasileiro de Desenvolvimento." Speech at Escola Superior de Guerra, Rio de Janeiro.

Sassen, Saskia. 1998. "On the Internet and Sovereignty." <http://www.law.indiana.edu/glsj/vol5/no2/9sas.html> (accessed July 2, 2000).

Scanlon, Thomas. 1972. "A Theory of Freedom of Expression." In *The Philosophy of Law,* ed. Ronald M. Dworkin, 153–171. Oxford: Oxford University Press.

Scannell, Paddy. 1989. "Public Service Broadcasting and Modern Public Life." *Media, Culture and Society* 11 (2): 135–166.

Schauer, Frederick. 1982. *Free Speech: A Philosophical Enquiry.* Cambridge: Cambridge University Press.

———. 1989. "The Aim and Target in Free Speech Methodology." *Northwestern University Law Review* 83: 562–568.

———. 1992. "The First Amendment as Ideology." *William & Mary Law Review* 33: 853–869.

———. 1993. "Free Speech and the Cultural Contingency of Constitutional Categories." *Cardozo Law Review* 14: 865–880.

———. 1997. "The Speech of Law and the Law of Speech." *Arkansas Law Review* 49: 687–702.

Schement, Jorge, I. Gonzales, P. Lum, and R. Valencia. 1984. "The International Flow of Television Programs." *Communication Research* 11 (2): 163–182.

Schiller, Herbert I. 1991. "Not Yet the Post-Imperialist Era." *Critical Studies in Mass Communication* 8: 13–28.

———. 1996. *Information Inequality: The Deepening Social Crisis in America.* New York: Routledge.

———. 2000. *Living in the Number One Country: Reflections from a Critic of American Empire.* New York: Seven Stories Press.

Schlesinger, Philip. 1987. "On National Identity: Some Conceptions and Misconceptions Criticized." *Social Science Information* 26 (2): 219–264.

———. 1991. *Media, State and Nation: Political Violence and Collective Identities.* London: Sage.

———. 1992. " 'Europeanness'— A New Cultural Battlefield?" *Innovation in Social Science Research* 5 (2): 11–23.

———. 1993 "Wishful Thinking: Cultural Politics, Media, and Collective Identities in Europe." *Journal of Communication* 43 (2): 6–17.

———. 1994a. "Collective Identities, Friends, Enemies." In *The Role of Stereotypes in International Relations,* ed. Jan Berting and Christiane Villain-Gandossi, 83–94. Rotterdam: RISBO.

———. 1994b. "National Identity as a Process of Cultural Management." In *Culture and Management in a Changing Europe,* ed. Annick Sjögren and Lena Janson, 71–78. Stockholm: Multicultural Center and Institute of International Business.

———. 1999. "Changing Spaces of Political Communication: The Case of the European Union." *Political Communication* 16 (3): 263–279.

Schlesinger, Philip, Rebecca E. Dobash, Russell P. Dobash, and C. Kay Weaver. 1992. *Women Viewing Violence.* London: BFI Publishing.

Schmitter, Philippe. 1985. "Neo Corporatism and the State." In *The Political Economy of Corporatism,* ed. Wyn Grant. New York: St. Martin's Press.

Screen Digest. 1993. "Tighter Times for Film Production." July: 153–160.

Seidman, Gay W. 1994. *Manufacturing Militance: Workers' Movements in Brazil and South Africa, 1970–1985.* Berkeley: University of California Press.

Selin, Sean. 1997. "Governing Cyberspace: The Need for an International Solution," *Gonzaga Law Review* 32: 365–388.

Seo, Jae-Jin. 1988. "Study on Social and Political Network of Korean Capitalist Class." *Korean Sociology* 22: 47–67. (in Korean)

Silj, Alessandro. 1992. "Domestic Markets and the European Market." In *The New Television in Europe,* ed. Alessandro Silj, 15–48. London: John Libbey.

Sinclair, John. 1994. "Televisa-ization and Globo-ization." Paper presented at the Latin American Studies Association, Washington, DC, September.

———. 1996. "Culture and Trade: Some Theoretical and Practical Considerations on 'Cultural Industries.' " In *Mass Media and Free Trade: Nafta and the Cultural Industries,* ed. Emile McAnany and Kenton Wilkinson. Austin: University of Texas.

———. 1999. *Latin American Television.* Oxford: Oxford University Press.

Singer, J. 1961. "The Level of Analysis Problem in International Relations." In *The International System: Theoretical Essays,* ed. K. Knorr and S. Verba. Princeton: Princeton University Press.

Singh, M. 1993. "New Economic Policy, Poverty and Self-Reliance." In *New Economic Policy: Reforms and Development,* ed. S. Prasad and J . Prasad. New Delhi: Mittal Publications.

Sinha, Nikhil. 1996. "The Political Economy of India's Telecommunications Reforms." *Telecommunications Policy* 20 (1): 23–38.

Skocpol, Theda. 1977. "Wallerstein's World Capitalist System: A Theoretical and Historical Critique," *American Journal of Sociology* 82 (5): 1075–1090.

———. 1985. "Bringing the State Back In: Current Research." In *Bringing the State Back In,* ed. Peter B. Evans, Dietrich Rueschemeyer, and Theda Skocpol. Cambridge: Cambridge University Press.

Smith v. Daily Mail Publishing Co. (1979) 443 U.S. 97.

Smith, S. 1988 "Paradigm Dominance in International Relations: The Development of International Relations as a Social Science." *Millennium: Journal of International Studies* 16 (2): 189–206.

Snidal, D. 1985. "The Limits of Hegemonic Stability Theory." *International Organization* 39 (4): 579–614.

Sodré, Muniz. 1977. *O Monopolia da Fala.* Petropolis: Editora Vozes.

———. 1978. "Interview." *Folha de São Paulo,* July 8, Folhetim.

Soma, John T., Thomas F. Muther, Jr., and Heidi M. L. Brissette. 1997. "Transnational Extradition for Computer Crimes: Are New Treaties and Laws Needed?" *Harvard Journal on Legislation* 34: 317–370.

Sparks, Colin. 1988. "The Popular Press and Political Democracy." *Media, Culture and Society* 10 (2): 209–223.

Sparks, Colin, with Anna Reading. 1998. *Communism, Capitalism, and the Mass Media.* London: Sage.

Splichal, Slavko. 1992. "Media Privatization and Democratization in Central-Eastern Europe." *Gazette* 49: 3–22.

———. 1993. "Post-Socialism and the Media: What Kind of Transition?" In *Media in Transition: An East-West Dialogue,* ed. Slavko Splichal and Ildiko Kovats, 5–32. Budapest: Research Group for Communication Studies.

Sreberny-Mohammadi, Annabelle, Dwayne Winseck, Jim McKenna, and Oliver Boyd-Barrett, eds. 1997. *Media in Global Context: A Reader.* London: Arnold.

Stein, Eric. 1986. "History Against Free Speech: The New German Law Against the 'Auschwitz'—and Other—'Lies.'" *Michigan Law Review* 85: 277–324.

Stevenson, R. L., and D. L. Shaw.1984. *Foreign News and the New World Information Order.* Ames: Iowa State University Press.

Strange, S. 1988. *States and Markets: An Introduction to International Political Economy.* London: Pinter.

Straubhaar, Joseph. 1981. "The Transformation of Cultural Dependency: The Decline of American Influence on the Brazilian Television Industry." Doctoral diss., Fletcher School of Law and Diplomacy, Tufts University.

———. 1984. "The Decline of American Influence on Brazilian Television." *Communication Research* 11 (2): 221–240.

———. 1988. "The Reflection of the Brazilian Political Opening in the Telenovela [Soap Opera], 1974–1985." *Studies in Latin American Popular Culture* 7: 59–76.

———. 1989. "Television and Video in the Transition from Military to Civilian Rule in Brazil." *Latin American Research Review* 24 (1): 140–154.

———. 1991a. "Beyond Media Imperialism: Asymmetrical Interdependence and Cultural Proximity." *Critical Studies in Mass Communication* (8): 1–11.

———. 1991b. "Class, Genre and the Regionalization of the Television Market in Latin America." *Journal of Communication* 41 (1): 53–69.

———. 1996. "The Electronic Media in Brazil." In *Communication in Latin America,* ed. Richard Cole, 217–243. Wilmington: Scholarly Resources.

———. Forthcoming. "Culture, Language and Social Class in the Globalization of Television." In *The Emerging Television Landscape: Globalization, Localization, or Something Else?* ed. Georgette Wang, Jan Servaes, and Anuraa Goonasekera. London: Routledge.

Straubhaar, J., C. Campbell, S. M. Youn, K. Champagnie, M. Elasmar, and L. Castellon. 1992. "The Emergence of a Latin American Market for Television Programs." Paper presented at the International Communication Association, Miami, Florida.

Straubhaar, Joseph, Antonio LaPastina, and Caçilda Rego. 2000. "TV Genres: Global Flows, Local Adaptations, and Hybridization." Paper presented at the International Communications Association, Acapulco.

Strauss, David A. 1991. "Persuasion, Autonomy, and Freedom of Expression." *Columbia Law Review* 91: 334–371.

Tassin, Etienne. 1992. "Europe: A Political Community?" In *Dimensions of Radical Democracy: Pluralism, Citizenship, Community*, ed. Chantal Mouffe, 169–192. London: Verso.

Terrett, Andrew. 1997. "A Lawyer's Introduction to the Internet." In *Law and the Internet: Regulating Cyberspace*, ed. Charlotte Waelde and Lillian Edwards, 13–26. Oxford: Hart.

Tomlinson, John. 1991. *Cultural Imperialism*. Baltimore, Md.: Johns Hopkins University Press.

———. 1997. "Cultural Globalization and Cultural Imperialism." In *International Communication and Globalization*, ed. Ali Mohammadi, 170–190. London: Sage.

Tunstall, Jeremy. 1977. *The Media Are American*. London: Constable.

Tunstall, Jeremy, and Michael Palmer. 1991. *Media Moguls*. London: Routledge.

Underhill, Geoffrey R. D. 1994. "Conceptualizing the Changing Global Order." In *Political Economy and the Changing Global Order*, ed. Richard Stubbs and Geoffrey R. D. Underhill, 17–44. New York: St. Martin's Press.

United Nations. 1948. "Universal Declaration of Human Rights." Reprinted in *Journal of International Law* 1949 (43) (Supp.): 127–132.

———. 1965. "Convention on the Elimination of All Forms of Racial Discrimination" (Dec. 21, 1965), 660 U.N.T.S. 195.

United States. 1998. Code of Federal Regulations. Title 47, Vol. 5, part 101. Washington: Government Printing Office. <http://www.frwebgate.access.gpo.gov/cgibin/multidb.cgi>

Valenti, Jack. 1993. "Expanding Competition in the International Market—An Industry Perspective." In *The International Market in Film and Television Programs*, ed. Eli M. Noam and Joel C. Millonzi, 147–150. Norwood, N.J.: Ablex.

Vasconcelos, Antonio-Pedro. 1994. Report by the Think Tank to the European Commissioner in charge of DGX, March.

Vazquez, Carlos Manuel. 1999. "Laughing at Treaties." *Columbia Law Review* 99: 2154–2217.

Veii, V. S. 1988. "Foreign Television Entertainment Programs Viewing and Cultural Imperialism: A Case Study of U.S. Television Entertainment Programs Viewing in Windhoek, Namibia." Ph.D. diss., Michigan State University, Department of Sociology.

Vick, Douglas W. 1998. "The Internet and the First Amendment." *Modern Law Review* 61: 414–421.

Vick, Douglas W., Linda Macpherson, and Sarah Cooper. 1999. "Universities, Defamation and the Internet." *Modern Law Review* 62: 58–78.

Vincent, Rickhard, Kaarle Nordenstreng, and Michael Traber. 1999. *Towards Equity in Global Communication*. Creskill, N.J.: Hampton.

Viotti, Paul R., and Mark V. Kauppi. 1993. *International Relations Theory: Realism, Pluralism, Globalism*, 2d ed. New York: Macmillan.

Wagnleitner, Reinhold, and Elaine Tyler May, eds. 2000. *Here, There, and Everywhere: The Foreign Politics of American Popular Culture*. Hanover: University Press of New England.

Waisbord, Silvio. 1995. "Leviathan Dreams: State and Broadcasting in Latin America." *The Communication Review* 1 (2): 201–226.

———. 1998. "The Ties that Still Bind: Media and National Cultures in Latin America." *Canadian Journal of Communication* 23: 381–401.

Wallerstein, Immanuel. 1974. *The Modern World System*, Volume 1. New York: Academic Press.

———. 1979. *The Capitalist World Economy: Essays*. Cambridge: Cambridge University Press.

———. 1980. *The Modern World System*, Volume 2. New York: Academic Press.

———. 1991. *Geopolitics and Geoculture—Essays on the Changing World System*. Cambridge: Cambridge University Press.

Walton, John, and David Seddon. 1994. *Free Markets and Food Riots: The Politics of Global Adjustment*. Oxford: Blackwell.

Waltz, K. 1979. *Theory of International Politics*. Reading, Mass.: Addison-Wesley.

Waterbury, John. 1992. "The Heart of the Matter? Public Enterprise and the Adjustment Process." In *The Politics of Economic Adjustment: International Constraints, Distributive Conflicts, and the State*, ed. Stephan Haggard and Robert R. Kaufman, 182–217. Princeton: Princeton University Press.

Waterman, Peter. 1991. "Social-Movement Unionism: A New Model for a New World." Working Paper Series No. 110. Institute of Social Studies: The Hague.

Waters, Malcolm. 1996. *Globalization*. London: Routledge.

Webster, D. 1984. "Direct Broadcast Satellites: Proximity, Sovereignty and National Identity." *Foreign Affairs* (Summer): 1161–1174.

Webster, Edward, and Glenn Adler. 1999. "Toward a Class Compromise in South Africa's 'Double Transition': Bargained Liberalization and the Consolidation of Democracy." *Politics & Society* 27: 347–385.

Wellington, Harry. 1979. "On Freedom of Expression." *Yale Law Journal* 88: 1105.

Wells, Christina E. 1997. "Reinvigorating Autonomy: Freedom and Responsibility in the Supreme Court's First Amendment Jurisprudence." *Harvard Civil Rights-Civil Liberties Law Review* 32: 159-196.

Wendt, Alexander. 1987. "The Agent Structure Problem in International Relations Theory." *International Organization*, 41 (3): 335–370.

———. 1991. "Bridging the Theory/Meta-Theory Gap in International Relations Theory." *Review of International Studies*, 17.

Wildman, Steven S., and Stephen E. Siwek. 1988. *International Trade in Films and Television Programs*. Cambridge, Mass.: Ballinger Publishing Co.

Williams, Glen, and Wallace Clement. 1989. *The New Canadian Political Economy*. Kingston, Ont.: McGill-Queen's University Press.

Williamson, John. 1994. "In Search of a Manual for Technopols." In *The Political Economy of Policy Reform*, ed. John Williamson, 11–28. Washington, D.C.: Institute for International Economics.

Wilske, Stephan, and Teresa Schiller. 1997. "International Jurisdiction in Cyberspace: Which States May Regulate the Internet?" *Federal Communications Law Journal* 50: 118–175.

Winseck, Dwayne. 1997. "The Shifting Contexts of International Communication: Possibilities for a New World Information and Communication Order." In *Democratizing Communication? Comparative Perspectives on Information and Power*, ed. Mashoed Bailie and Dwayne Winseck, 343–376. Cresskill, N.J.: Hampton Press.

———. 1998. *Reconvergence: A Political Economy of Telecommunications in Canada.* Cresskill, N.J.: Hampton Press.

Wolton, Dominique. 1990. *Eloge du Grand Public: Une Théorie Critique de la Télévision.* Paris: Flammarion.

———. 1993. *La Dernière Utopie: Naissance de l'Europe Démocratique.* Paris: Flammarion.

World Bank. 1995. World Bank Policy Research Report. *Bureaucrats in Business: The Economics and Politics of Government Ownership.* New York: Oxford University Press.

Wriston, Walter. 1992. *The Twilight of Sovereignty.* New York: Macmillan.

Wyplosz, Charles. 1998. "Globalized Financial Markets and Financial Crises." Paper presented at the conference on *Coping with Financial Crises in Developing Transition Countries: Regulatory and Supervisory Challenges in a New era of Global Finance*, organized by the Forum on Debt and Development. Amsterdam, March 16–17.

Yoon, Youngchul. 1994. "Political Economy of Television Broadcasting in South Korea." In *Elite Media amidst Mass Culture*, ed. Chie-Woon Kim, 191–213. Seoul: Nanam.

Yurdusev, A. 1993. "Level of Analysis and Unit of Analysis: A Case for Distinction." *Millennium: Journal of International Studies*, 22 (1): 77–88.

Zekos, Georgios. 1999. "Internet or Electronic Technology: A Threat to State Sovereignty." *Journal of Information, Law and Technology.* Available at <http://elj.warwick.ac.uk/jilt/99-3/zekos.html> (accessed 6 July 2000).

Zernetskaya, Olga. 1994. "Broadcasting Reform in Ukraine." *Media Development* 61 (1): 32–34.

Index

ABA. *See* Australian Broadcasting Authority (ABA)
access providers, xiv, 6, 9, 18, 22–23, 29
actors and actresses, 144–45
Adler, Glenn, 54
advertising, 86, 139, 143; audiovisual markets, 104; broadcast funding, 47; in Canadian magazines, 121; capital and media relationship in, 88; consumerism and, 101; as financial base for media, 152
African National Congress (ANC), 39, 43–53
agricultural sector, protection of, 72
agriculturists, 62–63
Algeria, 13, 14
Amado, Jorge, 147, 153
Ambedkar, Babasaheb, 61–62
"Americanization," 105–7
"Americanness," 106
Americans: compared to Canadians, 122; contrasted with Germans on views of offensive content, 28–29
Amnesty International, xiv
ANC. *See* African National Congress (ANC)
Anderson, Benedict, 153
anti-apartheid movement, 41, 42–44
antidiscrimination, 8
AOL/Time Warner merger, xi
apartheid, 37, 40–42, 158
Appadurai, Arjun, 136–37
audiences, 141, 144, 145–49, 151
audiovisual media, 102–5, 107, 113

audiovisual space, 106, 108–9, 110
Australia: censorship and, 21; Internet complaints, 26–28; Internet regulatory regime, 21–23, 31–33; origins of Internet legislation, 23–25; viewed as isolated, 30–32
Australian Broadcasting Authority (ABA), 22, 23–24, 26–29
Australian Democrats Party, 25

bankruptcy program, South Korea, 86–87, 89
Bardhan, P., 62
Bauman, Zygmunt, x
Bavaria, 10–11
BBC, xiv, 112–13
Behkler, Yochai, 19
Belarus, 18
Bell Canada, 126
Bertelsmann Foundation, 28, 105
Beto Rockefeller, 141
Beyond National Sovereignty: International Communication in the 1990s, 156–57
bilingualism, xiv, 122–23, 125, 130
Bishop, Mark, 25
Blainey, Geoffrey, 30
Block, F., 58
Bombay Club, India, 71
Boyd-Barrett, Oliver, xi
Brazil, 137–38; cultural capital and cultural proximity, 149–53; Internet access, 140; media policies, xiv; national television production, 142–49

185

About the Editors and Contributors

Seok-Kyeong Hong received a Ph.D. in Information and Communication Sciences from the University of Grenoble, France in 1995. She was a Senior Research Fellow at the Korean Broadcasting Commission from 1996–1999, and since 2000 has been Associate Professor at the Institute of Information and Communication Sciences of the University of Bordeaux.

Robert B. Horwitz is on the faculty in the Department of Communication at the University of California, San Diego. His research focuses on communication institutions and the state in the broad context of issues of democracy and development. Recent research follows two tracks: free speech issues and the changing nature of the public sphere, and the transformation of South African telecommunications. His publications include, among others, *The Irony of Regulatory Reform: The Deregulation of American Telecommunications* and *Communication and Democratic Reform in South Africa.*

Daeho Kim is Assistant Professor in the Department of Mass Communication and Information, Inha University, Korea. He received a B.A. and an M.A. from Seoul National University, Korea, and a Ph.D. from the University of Birmingham. His fields of research are broadcasting policy, convergence of broadcasting and telecommunications, and new media and culture.

Stephen D. McDowell is Associate Professor in the Department of Communication at Florida State University in Tallahassee. He has also taught at Michigan State University and Carleton University. His teaching and research interests include new communication technology and society, telecommunications policies, and communications policies in North America and India. He is the author of *Globalization, Liberalization and Policy Change: A Political Economy of India's Communications Sector.*

Nancy Morris is on the faculty of Temple University's Department of Broadcasting, Telecommunications and Mass Media. She is the author of

Puerto Rico: Culture, Politics, and Identity and articles about globalization, media, and identity.

Kaarle Nordenstreng is Professor in the Department of Journalism and Mass Communication at the University of Tampere, Finland. Among the books he has authored and coedited are *Television Traffic: A One-Way Street? The Mass Media Declaration of UNESCO, Towards Equity in Global Communication: MacBride Update*, and *International Media Monitoring*. He has lately focused on theories of democracy and ethics in relation to journalism and media.

Philip Schlesinger is Professor of Film and Media Studies and Director of the Media Research Institute at the University of Stirling, Scotland. He is also Professor in the Institute of Media and Communication at Oslo University, Norway, and joint editor of the journal *Media, Culture and Society*. His publications include *Media, State, and Nation* (as author), *International Media Research: A Critical Survey* and *Exploring their Limits: Europe's Changing Communication Environment* (as coeditor), and numerous articles.

Nikhil Sinha is Executive Vice President of the eFunds Corporation. Previously he was Assistant Professor in the Department of Radio-Television-Film and Associate Director of the Telecommunications and Information Policy Institute at the University of Texas, Austin. He has also worked in the Information and Broadcasting Ministry of the Government of India, as a consultant to the Informatics and Telecommunications Division of the World Bank, and as an advisor to the Indian Telecom Commission and the Indian Planning Commission. He has published numerous articles and book chapters on international regulatory and policy issues on telecommunications and information technology.

Joseph Straubhaar is Professor in the Department of Radio-Television-Film at the University of Texas, Austin. His work deals with broadcasting and global communication with particular emphasis on Latin America. He is the coauthor of *Communications Media in the Information Society* and coeditor of *Telecommunications Politics: Ownership and Control of the Information Highway in Developing Countries*.

Douglas W. Vick is Lecturer in Business Law at the University of Stirling, Scotland. Among his articles are "Universities, Defamation and the Internet," "Anglicizing Defamation Law in the European Union," and "The Internet and the First Amendment." He is currently working on a project assessing the effects of divisions within modern liberal thought on media regulation in the United States.

Silvio Waisbord is on the faculty in the Department of Journalism and Media Studies at Rutgers University. He is the author of *Watchdog Journalism in South America* and articles about journalism, broadcasting, and culture in Latin America.

Peter B. White is Associate Professor and Head of the Department of Media Studies and Director of the La Trobe University Online Media Program in Australia. He is a graduate of the University of Melbourne, the Newhouse School of Public Communications, Syracuse University, New York, and has worked in Australia and the United States in broadcasting and telecommunications policy, telecommunications privacy, and telecommunications strategy development. He was the Associate Director of the Monash Information and Communications Technology Centre.